LUM AND ABNER

NEW DIRECTIONS IN SOUTHERN HISTORY

SERIES EDITORS
Peter S. Carmichael, West Virginia University
Michele Gillespie, Wake Forest University
William A. Link, University of Florida

LUM AND ABNER

Rural America and the Golden Age of Radio

RANDAL L. HALL

THE UNIVERSITY PRESS OF KENTUCKY

Publication of this volume was made possible in part by a grant
from the National Endowment for the Humanities.

The University Press of Kentucky

Scholarly publisher for the Commonwealth,
serving Bellarmine University, Berea College, Centre College of Kentucky,
Eastern Kentucky University, The Filson Historical Society, Georgetown
College, Kentucky Historical Society, Kentucky State University, Morehead
State University, Murray State University, Northern Kentucky University,
Transylvania University, University of Kentucky, University of Louisville,
and Western Kentucky University.
All rights reserved.

Editorial and Sales Offices: The University Press of Kentucky
663 South Limestone Street, Lexington, Kentucky 40508-4008
www.kentuckypress.com

11 10 09 08 07   5 4 3 2 1

Library of Congress Cataloging-in-Publication Data

Hall, Randal L., 1971-
  Lum and Abner : rural America and the golden age of radio / Randal L.
Hall.
     p. cm. — (New directions in Southern history)
  ISBN 978-0-8131-2469-8 (hardcover : alk. paper)
  1. Lum and Abner (Radio program) I. Title.
  PN1991.77.L86H35 2007
  791.44'72—dc22   2007019780

This book is printed on acid-free recycled paper meeting the requirements of the
American National Standard for Permanence in Paper for Printed Library Materials.

Manufactured in the United States of America.

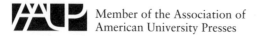 Member of the Association of
American University Presses

This work is dedicated to my parents,
Ernest John Hall and Mary Ann Radford Hall,
and to my wife, Naomi J. Hall.

Contents

Acknowledgments

I would like to thank Walter Beeker, Carlos Blanton, John Boles, David Brown, Fitz Brundage, Sandra J. Crump, Michele Gillespie, Joyce Harrison, Michele Hilmes, Tim Hollis, Richard Jackson, Scott Lauck, Bill Link, David Lubin, Duncan McCoy, Howell Smith, Melissa Walker, Ed Wilson, Ben Wise, one anonymous reader for the University Press of Kentucky, the participants in the Houston Area Southern Historians seminar at Rice University, and the participants in the Re:Visions II: Broadcasting Histories conference at the University of Central Lancashire. The history departments of Wake Forest University and Rice University generously provided financial support for research and for presentation of drafts of this work. Linda Pine, Jillian Barnett, and Shay Stiles provided helpful assistance in the Archives and Special Collections department of Ottenheimer Library at the University of Arkansas at Little Rock. The staff members of Fondren Library at Rice University—particularly Francine Arizmendez, Sarah Bentley, Angela Brown, Suellen Denton, DeAndrea Smither, and Randy Tibbits—have my appreciation for their stellar work.

INTRODUCTION

FROM 1931 UNTIL 1954 Chester "Chet" Lauck and Findley Norris "Tuffy" Goff gave voice to the village of Pine Ridge, Arkansas, on their popular radio comedy series, *Lum and Abner*.[1] The show is a rare example of a lasting national network program on rural themes. Even more unusual, it was set in the South and created by southerners. Until 1940 Lauck and Goff, who were natives of Arkansas, wrote the scripts, played the title roles, and provided the voices for an array of townspeople. Their humor tapped many standard comic devices, but the Pine Ridge setting gave the show a rich specificity. They based Pine Ridge on the rural hamlet of Waters, Arkansas, near their hometown. The citizens of Waters petitioned successfully in 1936 to change the name of the local post office to Pine Ridge, a campaign indicative of the community's support of the program. Thus, *Lum and Abner* sheds light on the creation and both the national and the local popular reception of an imaginative work over a period of years.[2] At a time when culturally influential Americans defined rural areas as a problem to be solved, *Lum and Abner* provided an important corrective to oversimplifications of rural life.

Since the 1960s, historians have worked to understand radio's role in the creation of American popular culture.[3] Yet knowledge of radio production and consumption in rural America, particularly in the South, remains lacking, even though an important mass audience had begun to form outside the nation's urban areas by the early 1930s. In April 1930 New Jersey led all states in the proportion of families owning radios—63 percent, compared

1

to 40.3 percent nationally. At the opposite extreme, 5.4 percent of families in Mississippi had radios. The region comprising Kentucky, Tennessee, Alabama, and Mississippi had the lowest regional average (12.3 percent), followed by the region encompassing Arkansas, Louisiana, Oklahoma, and Texas at 16.5 percent. The 1940 census likewise showed the southern states, plus Arizona and New Mexico, holding the bottom sixteen spots in a ranking of percentage of residences with radios, but by that point even in Mississippi, which ranked at the very bottom, 39.9 percent of residences had radios. Thus, the Great Depression coincided with the routinization of radio listening. Southerners, particularly in rural areas, owned fewer radios than residents of the rest of the country; however, they were an important and growing market.[4]

Fresh understanding of the rural aspect of radio broadcasting and, more broadly, the development of mass culture can best be achieved through intensive case studies of individual genres, stations, and programs. On the one hand, popular culture often dwelt on the negative side of rural America during the Depression. Hordes of novelists, photographers, filmmakers, and journalists used both written and visual media to depict sordid conditions in the countryside. On the other hand, at least a few rural and small-town dwellers used mass culture to gain a hearing for an alternative story of rural America. *Lum and Abner* told such a tale.

In the 1930s it was no easy task to get noticed among the many short-lived radio programs focusing on hillbillies and country life. As early as 1932 a reviewer evaluating the comedy *The Real Folks of Thompkins Corners* sighed, "This is another one of the long, long list of rural and country-town serials."[5] The trend grew even stronger as radios reached a wider spectrum of the rural population ("a new customer in every farmyard," glowed one trade publication).[6] Along with numerous performances of hillbilly music, comic programs, which were often set in the rural Northeast—for example, *Cracker Barrel Congress, The Stebbins Boys, Wilbur and Ezra, Happy Hollow, Sam and Joe, Uncle Ezra, Si and Elmer,* and *Eb and Zeb*—helped to fill the schedules of the networks and individual stations.[7] *Moonshine and Honeysuckle*, written by Lula Vollmer, a North Carolina native and successful Broadway playwright, gained critical notice during its run from 1930 to 1933 on NBC. *Variety* reported approvingly: "Miss Vo[l]lmer writes of the people of the moonshine belt, mountain folk with their own odd use of language, moral slant and conception of the outside world. This isn't new. It's nothing but our old chum, hillbilly. It's the treatment that counts."[8]

Popularity is difficult to quantify because the early audience ratings systems for radio were notoriously inexact. Many sponsors relied principally on sales figures and the response to on-air offers for free fan premiums to gauge listenership and advertising effectiveness. Others relied on telephone surveys of urban areas, an extreme disadvantage for a program such as *Lum and Abner*, which was likely to attract substantial listenership from rural areas and working-class households without telephones. Telephone access was particularly low during the depths of the Depression decade. However, one influential study concluded that the lower the "cultural level" of a radio listener, the more likely he or she was to listen to *Lum and Abner* (and this study also included only telephone surveys). Another contemporary study, which looked at media and the development of children, noted, "The dialogue (21–25 percent) of Amos 'n' Andy, Pick and Pat, Lum and Abner, and other funnybone ticklers again has but little cultural value and can rank only as simple amusement." A third academic survey of the time had a somewhat more supportive view of the program: "In similar fashion our city youngsters can be aroused to interest in rural life through comparing their limited experience of small towns with the concepts they glean from 'Lum and Abner.'" Throughout its run, though, *Lum and Abner* had respectable ratings, despite elite condescension toward the show and obstacles to accurate audience analysis. Lauck and Goff entered a crowded field, but their treatment of the subject stood out in revealing ways.[9]

By the early 1930s, radio broadcasting had become a thoroughly commercial enterprise, disappointing many idealistic observers who had hoped the new medium would primarily serve artistic, educational, or other public ends. In order to succeed, budding radio performers had to display an entrepreneurial streak.[10] This introductory essay traces Lauck and Goff's innovative ascent to radio stardom and explores the aspects of their show that allowed the two Arkansans to create a richly layered community of the imagination—a veritable gemeinschaft—that interpreted national concerns using a rural, overtly southern setting.[11]

Americans had long been of two minds about country life. Early in the century, romantic depictions of farm life coexisted with reform-oriented scientific planning within the Country Life Movement, a Progressive-era undertaking that acknowledged (and tried to improve) lackluster conditions among country dwellers. Lauck and Goff fashioned their work with an awareness of longtime nostalgia for the rural past, but they wholeheartedly endorsed a forward-looking focus on economic progress. Some of their listeners may have tuned in because hillbilly programming evoked appealing images of bygone rural life; others may have hoped to hear gothic tales of exotic hillbillies.[12] However, Lauck and Goff introduced both sets of listeners to two gentle old-timers who embraced economic growth and change. In doing so they created a vision immensely popular with listeners, urban and rural, southern and northern alike. Lauck and Goff, as Lum and Abner, broadcast a rural community that countered images of rural depravity, played with Americans' developing sense of nostalgia, and introduced rural values in step with the twentieth century and the Main Street middle-class mainstream. They reconciled the nation's conflicting images of the country.

At times the popularity of *Lum and Abner* surged ahead of the more famous contemporary serial *Amos 'n' Andy*, which generated both adoration and controversy for its depiction of black southerners who had migrated to the urban North. Lum and Abner dwelt in the South that Amos and Andy left behind, and each program captured essential truths about being on the margins of America in the Great Depression era. Lauck and Goff's characters dealt with the difficulty of being manly providers in a time of scarcity, of fighting for political representation amid corruption and pressing local needs, and of maintaining faith and neighborhood ties in times of social disjunction. They played out universal themes that crossed lines of race and locality.

Lauck and Goff grew up together in the town of Mena, situated at the edge of the Ouachita Mountains in western Arkansas. Their family lives embodied the new focus on commerce and industry that civic boosters in the South trumpeted following the Civil War. Both were Arkansas natives: Lauck was born in Alleene on February 9, 1902, and Goff in Cove on May 30, 1906. In 1911 or 1912 their parents moved from these tiny hamlets to the small town of Mena, where the two young boys became schoolmates and fast friends. The families worked their way to small-town business success as New South entrepreneurs. According to Lauck, his father "would buy timber throughout southwest Arkansas, put in a sawmill, cut out the timber and move to a new location. We always lived in sawmill shacks with no lighting except for oil lamps and wood stove heaters, but he kept growing until we moved to Mena, where he put in a big planing mill and at one time had 18 sawmills." The elder Lauck also served as president and later chairman of the board of Union Bank in Mena. Goff's father had made his way up through the commercial world and ran a successful wholesale grocery business. The two men's family backgrounds provided leisure for creativity and an abundance of material about the South, and their upbringing molded the two future showmen into determined businessmen as well.[13]

Following high school, the two had opportunities open to relatively few in the small-town South. Lauck had an ambition to be a political cartoonist. He enrolled at the Chicago Academy of Fine Arts in 1920. The lanky youth completed a two-year course of study in art and switched to the University of Arkansas, where he finished a degree in 1926. Lauck enjoyed college life—editing the humor magazine, studying journalism, developing a lifelong devotion to the Sigma Chi fraternity, and being a cheerleader for the Razorbacks. Goff enrolled at the University of Arkansas and joined Sigma Chi as well, but he transferred to the University of Oklahoma and completed his studies there in 1928. Lauck's publicity material later explained that after graduation he "progressed in the commercial art field, and soon had his own agency and was editor of a magazine in Texas." But the call of home was strong for both. Goff joined his father in the family's wholesale grocery business, and Lauck returned to Mena to work in a bank and then manage an automobile financing company owned in part by his father. Lauck was a charter member and president of the Lions Club, a toastmaster of the Polk County Possum Club (a civic group), a regular at the Elks Lodge, and a director of the local Chamber of Commerce. Both men got married to women from nearby in Arkansas, Lauck to a Hot Springs native in 1926 and Goff to a woman from Mena in 1929. They had achieved the emerging American dream. The pair settled into solid careers and occasionally entertained friends and local groups, sometimes in blackface, with their natural penchant for humor.[14]

The two old friends created the characters of Lum and Abner almost accidentally. In March 1931 the Mena Lions Club, with Lauck as president, staged a blackface minstrel act that included Lauck, Goff, and their fathers among the performers. "Chet and 'Tuffy' clowned through the whole performance in their usual manner, and were responsible for lots of the laughs and the usual good humor that prevailed," recorded the local paper.[15] In late April 1931 the Lions Club sponsored a broadcast for Polk County performers on KTHS in Hot Springs, a radio station operated by the Chamber of Commerce there. (Along with newspapers and educational institutions, Chambers of Commerce and other civic groups held many early station licenses.) Lauck and Goff drove to Hot Springs, planning to do a blackface act to go along with hillbilly music by other Mena performers. *Amos 'n' Andy* (originally *Sam 'n' Henry*) had taken America by storm in the late 1920s, helping to spawn mainstream Americans' infatuation with radio and inspiring a wave of imitators. On the drive to Hot Springs that Saturday morning, Lauck and Goff changed their minds about the subject of their act. Lauck remembered that trip vividly: "We had never seen a radio station. So we came over, and on our way over we decided we'd better not do blackface because *Amos and Andy* had just started and the Two Black Crows [another blackface act appearing on network variety shows] were tremendously popular." Instead Lauck and Goff decided to stand out by featuring two rural characters, thus showing the other side of the coin in American racial and ethnic politics. This side too could evoke exotic and interesting plots. "We had messed around with them [the two characters] a little bit just for our own amusement. So we went on the air not knowing what we were going to talk about: we adlibbed it. So we just kept those characters." Technical problems interrupted them only minutes into their broadcast debut, and the station invited them to perform again the following Sunday, April 26. Strong support from listeners then led the station to invite them back for *Lum Edwards and Abner Peabody's Weekly Visit* on several consecutive Sundays. Letters from Nebraska, Florida, Georgia, Illinois, and even Los Angeles, California, showed the young men's instant connection with listeners from all over the country and the exceptional geographical range of early AM radio stations.[16]

In designing a short serial comedy, Lauck and Goff fortunately chose a format that was waxing in popularity in the radio business. One report (coincidentally published soon after their opening effort in Hot Springs) claimed, "The tendency among radio advertisers, especially those using the larger chains, is to bring the former half hour and hour weekly down to a 15-minute program more times per week. The advertiser's attention has been called to the constant punch in being on the air six times a week with short snappy programs." Lauck and Goff's earliest programs clearly fit the bill, although the only clue to their content comes from the Mena newspaper: "The Mena entertainers are proving so popular they were announced to appear again next Sunday at which time they will tell about going to court at Little Rock, at which time they also expect to attend one of those 'girlie' shows they have heard about, and which will be done if possible without the knowledge of Mrs. Lum and Mrs. Abner." The rube in the city is an ancient comedic plot, but in their handling of it, Lauck and Goff touched fresh concerns both of rural listeners and of an urban audience that included many natives of rural areas. As they began to polish their newly discovered talent and gain a feel for how to please an audience, the two began to consider more prestigious outlets.[17]

Encouraged by the station manager at KTHS, Lauck and Goff and their wives traveled to Chicago in July 1931 for an audition with NBC. At this stage in radio's development, new talent often caught the ears of producers through such auditions, but apparently Lauck and Goff did not win immediate acceptance. A newspaper columnist later quoted an NBC sales department memo that discussed the audition: "There doesn't seem to be very much to say about these boys (Lum and Abner) except that they are a comedy team and impersonate a couple of farmers." Lauck recalled that they treated the process as a lark: "We thought that would be a fun trip anyway, so we went up there and fooled around for several days before we went to NBC, and finally we went down and set up an appointment for an audition." They got an offer to do their program on a sustaining basis (relatively low salaries and no long-term sponsorship), but hesitated. The next day an NBC official called to summon them for an audition with the Quaker Oats company. They signed a standard thirteen-week contract (managed by the influential Bill Hay, who also worked with the *Amos 'n' Andy* principals) and returned home to prepare cautiously for their new opportunity. "We didn't resign from our jobs, we took a leave of absence and went back up to Chicago," Lauck explained.[18]

For two weeks in late July and early August, *Lum and Abner* filled in for radio pioneers Gene and Glenn, vacationing hosts of the morning *Quaker Early Birds Program*. Beginning in late August, Lauck and Goff broadcast nationally over the NBC network in their own time slot for a month, but Quaker then ended their national broadcast and used them to reach a specific regional audience. The pair journeyed to Texas to make personal appearances as the Quaker Oats Greeters, and beginning on September 28 they broadcast *Lum and Abner* six days per week alternately from WFAA in Dallas and WBAP in Fort Worth, which were at the time sharing a frequency and dividing the airtime. Lauck and Goff were hailed upon arrival as "radio's finest portrayers of Southern rural characters," and the local newspaper noted with pride that this was the first time that a sponsor had moved an established network program to a local market. The signal from the two stations reached at least to Nebraska and Florida, though, and in cool weather as far as New York State.

Quaker ended its radio sponsorship near the end of 1931, and Lauck and Goff made their final broadcast from Fort Worth on December 26. The young men returned to the radio hotbed of Chicago and struggled through early 1932. Chicagoans remembered them as "the 'hill billies,' who filled in for Gene and Glenn . . . last summer." Lauck and Goff broadcast for NBC on a sustaining basis from WMAQ beginning January 11, sometimes three days per week and sometimes five, and in February they also began working on Saturday nights as end men "Chet" and "Tuff," using their limited blackface experience in Arkansas to be part of the *WENR Minstrels* program. Their network arrangement faded after the broadcast on June 4, despite Lauck and Goff's extraordinary appeal to their listeners for a fan-mail campaign to save the show. To no avail they mentioned their impending cancellation: "Now to tell you the truth, I bleave they'll send fer us to come back right chere, if a nuff of youns'll write in and tell em to. You know bout the only way they can tell up here wher you're likin our programs or not is by the number of letters they git about us." A trip to New York netted no new opportunities. *Lum and Abner* teetered on the brink of collapse until Lauck and Goff arranged to return to WBAP in Fort Worth beginning on August 1, 1932. There they remained, barely making ends meet, until a successful audition with network-owned affiliate station WTAM in Cleveland brought them back to NBC, at first only on WTAM but later on a growing number of NBC stations in the East and Midwest.[19]

Lum and Abner gained solid footing in Cleveland from the program's debut there on Thanksgiving Day in November 1932, and its rise to national success would not seriously waver again. Stations affiliated with NBC in the early 1930s could choose to fill time slots with local programs rather than purchasing particular network offerings, and WTAM's strong independent programming had led it frequently to clear space for its own material. As a result, NBC purchased WTAM in 1931 to gain control of its pool of talent and large midwestern listenership, and by August 1933 the Cleveland newspaper could boast that "WTAM here feeds more programs to the WEAF Net [the more important of the two NBC networks] than any other station in the chain outside of New York. Over 200 programs went out of WTAM over WEAF wires last month." Lauck and Goff took advantage of the stimulating environment, broadcasting two distinct episodes per day for the first few weeks. As they got their show under way in Cleveland, NBC also kept them in mind for bigger projects, inviting the pair to be part of a Christmas Day broadcast over the larger network. *Lum and Abner* quickly found an audience, and by February there were rumors of a commercial sponsor for the series.[20]

The program's next turning point occurred in late May 1933 when the Ford dealers of the Cleveland region (northern Ohio and part of Pennsylvania) became its long-sought sponsor. Automobile sales had just begun to bounce back from a dismal record in 1932, and radio stations also reported a boost in overall commercial sales. Lauck and Goff were perfectly positioned to ride the wave of successful sales figures in the coming months. The Ford dealers immediately put them to work making appearances, and they attracted wider attention. An audition over the NBC network for a reported "587 Ford dealers of some sixteen eastern cities" led to a network contract (reportedly bringing in $800,000 for NBC). On July 3, NBC launched the program from WTAM to affiliates in the East and Midwest and featured a guest appearance by Graham

McNamee, a star announcer. More than twenty stations signed on, and network executives sent congratulations.[21] NBC and the Ford dealers quickly developed confidence in the ability of the rustic comics to appeal to both rural and urban listeners.

Beginning on July 8 the Ford Motor Company sponsored a week-long exposition in Cleveland's Public Hall to highlight the company's massive contribution to the area's economy through parts suppliers in Ohio. Every night Lauck and Goff broadcast from the exposition, in company with a large number of visiting NBC stars, and a total of over 190,000 people attended the events. With such a well-supported launch, *Lum and Abner* became a fixture in Cleveland for a time. Lauck claimed that during their first thirteen-week run with Ford, the greater Cleveland region "jumped from 18th place to 5th in national sales."[22] In the summer of 1933 *Lum and Abner* finally grabbed national kudos.[23] Lauck and Goff's creative minds and footloose entrepreneurialism had begun to pay dividends.

New York's *Variety* magazine acknowledged the success of the show in July 1933: "After knocking about through the south and middlewest for several years without making much of an impression, Lauck and Goff recently sold themselves and their rural background act to the Ford distributor for the Cleveland district, with WTAM as the outlet. The team did an unusually fast click locally, and the results garnered by the Cleveland Ford dealers made it no hard task for NBC to sell Ford reps in 20 other cities on the idea of hooking in on the Lum and Abner program." By October 1933 the fan magazine *Radio News* could report that "a new series of rural skits which shows promise of becoming a radio sensation is the 'Lum and Abner, Ford Dealers of the Air,' sketch which is heard over NBC each night, excepting Saturdays and Sundays." That same month an even-more-influential fan publication, *Radio Guide*, featured *Lum and Abner*: "The thousands in the teeming streets of Manhattan, Chicago, Detroit, Philadelphia, and the other large and bustling cities of the country have come to love the homely wisdom of Lum and Abner. . . . And still other thousands, scattered more widely over the rural sections that lie between the cities love Lum and Abner, too." The show stormed Washington, D.C., for a week of broadcasts in October, marked by an episode on Friday the 13th in which Lum was to marry his sweetheart Eva-lena. (Of course the wedding was foiled, by Lum's arrest on mis-guided charges of embezzlement of public funds.) The performers drew a capacity crowd of six thousand spectators for the special broadcast, which was complete with a large, fully costumed cast provided by NBC. The following month even the *New York Times* took note when Lauck and Goff visited New York to air a pro-gram as part of the opening week of broadcasts from NBC's new Radio City facility. Lauck told the *New York Times* reporter, "We receive an average of 15,000 letters a week. One week we opened 23,000 letters. And in small towns of about 350 people petitions have been drawn up listing the names of every one in the village, from the Mayor down to the youngsters. But we also get many let-ters from urban listeners."[24]

In a promotional newspaper, the *Pine Ridge News*, NBC and *Lum and Abner* informed Ford dealers in November 1933 that the Arnold Research Service of New York City "took a section of New England and made a total of 5016 telephone calls during the broadcasting period of the Ford program." Of those listening to the radio during broadcasts on Tuesday, Wednesday, and Thurs-day, "46% of the radio audience were tuned in on Ford." The network claimed that "this New England audience may be taken as a cross section of the radio listeners covered by the NBC net-work—and would indicate that a substantial half of the radio sets turned on favor the Ford program presented by Lum and Abner." The network also claimed that *Lum and Abner* generated a record 150,000 entries for a contest giving away a new Ford V-8 sedan.[25]

The show's contract with Ford ceased at the end of December 1933 (when Ford decided instead to sponsor twice-weekly broad-casts of Fred Waring's orchestra), but WTAM on its own sustained *Lum and Abner* four days per week until February 1, 1934. The team then made a series of vaudeville-style appearances in cities such as Indianapolis and Louisville as they searched for the right new opportunity.[26] This time, though, Lauck and Goff had little trouble selling their act to a new sponsor. William Horlick bought the series to promote his Horlick's Malted Milk Corporation in Racine, Wisconsin. (Emboldened by a fan letter from Horlick, Lauck and Goff reportedly bypassed the normal protocol of approaching an advertising agency and went to see Horlick personally at his home to initiate the deal.) Unable to get the network arrangement he wanted, Horlick arranged for *Lum and Abner* to be broadcast only from powerful WCCO in Minneapolis for more than two months, at which point the program joined an infant network—with important affiliates in Chicago, Cincinnati, New York, and Detroit—that would become the Mutual Broadcasting System. Their listenership on the small network responded enthusiastically, sending 350,000 replies when Lauck and Goff offered a free copy of the *Pine Ridge News* tabloid. In September 1935 Horlick gained a spot for them on the national NBC Blue network, where they remained a staple of NBC's lineup until 1938 (after which they jumped to other national networks). Lauck recalled that their work brought excellent results for the malted milk manufacturer: "When Lum and Abner started broadcasting for Horlicks, their plant was running 3 days a week and [they] were 6th in sales among other brands of malted milk. Within 90 days they were running the plant 6 days a week and in 6 months they were running the plant in Racine, Wisconsin, day and night." Lauck and Goff had achieved national fame and clear commercial influence.[27] Fans could find in the program not only reassuring images of rural stability but also plots that moved rural hayseeds into the national mainstream. But Lauck and Goff achieved this profitable combination only after some initial experimentation with the program's structure.

The plot of *Lum and Abner* evolved somewhat between 1931 and 1934, when it assumed the basic form it would have for the rest of its run. Initially the two old-timers, each of whom owned a farm, served as justice of the peace and constable and spent a good deal of time loafing at Dick Huddleston's store. Under the Ford sponsorship, the characters added to their duties the proprietorship of the Pine Ridge Ford dealership, and the show sometimes ran with the subtitle "Ford Dealers of the Air." But it was as rural merchants that they became memorable. By February 1933 they not only were fulfilling their civic duties but also were working as storekeepers (after a competing program about rural New England store owners, *The Stebbins Boys*, went off the air). Lauck remembered that he and Goff enlisted their listeners' help in naming the new establishment: "When the show was still young, we didn't have a name for the store, so Tuffy and I . . . had a contest to name the store. Well, we already had the store in the show, and we had that tablet where people wrote down what they had bought so the boys could bill them later, so about five people sent in 'Jot It Down Store.' That was the best name, but we didn't want to have to pay five first prizes, so we gave it to one person who had suggested 'Jot 'em Down.'" Lum and Abner's work as store proprietors remained the show's foundation for more than two decades.[28] Their role as entrepreneurial businessmen perfectly reflected Lauck and Goff's family and personal experiences and the nature of their determined climb to success in radio.

Although radio was young, some model programs already existed. The prototype of the comic radio series during the early 1930s was *Amos 'n' Andy*. In January 1926 Freeman Gosden and Charles Correll had completed the transition from minstrelsy to radio and had begun their phenomenal rise as *Sam 'n' Henry* over WGN in Chicago. In March 1928 they switched to the cross-town rival station WMAQ, renamed the characters, and as Amos and Andy established the patterns of early radio comedy. By the time *Lum and Abner* debuted, other important series, such as *The Rise of the Goldbergs*, had already latched onto the new method of telling stories serially over the air, and the subtle, long-lasting *Vic and Sade*, one of Lauck's all-time favorites among the competition, soon followed. Jim and Marian Jordan, who would create *Fib-

ber McGee and Molly in 1935, had also been at work on various projects since the mid-1920s. Between 1931 and 1933 the comedians who would dominate the decade—Ed Wynn, Fred Allen, Jack Benny, and George Burns and Gracie Allen—joined the airwaves. Lauck and Goff seized the latest trends but gave them a fresh twist and a new setting in the South.[29]

An important part of 1930s radio comedy was what one historian labels "linguistic slapstick." The scholar Susan J. Douglas explains that "linguistic rebellion, even anarchy, reigned supreme." This "verbal dueling," a new version of vaudeville-style routines, suggested that "radio comedy was enacting much larger dramas about competition, authority, fairness, and hope during the greatest crisis of American capitalism, the Great Depression." For some programs, racial or ethnic stereotypes provided the fodder for malapropisms and misunderstandings, while on many shows during the 1930s it was the so-called dizzy dame who mutilated the language. Jane on *The Easy Aces*, Gracie of *Burns and Allen*, and Mary on Jack Benny's programs fit this description. The verbal stumblers seemingly were the dumb ones, but often these women or ethnic characters deflated and undermined the dominant characters in ways that left power relationships uncertain.[30]

On *Lum and Abner* this sort of verbal comedy took the form of "old Edards sayings." Lum typically seized the role of straight man, often a bit pompous and always gently frustrated at the seeming ineptness of Abner. Abner, in contrast, operated with a literalist mind. Like the fundamentalists so familiar in the American imagination after the radio broadcasts of the 1925 Scopes Trial, he took words at their face value. Lum would lay out a proverbial statement, a so-called old saying, to show off his wisdom, and Abner would become confused. The following unhurried dialogue from 1934 typifies the linguistic element of Lum and Abner's comedy. Here, they debate the motives of a boastful detective visiting Pine Ridge:

Lum: Jist recollect that old Edards sayin. A barkin dog seldom bites.

Abner: Huh?

Lum: I say a barkin dog seldom bites.

Abner: Oh I was still talkin bout that feller Looney, the detecitive.

Lum: I was too. I jist said a barkin dog seldom bites.

Abner: Oh . . . I dont know bout that though Lum. Old Lead that dog of mine barks at everything that comes on the place and anybody that dont think he'll bit jist orter try to come in that yard ofa night.

Lum: Well thats a old sayin of mine. If that dog of yours barks he wont bite.

Abner: Thats jist all you know bout it. I know I've saw him. He might nigh takend a leg offen Mose Moots here a while back.

On another show from 1934 Lum and Abner wonder if the devious Squire Skimp will accidentally give himself away as the villainous architect of their latest misfortune. Lum says hopefully, "Well jist give him anuff rope and he'll hang his sef Abner." Abner hopefully but guiltily begins calculating the necessary length: "Course I reckon hit'd depend on wher he hung hisef from. Now if he'd pick a limb clost to the ground it ortent to take hardly any. Ten foot ort to be a nuff ortent it?"[31]

This sort of wordplay placed them in the mainstream of comic linguistic manipulation, but the show succeeded for a number of other reasons that set it apart from its many competitors. In February 1933 Lauck and Goff used a significant innovation to attract new listeners: they added a night of hillbilly and other popular music into their comic serial. The two creative mediums meshed perfectly. On Saturday, February 18, they broadcast their first Old Time Sociable at the desirable 9:00 P.M. time slot. Their weekday program ran for fifteen minutes at 6:15 P.M. (although the time would vary later), but they now had a half hour on Saturday nights to add a variety show of music and comedy, conceived as a schoolhouse gathering in Pine Ridge emceed by Lum and Abner and broadcast to the community over the shared telephone line (a practice that actually took place in rural America). By the second outing of the sociable, Lauck and Goff had formed the Pine Ridge String Band to anchor the program amid a range of musical guest stars. Eight hundred listeners overflowed the WTAM studio to watch the broadcast of a sociable in early March, forcing Lauck and Goff to do a second performance for those denied entrance to the actual broadcast. In subsequent weeks they moved to a larger auditorium away from the studio and charged twenty-five cents for admission. Even the local radio columnist, always skeptical of programs with a rural bent, acknowledged the popularity and charm of the sociables: "Remember the 'Old Fashioned Singing School' of your small town days? It was one of those affairs with school room background and rural costumes, by crackety. . . . All the setting lacked was the old gaslight." The sociable later moved to Friday nights, and until the end of 1933, when it was dropped at the close of Ford's sponsorship, it was important to the overall success of *Lum and Abner*.[32]

Variety magazine attributed some of the program's initial success to the addition of the weekly variety show: "It is obvious that the script phase of their show has only in small measure, if any, been responsible for their clicking in the Cleveland area. What undoubtedly has put them over is the Friday night variety show. Combined here is adroit routining, nicely balanced and good entertainment and a touch of the novel. . . . As an all around variety bill for mike purposes this same Friday night spasm had practically all that it takes to hold and beguile the average attention." *Variety* wrongly dismissed the serial portion of *Lum and Abner*; however, the reviewer rightly identified the sociable as a crucial part of the show's early development.[33]

The addition of the Old Time Sociable (sometimes called the Friday Night Sociable) to their established plot-driven series allowed Lauck and Goff to appeal simultaneously to their listeners' love of both rustic comedy and, importantly, the new hillbilly music. One radio columnist exclaimed, "Do Clevelanders go for the hillbilly fiddler, jug band, dialect humor? Yowsah." Such entertainment captured midwesterners' imagination throughout the decade. Later in the thirties, the sociologists Robert S. and Helen Merrell Lynd found that the pseudonymous Middletown (Muncie, Indiana) also embraced hillbilly programming: "Four-fifths of local listeners were said in 1935 to prefer 'popular' and 'hillbilly' music. As many as 12,700 'fan letters' have been received in a single week commending these 'hillbilly' programs, whereas local people who prefer symphonic music rarely send in 'fan' mail. A commercial user recently received only four responses from an organ program, as against 246 from a 'hillbilly' program."[34]

The Pine Ridge String Band and the Milk Maids anchored the Old Time Sociable. Although often associated with its southern or Appalachian origins, commercial country music from its inception attracted droves of midwestern listeners; it was one of the first twentieth-century formats in which creative rural residents earned national attention. Radio broadcasts of vaudeville-style barn dances—varied programs of live music simulating rural community gatherings—began at least as early as January 1923 on WBAP (the Fort Worth station that helped keep *Lum and Abner* on the air in 1931). In 1924 WLS in Chicago began its long-lasting *National Barn Dance*, giving farmers throughout the Midwest an array of pop, folk, and hillbilly music, hymns, and comedy, with regulars such as Arkie the Arkansas Woodchopper. The owner of the *Prairie Farmer*, a midwestern agricultural newspaper, bought WLS in 1928, reaffirming the regional importance of rural programming. Under the guidance of a former member of the *National Barn Dance* cast (Indiana native George D. Hay), WSM in Nashville started the *WSM Barn Dance* program in 1925 and renamed it the *Grand Ole Opry* in 1927. It too featured both music and comedy (and helped Nashville grow into the center of the country music world). WSB in Atlanta had a similar program, as did stations such as WOS in Jefferson City, Missouri. Wisconsin farmers beseeched Madison's lofty WHA for more banjo and fiddle music. Moreover, by 1933 the national networks, drawing on performers from the dying vaudeville industry, had turned to comic variety and amateur programs of all sorts in order to win back an overall listenership that had peaked in 1931 and then stabilized as the public grew accustomed to radio. With their Friday Night Sociable, Lauck and Goff had the perfect way to take part in several trends—a mixture of hillbilly and popular music, variety programming, and rural appeal—without disrupting their serial format.[35]

A reviewer listed some of the acts: "For the first (9) of the sociables broadcast over the hookup the Lum and Abner team imported Annie, Judy and Zeke and Major, Sharp and Minor, two harmony teams from the regular New York NBC list." Comic Jerry Hausner performed on the sociable and recalled that for one show "they had a trio called the Dritzen Boys, Scandinavian folk singers . . . and they had a trio called Annie, Judy and Zeke, who turned out to be Zeke Manners (a big star later on) and Judy Canova . . . and there was a girl singer by the name of Frances Langford." Langford would become well known for both singing and acting and later would costar in a *Lum and Abner* film. The inclusion of Canova is also significant because early on she was stereotyped as a rural character, and later she had a series of hillbilly films and her own rube program, the *Judy Canova Show*, in which she had "migrated to Hollywood from a hillbilly hamlet called Cactus Junction." From July through December 1933, the radio columnist for the *Cleveland Plain Dealer* often listed the lineup for each week's sociable. Some other acts included Cleveland hillbilly musician Pie Plant Pete, minstrel performer Al Bernard, tenor Jimmy Melton, newsman Lowell Thomas, singers Arlene Jackson, Ralph Kirbery, Johnny Marvin, and the Three X Sisters, and eleven-year-old musical sensation Mary Small. The array was grounded in hillbilly imagery but cosmopolitan enough for a broad audience.[36]

Louis M. Jones, a country musician who later became famous on television as *Hee Haw*'s Grandpa Jones, played in the Pine Ridge String Band. His reminiscences preserve a sense of excitement about the special editions of the *Lum and Abner* program:

"Though the sponsors really aimed the show at residents of Ohio and Pennsylvania, it would be heard on 44 different stations. . . . It would really be the big time." Jones earned ten dollars per program, and the work extended beyond the weekly broadcast. He recalled, "I played guitar and sang solos; Joe [Troyan, also well known later in country music circles], besides playing harmonica in the band, did all the imitations of farm animals needed for the radio show's sound effects. We did a lot of live theater dates with Lum and Abner as well."[37] Occasionally the live broadcast on Friday night originated from a city other than Cleveland. On November 10, 1933, ten thousand people attended the Cadie Tabernacle in Indianapolis to serve as the crowd in the imaginary Pine Ridge Schoolhouse. Like the *National Barn Dance* and other such programs, Lauck and Goff's Friday night show included popular music as well as the string band, appealing to the broadest audience possible. In Indianapolis, for example, the tabernacle's large choir joined Stubby Gordon's Dance Orchestra, singer Irene Beasley ("the famous songbird of the South"), Chicago's Maple City Four, and other acts, all pitched justifiably as "famous stars of the air and of Broadway." When *Lum and Abner* expanded beyond WTAM to the network, NBC began funneling widely known stars from other programs to the sociable and testing promising performers whom the network was considering as potential anchors of new musical programs (trying out such performers on the show was a service that, in the absence of more reliable measures of the listening audience, provided one measure of the show's popularity and significance).[38]

Lum and Abner offered a mix of popular music, hillbilly music, and rube comedy designed to sate any midwesterner's listening appetite, but the duo's popularity also rested on a social transformation gripping the South and the Midwest. Southern whites migrated to midwestern (and northeastern) industrial cities in great numbers during the 1920s and 1930s. Often, families returned to the South after accumulating some savings or when jobs became scarce, only to return to northern cities later. Others moved to the city and stayed. These new urban dwellers maintained close ties to home, visiting often via newly improved roads, bus services, and their own automobiles, purchased in a flush of excitement when they became industrial wage earners. In their restlessness they would have spread the word about the radio programs they enjoyed; they were the foot soldiers who carried *Lum and Abner* into their home region. Close to their rural background, but perhaps sufficiently separated from it to allow for a twinge of nostalgia, these new urban midwesterners could use the program to weld together the disparate aspects of their modern life. Moreover, they made an excellent target group for the program's sponsor, Ford.[39] The sociable and the Midwest contributed in crucial ways to *Lum and Abner*'s gradual rise; however, the show soon appealed to an even more expansive audience.

Lum and Abner tapped into the deep-seated concerns of all Americans during the 1930s: the two comics gained a loyal audience by presenting an attractive vision of how to ameliorate rising national concern about community life. Sociologists were focusing attention on the evolution of community—particularly rural community—at the time that *Lum and Abner* emerged. In 1929 the Lynds had published their groundbreaking study of Middletown, and studies of not only specific communities but also the idea of community had a great deal of intellectual momentum in the early 1930s. Pointing out that the Great Depression had led many people to return to farms (in a nation that the 1920 census had revealed for the first time to be predominately urban), two sociologists in 1933 analyzed a hamlet in eastern Illinois to learn more about rural community life. Their conclusions seem rather idealistic, but the ideals run parallel to the imaginary community that Lauck and Goff were simultaneously creating. The scholars wrote, "The homogeneity of the people, the high moral standards, the religious idealism, and the firmly rooted mores and traditions are largely responsible for the solidarity of the community and the comparative absence of social maladjustment. The community is a primary group in the true sense of the term. The contacts are intimate and face-to-face, and the people identify themselves with the area. They are concerned about the welfare of their community and defend their institutions." In theory, small communities offered a vision of stability in a time of profound uncertainty: "The rural community, whether centered in a hamlet or a village, has a unity seldom found in city areas. It possesses the essential social and economic resources for possible independent existence if properly organized. However, modern conditions seldom permit a self-sufficient life. Rural communities with good schools, churches, recreation provisions, trade facilities, and the necessary governmental and welfare agencies can supply the main necessities of life and maintain the communal existence with little disorganization. The village is inseparable from the surrounding hinterland."[40]

Another rural theorist in 1932 enumerated similar components of a healthy rural community, again largely taking the Midwest and Northeast, *Lum and Abner*'s first important fan bases, as the norms. He explained, "The village community . . . saw the rise of institutions, the church, the school, the market, and it is the desire for these institutions which brings together the dispersed farmers. . . . The very isolation of the separate homesteads stimulates a desire for new forms of association, such as the grange, the lodge, the motion picture, the library, the coöperative association, which are possible only with more than a neighborhood constituency and which naturally arise at the common meeting point in the village."[41]

Ironically, in the South a group of intellectuals who steadfastly opposed sociological methods voiced a similar concern that the way of life in rural villages was under siege. "Twelve Southerners" centered around Vanderbilt University—including such writers as Robert Penn Warren, John Crowe Ransom, and Donald Davidson—published the anti-industrialist agrarian manifesto *I'll Take My Stand* in 1930. These so-called agrarians wailed plaintively, "How may the little agrarian community resist the Chamber of Commerce of its county seat, which is always trying to import some foreign industry that cannot be assimilated to the life-pattern of the community?"[42]

The shared longing for community provided little room for diversity of opinion and interest on fundamental questions. It was an appealing outlook for middle-class observers who were frightened in the early thirties by the depredations of big business, on the one hand, and the potential for lower-class radicalism, on the other. These were people who would also recall the frightening influx of foreign immigrants in the preceding decades. *Lum and Abner* captured the spirit of the times by providing a reassuring voice that creatively and warmly affirmed both stable rural life in an agricultural vein and a small-town Main Street existence. In a sense, Lauck and Goff straddled the divide between the agrarian idealists and the sociologists, finding fertile soil in the common ground of national concern about community life in troubled times. Although Lum and Abner constantly worked for the civic and commercial development of Pine Ridge, the earliest national reviews emphasized the rural authenticity Lauck and Goff brought to the airwaves. *Radio News* noted, "They claim to bring to their broadcasts the authentic color of the rural community in which they grew up together." The *New York Times* explained after an interview with Lauck that he had "lived close enough to the type of people he plays on the air to portray them realistically." In 1937 Lauck and Goff were still emphasizing their authenticity. Lauck told an interviewer, "The native friendliness of rural America is appealing in itself. The simple philosophy of the Arkansas hills, genuine and unadorned, is very interesting. . . . We make a serious effort to re-create living characters in the territory where we were born."[43]

Early in the show's development, Lauck and Goff briefly explored a dark, conflict-ridden source of comedy—the violence that was often a part of political life in their home region. In one series of episodes in 1932, Abner, the constable, is afraid to arrest Oscar Fields, a poverty-ridden local tough who Abner knows robbed Dick Huddleston's store. Huddleston eventually decides not to press charges because he feels sorry for Fields, thereby easing the class-based tension with paternalistic salve.[44]

In episodes later in the same year, Abner decides to run for sheriff of the county against incumbent Snake Hogan. Abner runs as a Demopublican in order to appeal to everyone. He and Lum make a campaign announcement on WABL, the "Voice of the Ouachitas" in the county seat; and they paint campaign slogans on a sandwich-board advertisement as well as on the side of a very large horse named John Doe. However, Abner learns that Hogan is not at all open to legitimate competition:

> Lum: They was a couple of fellers come out agin him onct and fore the lection come off, they both showed up a missin. Aint nobody run agin him since.
> Abner: Well what become of em, Lum?
> Lum: Thats the strange part about it, nobody ever knowed. They've never been seen or heard of since.

Abner responds by having his sandwich-board advertisement constructed of iron (he nicknames it Old Iron Sides). When Lum and Abner run a contest to determine Abner's campaign slogan, Snake Hogan enters: "Here lies Abner Peabody in his last restin place, / He made the mistake of runnin agin Snake Hogan in the sheriffs race." Snake eventually arrives to murder Abner, but Lum and Abner's young friend Cedric Weehunt saves the day by getting the drop on Snake with a shotgun. Abner later withdraws from the race after Snake Hogan offers him a bribe. Abner accepts only enough of it to pay a mortgage that Lum has taken in order to pay for Abner's campaign advertising; he thus saves Lum from losing his land. Lauck and Goff reworked this general plot during December 1933 and January 1934, but raw conflict would seldom recur as their source of comedy.[45]

At the nadir of the Great Depression, however, their show may have reflected a broader lack of faith in the integrity of politics and in government's capacity to aid far-flung hamlets like Pine Ridge.

Indeed, a great deal of political power in the rural South of the time did belong to the county-seat elites. Lauck and Goff's depiction of corrupt local politics drew on reality. Unable to change macro-level policy, their characters tried to better local conditions with pragmatic community leadership rather than with radical change. While deeply critical of corruption, their argument was ultimately a conservative one, based on the notion that government could do only so much. Keeping a farm trumped abstract political crusades.

In this early stage of the program, the lack of a sponsor allowed Lauck and Goff to address other controversial topics in addition to politics. On religion, for example, Abner complains at one point that he should go to church, but "hit jist looks like they's so many hypocrits in the church here of late I jist hate to attend." Likewise Lum and Abner scored corporations as they made arrangements to sell stock in their 14 Karet Gold Mining Company. In one episode Lum assures Abner that they will not share the profits with any stockholders they can get to support them: "Why thats all took up by the ossifers and pardners and sich as that. You see they deevide it all up twixt em and then if they got any left over why they jist raise all of ems salaries. Them that jist owns stock dont never git none of it." Many investors who were devastated by the crash of 1929 and the ensuing economic depression would surely have recognized these sentiments.[46]

Later, as their audience expanded and they became more skilled at subtle comedy, Lauck and Goff almost never addressed such potentially controversial subjects with an overtly critical voice. Religion nearly disappeared from the show, and politics never again involved so much violence. The community of Pine Ridge quickly became a broadly appealing model of the national self-image, a solid community of civic-minded entrepreneurs. To be popular (and lucrative), a radio program needed an affirmative outlook, and social and political critiques had to be offered gently. The promise of political change under a new presidential administration in 1933 may well have brought a somewhat brighter outlook to the show as well as to the nation.

In August 1932 Lauck and Goff released a short book that out-
lined the principal people and institutions of Pine Ridge. While
struggling to continue broadcasting on WBAP in Fort Worth, they
publicized the book on the air and sustained themselves with the
profits. *Lum and Abner and Their Friends from Pine Ridge* provides a blueprint to the permanent locale of their imagination. It
reveals a community in which anxious white Americans of the
Great Depression found stability and order that matched the most
idealistic hopes of specialists in rural sociology (and perhaps even
of the Vanderbilt agrarians). Lauck and Goff explain their characters' values in the foreword: "In times like these, when so many
of us are losing faith and becoming disillusioned, there is a great
lesson to be learned by turning to these purveyors of true Americanism for inspiration. Here is a people who are content to eke
out an existence and live their lives undaunted by the depression's
hardships that have filled the rest of the world with consternation.
The authors in writing of and portraying these characters desire
to picture to their readers and listeners a type of true American
citizenship that is being rapidly absorbed by our so-called modern
civilization." In describing Dick Huddleston's store and the office
housing the constable and justice of the peace, Lauck and Goff
construct the settings in which their Americanism can come to life.
At this stage of the program, Lum served as justice of the peace
and president of the school board, while Abner acted as constable.
In their office, "they often take recess from the treadmill of labor
to discuss the 'goins on' of the community."[47] But the real positive
authority of the community lay in Dick's store (and later the Jot
'Em Down Store, once Lum and Abner became merchants):

Dick's store is more than just a store; it is the hub of all activ-
ity in the community, a gathering place for those tired souls
who can find a few spare moments from their daily routine
to hear the news of the outside world. Here you may find
Lum and Abner and their friends, back by the stove near the
cracker barrel, discussing politics, "meetin' matters," how

best the Government should be run and many other grave and important questions of the day. Every Thursday the county weekly paper arrives and upon this occasion, Dick Huddleston reads aloud, to a group of attentive listeners, together, the news with comments and explanations. Many of the scenes in the daily episodes of Lum and Abner are laid within this old building.[48]

In describing the people of Pine Ridge, Lauck and Goff continued to project an illusion of verisimilitude. As one historian has explained (in reference to folk music), "middle-class Americans were drawn to people who seemed to exist outside the modern industrial world, able to survive independent of its inhumane economy and not lulled by its superficial luxuries." Profitable cultural productions needed to tap into this "cult of authenticity."[49] Oscar Plaster, a photographer in Mena, accompanied the two performers to the hamlet of Waters (about eighteen miles east of Mena), from which they had drawn the inspiration for many of the characters in the program. Goff's father had long been close to the real Dick Huddleston, who was a faithful customer of the elder Goff's wholesale house in Waters, and Lauck's father was also well acquainted with the rural storekeeper by virtue of traveling through Waters while in the lumber business. The younger Lauck and Goff had come to know Huddleston and the residents of the Waters area through their own business careers. Lauck and Goff asked local people to pose for the photographer Plaster and then used those photographs to illustrate the corresponding fictional residents of Pine Ridge. (Only Dick Huddleston's real name was used extensively on the program and in the book, a distinction that he would capitalize on later.) The list of Pine Ridge's residents closely parallels sociological compilations of the roles to be filled in a healthy rural community. Abner's wife Elizabeth "takes to work jist as willin as the ordinary run of wimen does to buyin a hat," and her work included not only doing farm chores but also keeping a meticulously clean home with flowers and "the best swept yard they are in the cammunity." The Huddlestons also earned respectability in both public and private arenas:

> If you was tryin to name the leader of the cammunity you wouldn't have to look no further'n Dick fer he's allus the first un to put his name down on anything that's better'n the cammunity and ginerally allus leads out at the casket makins. The Cirkit Rider ordinary puts up at his place twiset as long as he does anywhere else fer his woman sets as fine a board as abody ever drawed a chair to and is jist as hospital as can be. She takes a turible big hand in meetin matters and is the backbone of the missionary.

While Abner's daughter seemed likely to become a local school-teacher even without a college education, Dick's daughter had gone to college. Striving for respectability was a characteristic that marked Pine Ridge's leading citizens, and a sense of community betterment was essential to their standing.[50]

A number of other characters filled out the Pine Ridge community. Squire Skimp, whose self-seeking business schemes would always ensnare Lum and Abner (at least temporarily), came from Missouri, and the fact that he "aint lived in our cammunity long" was noteworthy. Grandpappy Spears, a long-winded but amiable storyteller and a crack combatant at checkers, and his saintly wife Aunt Charity, who was skilled at folk medicine and midwifery, remained fixtures on the program. Sister Simpson, the mostly good-hearted town busybody, would "leave her clothes in the warsh biler any time to go out and see how many signers she can git on a pititin to git a law passed to make everbody keep their cows and pigs shet up or sompin else equal as outlandish." Discussions of their roles in church established the presumption that even Pine Ridge roustabouts attended religious services. Perhaps the most pure-hearted character was the ever-present, somewhat dim (because he was "kicked in the head by a mule when he was a kid of a boy") young man named Cedric Weehunt, who could do all manner of chores and thus kept "turible busy a heppin thissen and thatten all over the cammunity."[51]

Lauck and Goff provided voices for Lum, Abner, Grandpappy, Squire, Dick, Cedric, and others. Women almost never appeared on the air, instead being vividly depicted through the men's conversations. Many early radio serials incorporated the gender conflicts of the 1930s, often leaving the resolution ambiguous, open to the interpretation of the listener. *Lum and Abner* simultaneously upheld and subverted conservative gender conventions. Elizabeth Peabody worked admirably hard not only at housecleaning but also at farm work, but she "never goes nowhar." Her place was at home, and while daughter Pearl might one day teach school for a while, she would "make some man a awful good companyon fer life." Veteran schoolteacher Evalena Schultz kept strict order in school, as expected, but she could undermine other small-town and rural assumptions about women's proper role: "They's some that claims that Evalener uses artyfishal favorin and cullorin to make herself look and smell so good but, be that as it may, she's bout as restful to the eye as any woman you'd want to see." She had power over the school-board members (including her sometimes-beau Lum), but the influence was based in part on her feminine appeal. She managed to maintain her position on the fine line of acceptability: "While she's got more book larnin than's good fer a woman to have in her head, she aint the least bit uppish in her ways like some is that's had a smart deal of eddication thataway." Squire Skimp's fetching daughter Bular also exercised some power as a model for women as consumers. "The only thing agin Bular a comin to Pine Ridge is, she's so stylish she's made a smart deal of the wimin fokes unsatisfyed with the clothes their men has been buyin em."[52] Listeners could choose how to interpret the women to whom the men gave voice—for example, whether to cheer Evalena's education or welcome Elizabeth's domestic virtue.

In 1937 Goff explained that he and Lauck were initially criticized for not including women characters to provide a "sex angle" on the show, but Goff provided a pragmatic reason behind the lack of women in speaking roles: "We were almost sold on the suggestion ourselves. For a solid week we auditioned every actress we could locate. They all sounded the same. That is to say, different. Different from the women of Pine Ridge. If the listeners accepted any of those characters as authentic, they'd simply have to believe that we were phonies." In a 1937 episode, temporary character Spud Gandel, a northeastern urbanite who ended up in Pine Ridge as a partner of Lum and Abner in a lunchroom, complains to Lum that it is a shame that local women have to do agricultural work. Lum explains to Gandel, "Whenever you hear somebody feelin sorry fer these wimen that hep their husbands scratch out a livin on these hillside farms around here, you can jist tell em they dont know what they're talkin about. If the truth was knowed nine times out of ten they're a heap happier'n them thats feelin sorry fer em." Again, this depiction of women could be seen as empowering working farmwives or as manipulatively voicing happiness for oppressed women. The exchange also reflects a certain frustration with the burgeoning literature of the 1930s by authors such as Erskine Caldwell, works that depicted the depravities and exploitation of southern poor farmers.[53]

The near absence of women also allowed Lum and Abner to maintain their manliness. Regular appearances by a woman character, particularly a strong, sensible one, would have left the two old men looking weak, rather than sympathetically comic. In situations such as their fearful encounters with Oscar Fields and Snake Hogan, Lum and Abner already walked the boundaries of acceptable manhood. They could be frightened of the toughs, however, as long as they could maintain face in the community, particularly with the women of Pine Ridge. Women and men in the listening audience for various episodes—especially urban migrants adjusting to new gender roles in industrial settings—might have laughed for different reasons as the two old characters sought to cover up fear, failure, or duplicity. Men struggling to earn a living likely found release in the dogged perseverance of Lum and Abner, while women might have found it easier to laugh at the failings of fictional men than at their own companions.

While women perhaps pushed at the limits of peaceful homogeneity in Pine Ridge, the presence of African Americans might have actually disrupted the community's cohesion in the ears of white radio listeners, who likely made up the bulk of the program's audience. Sociologists of the 1930s, at times using the racist assumptions then prevalent in much of academia, noted that racial repression had prevented the South from having the organic unity supposedly enjoyed by communities elsewhere. The plantation system and slavery had mandated a dispersed population with no middle class, a group "which is always the mainstay of community life." One northern social scientist noted in 1932 that "there has been small chance for the development of the community throughout the South," elaborating that "the possibilities of community life are most difficult in the Black Belt, where the whites are so outnumbered that there are too few of them to support local institutions, in the sense of a local area like a township." When white social scientists did turn to investigations of black community life, the academics still regarded blacks as a negative counterpoint to the normal, an ominous minor chord blaring into the harmony of American life. Gunnar Myrdal studied "the Negro community as a pathological form of an American community," for example. (Of course, black social scientists of the time, including the eminent Charles S. Johnson, studied black communities without starting from the same racist assumptions.)[54]

Lauck and Goff positioned their distinctively southern community as part of the national white mainstream by keeping it free of blacks. They could do so without departing from narrowly defined reality because their region of Arkansas—the Ouachita highlands—had a minuscule population of blacks in comparison to many southern subregions. In 1930, Polk County, which includes Mena, had a total population of 14,857, of whom 3 were African Americans. Neighboring Montgomery County, home to the hamlet of Waters near the Polk County line, had 136 blacks among its

10,768 residents. (For comparison, more than 18 percent of the 2.6 million residents of Arkansas were black.) A report on 1932 Mena noted that "for many years there have been no negro residents of the city, or in the adjacent territory." The writer considered the paucity of blacks to be due in part to an intimidating lynching that took place in Mena on February 20, 1901, only a few years after the railroad arrived and the town was created.[55] The topic of racial violence was easily avoided in homogeneous Pine Ridge, but violence as a political tool emerges in the scripts when a local tough gathers a mob and threatens to lynch Abner.

Lauck and Goff depicted a racial innocence that went beyond even whites' demographic dominance, however. In one early program Lum is filling out a standardized form:

> Lum: What nationality? Meanin I reckon if you're a indian or irshman or german or what.
> Abner: You aint nuthin air you?
> Lum: Nope, I'm jist a Arkansawer. I reckon though I ort to put somethin down ther to make it look right.
> Abner: Put down ther that yer a chinese.
> Lum: I dont look like no chinese. I'll jist say I'm a Arkansawer. Now lets see. Next un here is Race.
> Abner: Race?
> Lum: Yea, jist plain race. R A C E question mark.
> Abner: What kind a race they talkin bout foot racin or horse racin?
> Lum: I dont know I'm jist goin to set down "no" here.
> Abner: Read anothern.

Pine Ridge's purported racial homogeneity allowed Lauck and Goff to depict it as a community that met the fond hopes of whites in a segregated nation. As one feature writer remarked, "It might be anywhere between Maine and California."[56] At the same time, the hill country setting allowed listeners to regard Pine Ridge as a rustic, exotic locale. Lauck and Goff embraced the hillbilly label for the program but deftly undermined some of the negative, harmful aspects of this already-aged white stereotype.

In the early twentieth century, some Americans projected their own anxiety about urbanization onto a distorted fabrication—the southern hillbilly, seen as a degraded but authentic, natural man in a type of organic community that had virtually ceased to exist elsewhere. Novelists and reformers at the turn of the century saw in the southern mountains a population free of the worrisome qualities of immigrants and the weakness of urban dwellers. Frequently labeled as the contemporary ancestors of the rest of America, southern mountaineers became a topic of national fascination for their seeming ethnic purity and raw independence. Some hillbillies in early films were vicious beasts, but in other characterizations the figure was one of low comedy, a projection of broken social taboos about work, hygiene, and social conduct. The widespread seizure of the term *hillbilly* became ever more commercialized in the 1920s with the rise of hillbilly music (later called country music once the negative aspects of hillbilly imagery became limiting in the 1940s). National purveyors of the hillbilly image usually conflated the southern Appalachians and the Ozark Mountains of Arkansas and Missouri. Although the fictional Pine Ridge and its geographic counterparts lay in the little-noticed Ouachita Mountains, just south of the Ozarks, the power of the Ozark hillbilly image swept aside the distinction. Lum and Abner were "those Ozark hillbilly philosophers" to most of their listening public.[57]

Not until 1934 did the physical image of the mountaineer begin to take a standardized graphic form. In that year Paul Webb began his long-running series of *Esquire* magazine cartoons, *The Mountain Boys;* Billy DeBeck added Snuffy Smith to his *Barney Google* comic strip; and Al Capp began the famous *L'il Abner* comic strip. (One cannot be sure whether Capp, a New Yorker, adapted the name of his strip from *Lum and Abner*, which was already widely heard in the Northeast by July 1933.) From sources such as these, Americans came to see hillbillies as stooped men

with long beards (often in their underwear and carrying a moonshine jug and an old-fashioned rifle) and as frumpy, downtrod-
den older women or buxom, innocently sexual younger women.
Animal traits often marked these cartoon hillbillies at their more
primitive moments.[58]

Lum and Abner used the hillbilly figure, but they recast the hillbilly as a likable, forward-looking, still authentic, yet recognizably
American icon. The program redefined what it meant to be au-
thentically rural. Trained as a cartoonist, Lauck drew illustrations
of each character in the 1932 guide to the program. His cartoons
fit the program's overall theme of using the southern mountains
as a setting while simultaneously destabilizing the negative stereotypes that often went with that location. Lauck drew Lum as a
tall, slender, upright man, not at all like the degenerate hillbillies
stereotyped in L'il Abner and The Mountain Boys. Lum, as would
befit a man of civic importance and entrepreneurial instincts,
wears nice pants, a closed collar, and a vest. He sports only a long,
well-groomed mustache. The shorter Abner likewise dresses with
a closed collar and vest, and he has a small goatee. Squire Skimp
has similar clothing, but the addition of a watch chain alludes to
his desire for higher status. None have the flowing beards, decay-
ing clothing, slouched hats, and hunched postures that would soon
be de rigueur in hillbilly imagery. Likewise, the drawings of the
supporting characters in the 1932 booklet feature traits that are
more realistic. Farmers and laborers such as Cedric Weehunt wear
overalls, but they have clean-cut features. The accompanying photographs of Waters residents link the imagery and reality. All look
clean and respectable, with one exception, who modeled without
shoes (although the corresponding character, Ezra Seestrunk, is
written up positively as a fine fellow and "a class leader in Sunday skoole"). Lauck and Goff donned makeup and costumes for
the 1932 photographs and created an image that remained largely
consistent thereafter. They matched their cartoons and their mod-
els from Waters; both were well dressed and looked like fully the
respectable hamlet leaders they depicted—with shined shoes, col-

lars, vests, and slacks. Simultaneously, though, the dialect in which Lauck and Goff wrote the booklet and conducted the show tapped the sense of mountain exoticism, giving the program its regional flavor.

More forcefully than graphic images and photographs, the programs themselves craftily undermined national expectations of southern hillbillies. On one episode, as Abner relaxes with the newspaper, he overtly makes fun of the Snuffy Smith comic strip character: "Looky there. Him and his nabors is having a feud with one another. . . . I'll swan that Snuffy is the backwoodsiest somebody I ever seen in my life."[59] The tension between the stereotypes and the actual episodes accounts in part for the show's lasting popularity throughout the country. Lauck explained in 1937 that he and Goff tried "to make our program amusing through the situations we build up rather than through the ignorance or obtuseness of any character." Lauck posited that "the simple philosophy of the Arkansas hills, genuine and unadorned, is very interesting."[60] In Lauck and Goff's handling, that worldview took in many traits not normally associated with southern mountaineers. Despite the strong accents and humorous verbal idiocy, the plots of the program reveal a strong current of commercialism in the old storekeepers. Far from being lazy or out of step with modernity, Lum and Abner constantly sought new financial opportunities, many of them in complete harmony with the latest American trends. And even though the ventures often resulted in hilarious missteps, the old fellows' motivated, boosterish outlook flies in the face of conventional wisdom about hillbillies. Investigating those comic entrepreneurial ventures uncovers some often-ignored aspects of the relationship between popular culture and rural imagery.

Only recently have historians extensively explored the beginnings of tourism in the rural South. They have found that civic boosters and business-oriented promoters pushed tourism even before World War II, in areas far beyond the typical destinations of Florida and the newly formed national parks in the Appalachians. Although tourism would work its greatest economic transformations following 1945, health resorts had long attracted streams of visitors from distant points. The Ozarks Playground Association, for example, had formed in Eureka Springs, Arkansas, in 1919 with the guidance of a Rotary club.[61] Lauck and Goff had a specimen of tourism just outside Mena as well. The town of Mena had begun with the construction of a railroad through the area in the 1890s, and in June 1898 the railroad owner opened the Queen Wilhelmina Inn as a health resort atop nearby Rich Mountain. Although the business was abandoned by the 1930s, the building remained, and local people had not forgotten its significance.[62] Lauck and Goff quickly introduced the idea of tourism into their series. On the Friday Night Sociable, Lum and Abner accounted for the presence of Hollywood and Broadway stars at a Pine Ridge function by depicting them as guests at the local resort hotel.[63] In episodes from September 1933 the two old fellows help their friend Grandpappy Spears make plans to develop the health-giving potential of the water from a spring on his farm and to avoid the schemes of two devious competitors.[64] And scripts from July 1934 show Lum and Abner themselves running the Mountain View Hotel in addition to their store (and dealing with the comic complications provided by a gang of jewel thieves hiding out at the hotel).[65]

Moreover, in the 1930s, national images of rural southerners and hillbillies certainly did not acknowledge the extent to which the oil business had affected some areas of the southern states. Lauck and Goff, however, worked this progressive side of the southern economy into their plots. The most famous oil discovery in the South came in 1901 at the Spindletop gusher near Beaumont, Texas, but additional large deposits of oil were found in the 1920s in various southern locales, including Oklahoma, Louisiana, and southwest Arkansas, only a few dozen miles from Mena and Waters. Prospectors even drilled test wells in Mena, although they found no oil.[66] With this business boom in mind, Lauck and Goff added an oil craze to the program in late 1934 and early 1935. Naturally, the oil found in Pine Ridge bubbled up only because a local resident had drilled into a pipeline that had been buried in the area years earlier. Despite the comic outcome, though, listeners would have become more aware of the excitement for such modern business opportunities in the rural trans-Mississippi region.[67]

While Lum and Abner's bumbling natures and outlandish verbal humor made the series lively and a bit exotic for many Americans, Lauck and Goff nonetheless kept Pine Ridge in the national mainstream in ways beyond oil and tourism. With the store as their central concern, they branched into various other (always comic) money-making enterprises during the program's early years, including a matrimonial bureau, selling flashlights, and distributing shares (in conjunction with Squire Skimp) to develop a silver mine in Arizona.[68] At other times they created the Polk County Rubber Company (to market Abner's rubber recipe of "sweet gum and stretch-berries and pine rosen and a little bit of tar") and the 14 Karet Gold Mining Company, which did not pan out.[69] The humor of the program came through their struggles to survive the trickery of various schemers, including local ones such as Squire Skimp, outsiders with dubious motives, and Lum's own fiscal braggadocio. Naturally, Lum and Abner always landed on their feet in one way or another. Sometimes their businesses involved visibly modern cultural undertakings. In 1935, for instance, they opened a movie theater (it later burned down). In the 1930s a movie house helped define a small town as being in step with modernity, and large circuses still traveled the railroads throughout the country, bringing wonders and spectacles even to small towns. A circus passing through Pine Ridge ended up under the ownership of Lum and Abner, who operated it with the help of Squire Skimp for a time in Pine Ridge and surrounding towns. And in 1936 Lum and Abner accidentally developed a new pesticide that effectively treated the infestation of boll weevils attacking southern cotton plants. Modern chemical pesticides were a dream of agricultural progressives at the time and would later aid the transition to post–World War II agribusiness.

In these plotlines, economic reality, commercial desires, and mass culture merged in unexpected ways.[70]

Commerce, civic interest, and popular culture combined even more explicitly in an unusual event that brought a fictional construct to life. Pine Ridge became a real place. In April 1936 Lauck and Goff received an unprecedented endorsement of their program's popularity and authenticity. In January of that year, Dick Huddleston, the real-life storekeeper in Waters, began a drive to change his community's name to Pine Ridge. Huddleston might have gotten the idea on Christmas Eve and Christmas Day 1935, when he hosted gatherings at a local church to listen to *Lum and Abner*'s annual Christmas broadcast and to distribute gifts to needy members of the community (made possible by a sizable gift from an anonymous donor). The community's imagination had clearly incorporated the on-air Pine Ridge quite fully by then. The Christmas episode of that year attracted national attention because the birth of a child in a barn in the Waters area (the couple's house had burned) paralleled some of the show's plotline, including the child's family name. The news report noted, "Lum and Abner themselves did not know they were dramatizing the truth until Dick Huddleston, the general storekeeper in Waters, wrote them about the true-life advent of the little Garrett son. It was then that the amazing parallelism between a radio prophecy and reality came to light. It made Lum and Abner gasp, but there was the birth certificate to prove Dick Huddleston's letter."[71]

Early in the new year, Huddleston and "upwards of 400" other area residents signed a petition asking federal postal officials to change the name of the local post office (the community was not incorporated, so only the postal designation needed to be changed). With assistance from the area's congressional representative, Ben Cravens (and possibly William Horlick, head of *Lum and Abner*'s sponsor, Horlick's Malted Milk Corporation), Huddleston and the petitioners received their wish. On April 26, 1936, the fifth anniversary of the program's debut, a crowd of thousands gathered in front of the state capitol in Little Rock to witness Governor J. Marion Futrell lead a ceremony marking the name change. NBC broadcast the event around the country, the Hot Springs Chamber of Commerce provided a birthday cake, and Futrell declared Lum and Abner Day throughout Arkansas. The governor praised Lauck and Goff lavishly, hoping that the name change "would show in part that Arkansas truly appreciates the work of these two boys of ours." Goff relished the moment, recalling that not long before, he had been selling groceries to Huddleston. He gushed, "During the five years that we've been on the air we have always felt that the audience here in Arkansas was right along with us all the time."[72]

Renaming Waters required both civic and governmental endorsement of Lauck and Goff's imaginary postage stamp of soil. In 1941 a writer for the Federal Writers' Project of the Work Projects Administration succinctly described Pine Ridge and its close relationship with *Lum and Abner*: "The name of PINE RIDGE . . . (840 alt., 45 pop.), results from the fact that the town is an example of life imitating art. . . . As the genuinely Arkansan and the conventionally vaudevillian were blended on the Lum [and] Abner program, so the actual mountain town of Waters attempted to adapt itself to the traditional Broadway conception of the Arkansas hill country. Tourists were interested; the village's backwardness became a commercial asset. Eventually, the process reached its climax when the people of Waters changed their town's name to Pine Ridge." The writer also pointed out that the name change did not exhaust local enthusiasm:

> The self-consciousness of Pine Ridge manifests itself at the village's edge in such signs as "Drive Keerful," "Don't Hit Our Young'uns," and "You-all Hurry Back"—locutions which nearly all Arkansas hill people use daily but would never dream of putting in print. The weather-beaten crossroads store, otherwise like hundreds of others, sells souvenir photographs, knives, pipes, and pottery, along with the customary lamp wicks, soap kettles, work shoes, women's

dresses, and harness. Dick Huddleston, the proprietor and a leading figure in the broadcasts, keeps a register of all visitors. A few dozen yards away on the Ouachita is a tourist camp and fishing lodge, with rowboats named for Lum and Abner and their characters.

Lauck and Goff's hometown of Mena (population four thousand), the county seat frequently mentioned in the program, also worked to capitalize on their fame. The town erected two large signs, labeling itself "The Home of Lum and Abner." Lauck and Goff kept close ties there in the 1930s—for example, by donating to the local hospital. (Listeners from around the nation likewise sought the commercial and community benefits of the program by naming businesses after the Jot 'Em Down Store. In September 1937 Lauck and Goff granted permission for the name to be used for what was reportedly "the 100th real grocery store in America bearing the name coined by the comics.")[73]

The strategic repositioning of the town reflects the parallel values demonstrated by the *Lum and Abner* characters and the residents of Arkansas and Pine Ridge.[74] Lum and Abner constantly sought to advance both their own interests and the civic good of the imaginary Pine Ridge. In the written descriptions of the program, Lauck and Goff portrayed in a positive light those characters who kept the community's well-being foremost in mind. Governor Futrell pursued similar goals by publicizing Arkansas's 1936 state centennial during the renaming ceremony in Little Rock, and the Arkansas Centennial Commission helped to sponsor the broadcast of the renaming. Along comparable lines, the real Dick Huddleston used his moment in the limelight to invite listeners on NBC to tour Arkansas and the new Pine Ridge: "I want to take this opportunity to extend to you an invitation sometime when you're traveling down through our mountain country over the good roads the highway department are improving for us to take time to visit Pine Ridge and view some of the scenery that's in our wonderful Ouachita National Forest and catch a few of those bass that are so plentiful in our beautiful mountain streams."[75]

Huddleston, who owned a fishing camp with tourist cabins in addition to his store, would later become known as the state's goodwill ambassador. He hosted a continual stream of visitors to Pine Ridge, and before World War II, with the support of Lauck and Goff, he toured nationally with country music bands and performers from Pine Ridge as a way to promote the area's tourist potential as well as the program. According to a news report in July 1937, "There were 212 visitors in Pine Ridge the past week from the following states: Oklahoma, Kansas, Ohio, Texas, Georgia, Louisiana, Alabama, Mississippi, Kentucky, Missouri, Rhode Island, New Mexico, California, Arizona, Michigan and Illinois." Huddleston would sometimes be on the road for months at a time with the Pine Ridge Silver Cornet Band (named for a band on the program that supported Lum's bid for president in 1936 on the Demopublican ticket); and the Midwest received especially intensive coverage because of its particular potential for tourism in Arkansas. One Indiana woman wrote to the Mena newspaper after seeing Huddleston and the group, "He is really doing a big thing up here, appearing with a fine 'show,' and you folks down there are going to reap the benefits in increased good-will, interest and visitors to your good state, Arkansas." Huddleston concluded in 1960 that his stage show had performed at nearly 150 state and county fairs around the nation. On one occasion he even addressed the state legislature of Indiana. Huddleston's daughter recalled that *Lum and Abner* paid half of Huddleston's salary on these trips (and Lauck and Goff sometimes joined the stage shows), while the state of Arkansas paid the other half.[76]

Arkansans were acutely aware of the need to improve the state's national image. A *Vanity Fair* writer in 1933 snidely reported, "When the tide of civilization swept westward it detoured Arkansas."[77] Clearly many people believed that *Lum and Abner* could help to better the nation's outlook on the duo's home state. Even on its road maps, the state of Arkansas officially welcomed the good publicity from *Lum and Abner*. The highway commission noted in October 1936, "While we Arkansans bitterly resented Opie Read's 'Arkansas Hill Billy' stories, we have listened to the dramatization of our mountaineer characters by Lum and Abner with amused interest and even appreciation."[78] One listener explained in 1936: "The boys have never changed the basic idea of their act, which is to portray characters that they have known in real life and love. They guard against anything that might be construed by anybody as ridicule of their characters."[79] In contrast, Bob Burns, another famous Arkansas comic, earned cheap laughs by playing up the negative vision of hillbillies. Most Arkansans understood the sometimes subtle difference. A native of Van Buren (in the Ozarks) who was educated as a civil engineer, Burns turned a mediocre career in show business, including blackface, vaudeville, and carnival work, into stardom in January 1936, when he joined Bing Crosby in Hollywood as a full-time member of the cast of Crosby's *Kraft Music Hall* show. (Burns was down to only fifty dollars in resources in the summer of 1935, but he earned four hundred thousand dollars in 1937.) He played the bazooka, a primitive musical instrument that he had invented, and revived the Arkansas Traveler, an itinerant outsider relating tall tales of primitive locals whom he encountered in the state. This not-so-complimentary figure had long been a part of Arkansas's backwoods image, and Burns employed the stereotype while spinning yarns about outlandish (and fictional) hillbilly relatives back home—characters such as Aunt Doody, Uncle Slug, and Grandpa Snazzy. With Paramount, he also made four films with like themes between 1937 and 1940. From 1941 until 1947 he had his own hit weekly show as the Arkansas Traveler and made additional movies. He quickly became known as the Ozark Sage.[80]

Those allegedly picturesque folks back in Arkansas responded with mixed emotions. Van Buren, Burns's hometown, embraced him with civic pride and used his popularity to appeal to tourists. The town's Junior Chamber of Commerce published a promotional pamphlet purporting to be "an approved guide to the Bob Burns country." It led visitors to Burns's boyhood home and announced that "all paved highways in the Southwest lead to the Bob Burns and Arkansas Traveler country."[81] The rest of Arkansas had a more ambivalent view. One person recalled to Chester Lauck that his generation "appreciated your and Mr. Goff's characterizations of rural Arkansas (although many of us felt that Bob Burns was making fun of us, instead of laughing with us)." A writer with the Work Projects Administration detected an undercurrent of resentment toward Burns, noting that "some Arkansans feel that Burns does the State a disservice in helping to perpetuate the fable of the hill-billy in connection with it."[82] A number of letters written to the *Little Rock Arkansas Gazette* in 1936 also took Burns to task for perpetuating negative images of Arkansas hillbillies. For a special centennial issue of the newspaper the same year, the Piggly Wiggly grocery store chain ran an ad assuring readers and visitors that "all those stories that Bob Burns tells on Bing Crosby's program aren't true."[83] The mixed response to Burns simply underscores the firmer ideological connections between the *Lum and Abner* characters and their audience, which resulted in consistent local and national acclaim for the program. Rural radio listeners clearly valued more than the rube comedy. Real concerns and mass culture mingled in the dialogue between Lauck and Goff and their many fans back home and across the nation.

The renaming celebration in April 1936 marked the early stage of Lauck and Goff's period of greatest renown. Their plotlines subsequently followed a stable course, sometimes even repeating ideas from the earliest period of the show, and the program's fan base remained solid until the explosive growth of television in the years following World War II. In January 1937, Lauck and Goff, like many radio stars, moved with their families from Chicago to Hollywood, once NBC began radio production there. In July 1937 the readers of the popular *Radio Guide* voted Lauck and Goff in fourth place among comedians in a national vote to select the "Star of Stars" (Lauck and Goff trailed only Jack Benny, Eddie Cantor, and Milton Berle, and they were ahead of Fred Allen, the

Amos 'n' Andy duo, and George Burns and Gracie Allen). The pair continued to write all their own scripts until March 1940, when they temporarily suspended the radio series to make the first of six movies that they would release by 1946. Returning to the air in May 1941, they hired scriptwriters as they juggled radio, films, and stardom.[84]

Only gradually did *Lum and Abner* decline in quality and popularity. Through the war and several years thereafter, Lauck and Goff enjoyed considerable celebrity; like most network stars, they supported various wartime government propaganda efforts, which reinforced their place before the public eye.[85] Fan magazines featured details about their holiday parties and Lauck's hobby as the owner of racehorses. Both families bought large ranches to enjoy (and to keep alive their rural ties). As their popularity slipped with the advent of television, Lauck and Goff worked vigorously to keep the program on the air. They varied networks and time slots, briefly brought back their variety format, and used syndication. After a gap from April 1950 to February 1953, during which they created television pilots (filmed in Yugoslavia), they stayed on the air until May 1954. Goff's chronic health problems and the generally poor quality of the television pilots doomed their hopes to enter early television (although as late as 1962 the ABC network seriously considered reviving *Lum and Abner* as a series for the small screen). The three half-hour pilot episodes were cobbled together as their seventh and last film in 1955. Goff retired in California (although he did some real-estate development and made guest appearances on *Lum and Abner*'s spiritual heirs, *The Andy Griffith Show* and *Gomer Pyle, USMC*). Lauck sold his ranch in Nevada and moved to Houston to work for Continental Oil Company. He traveled widely as a speaker (often on pro-business political themes) and did advertisements (as Lum) for Conoco until retiring to Hot Springs, his wife's hometown, in 1967. Goff died in 1978, and Lauck followed in 1980.[86] Although their program retained a small, loyal following in syndication, their once-obvious appeal—an important part of the intellectual and cultural history of rural America—had grown obscure by the time of their deaths.

Lauck and Goff had entertained radio listeners at a peculiar moment in time, an era when economic depression forced Americans to think hard about the contrast between the nation's prized rural past and its comparatively bleak rural present. The rural dwellers of the 1930s and 1940s had to come to terms with their demographic decline and America's ever-growing commercial popular culture, which generally emanated from flourishing urban centers. Foreign-language and ethnic radio stations eased immigrants' entry into the dominant urban culture. *Amos 'n' Andy* on the radio, films by black directors like Oscar Micheaux, and so-called race records by black artists helped blacks, who were caught up in migrating to cities, to adjust to their new surroundings and, not incidentally, to become consumers of popular culture. *Lum and Abner* nourished many white rural Americans during the same transition. Even as their lives were alternately romanticized and vilified, they began to immerse themselves in America's popular culture, changing it and being changed by it, accepting it, yet resisting some of its messages. Urban listeners, on the other hand, could appreciate an on-air rural life that gave the lie to the stereotypical depictions prevalent at the time. Huddled before their radios in townhouses, farmhouses, and cabins alike, millions of listeners listened to the same broadcasts, but what they heard in the stories reflected their perspective on rural America.

NOTES

1. Surviving episodes of the program have been broadcast in syndication since the 1960s. Much of early radio in general has been preserved only through the work of fans, amateur historians, and former participants. In 1984 fans formed the National Lum and Abner Society (NLAS), which meets most years in Mena, Arkansas, and publishes four issues (six until recently) per year of the *Jot 'Em Down Journal* (hereafter *JEDJ*), featuring interviews, reprinted original material, and carefully researched popular articles on every aspect of the program. The NLAS also has col-

lected and published a number of the program's scripts, and the organization provides cassette copies of all programs for which recordings are known to exist, with the exception of the four episodes from July 28 and 31 and August 1 and 2, 1933, which are in the NBC Radio Collection of the Motion Picture, Broadcasting, and Recorded Sound Division, Library of Congress, Washington, D.C. The most complete collection of scripts belongs to Duncan McCoy, a private collector in Houston, Texas, who has the only extant copies of most of the scripts from 1932 through 1935. He has graciously allowed me to use them in my research and to copy the ones reproduced in this book. Citations hereinafter will refer to the McCoy collection when appropriate.

2. On the challenge of understanding the reaction of mass audiences to cultural works, see Gregory A. Waller, "Hillbilly Music and Will Rogers: Small-town Picture Shows in the 1930s," in *American Movie Audiences: From the Turn of the Century to the Early Sound Era*, ed. Melvyn Stokes and Richard Maltby (London: BFI Publishing, 1999), 164–79; Lawrence W. Levine, "The Folklore of Industrial Society: Popular Culture and Its Audiences," *American Historical Review* 97 (December 1992): 1369–99; and Kristine M. McCusker, "'Dear Radio Friend': Listener Mail and the *National Barn Dance*, 1931–1941," *American Studies* 39 (Summer 1998): 173–95.

3. Classic studies of radio history include Erik Barnouw, *A History of Broadcasting in the United States: A Tower in Babel, Volume 1—to 1933* (New York: Oxford University Press, 1966); Barnouw, *A History of Broadcasting in the United States: The Golden Web, Volume II—1933 to 1953* (New York: Oxford University Press, 1968); J. Fred MacDonald, *Don't Touch That Dial! Radio Programming in American Life, 1920–1960* (Chicago: Nelson-Hall, 1979); Arthur F. Wertheim, *Radio Comedy* (New York: Oxford University Press, 1979); and Wertheim, "Relieving Social Tensions: Radio Comedy and the Great Depression," *Journal of Popular Culture* 10 (Winter 1976): 501–19. See also a special issue devoted to radio by the *Journal of Popular Culture* 12 (Fall 1979); and Félix F. Gutiérrez and Jorge Reina Schement, *Spanish-Language Radio in the Southwestern United States* (Austin: Center for Mexican American Studies, University of Texas, 1979), chap. 1. MacDonald and Wertheim tend to characterize 1930s programs as diversionary relief and a source of order and affirmation for Americans beset by the Great Depression. Only in the last decade or so have scholars moved beyond the few pioneering narratives of radio history that broadly blazed the way in the 1960s and 1970s. Recent writers hear even more in these shows. For example, Melvin Patrick Ely explored the racial subtleties of the *Amos 'n' Andy*

program and Americans' reactions to it. Ely, *The Adventures of Amos 'n' Andy: A Social History of an American Phenomenon*, rev. ed. (1991; repr., Charlottesville: University Press of Virginia, 2001). Susan J. Douglas, Michele Hilmes, Margaret T. Mcfadden, and Mary Murphy have pushed toward an understanding of the gendered dimension of 1930s programming, while they and others have also situated radio in the context of American capitalism and national identity during the Great Depression. See Douglas, *Listening In: Radio and the American Imagination, from Amos 'n' Andy and Edward R. Murrow to Wolfman Jack and Howard Stern* (New York: Times Books, 1999), esp. chap. 5; Hilmes, *Hollywood and Broadcasting: From Radio to Cable* (Urbana: University of Illinois Press, 1990); Hilmes, *Radio Voices: American Broadcasting, 1922–1952* (Minneapolis: University of Minnesota Press, 1997); McFadden, "'America's Boy Friend Who Can't Get a Date': Gender, Race, and the Cultural Work of the Jack Benny Program, 1932–1946," *Journal of American History* 80 (June 1993): 113–34; McFadden, "'Anything Goes': Gender and Knowledge in the Comic Popular Culture of the 1930s" (doctoral dissertation, Yale University, 1996); and Murphy, *Mining Cultures: Men, Women, and Leisure in Butte, 1914–1941* (Urbana: University of Illinois Press, 1997), chap. 6. Immigration historians and scholars of country music have begun to tease out the local and regional specificity of the medium. On immigrants and mass culture, including radio, see Lizabeth Cohen, *Making a New Deal: Industrial Workers in Chicago, 1919–1939* (Cambridge: Cambridge University Press, 1990), chap. 3; and George J. Sánchez, *Becoming Mexican American: Ethnicity, Culture, and Identity in Chicano Los Angeles, 1900–1945* (New York: Oxford University Press, 1993), chap. 8. On radio, country music, and the South, see Pamela Grundy, "From *Il Trovatore* to the Crazy Mountaineers: The Rise and Fall of Elevated Culture on WBT-Charlotte, 1922–1930," *Southern Cultures* 1 (Fall 1994): 51–74; Grundy, "'We Always Tried to Be Good People': Respectability, Crazy Water Crystals, and Hillbilly Music on the Air, 1933–1935," *Journal of American History* 81 (March 1995): 1591–620; Jacquelyn Dowd Hall, James Leloudis, Robert Korstad, Mary Murphy, Lu Ann Jones, and Christopher B. Daly, *Like a Family: The Making of a Southern Cotton Mill World*, rev. ed. (1987; repr., New York: W. W. Norton and Company, 1989), chap. 5; and Bill C. Malone, *Country Music, U.S.A.*, rev. ed., (1968; repr., Austin: University of Texas Press, 1985), chaps. 2–4. The field has begun to mature further as a number of young scholars have settled on topics related to radio broadcasting. See the many fine essays in Michele Hilmes and Jason Loviglio, eds., *Radio Reader: Essays in the Cultural History of Radio* (New York: Routledge, 2002).

4. One study narrowed the focus from radio ownership across the states generally to ownership in rural areas in particular. Conducted in October and November 1937, it found that nearly half of American families lived in rural areas (i.e., in communities with less than 2,500 people). The researchers divided the country into nine districts. The percentage of rural families owning radios was lowest in the East South Central (51 percent), West South Central (52 percent), and South Atlantic (54 percent) regions. Next lowest was the Mountain region at 72 percent. See "Radio Still Has 60% of the Country to Sell," *Business Week*, December 9, 1931, 12; "Rural America's Receivers: National Networks' Question Unearths Gigantic Market," *Newsweek*, March 6, 1939, 29–30; Edgar A. Schuler, *Survey of Radio Listeners in Louisiana* (Baton Rouge: General Extension Division, Louisiana State University, 1943), 60–61; and Steve Craig, "How America Adopted Radio: Demographic Differences in Set Ownership Reported in the 1930–1950 U.S. Censuses," *Journal of Broadcasting and Electronic Media* 48 (June 2004): 179–95. For a detailed study of one southern station, see C. Joseph Pusateri, *Enterprise in Radio: WWL and the Business of Broadcasting in America* (Washington, D.C.: University Press of America, 1980). Older fact-filled chronicles tracing the growth of radio broadcasting in the region include Wesley Herndon Wallace, "The Development of Broadcasting in North Carolina, 1922–1948" (doctoral dissertation, Duke University, 1962); and Barnwell Rhett Turnipseed III, "The Development of Broadcasting in Georgia, 1922–1959" (master's thesis, University of Georgia, 1960). Both Wallace and Turnipseed took part in the early radio industry. See also the excellent essay by Derek Vaillant, "Bare-Knuckled Broadcasting: Enlisting Manly Respectability and Racial Paternalism in the Battle against Chain Stores, Chain Stations, and the Federal Radio Commission on Louisiana's KWKH, 1924–33," *Radio Journal* 1, no. 3 (2004): 193–211.

5. *Variety*, February 9, 1932, 52. See also Ronald R. Kline, *Consumers in the Country: Technology and Social Change in Rural America* (Baltimore: Johns Hopkins University Press, 2000), chap. 4.

6. E. E. Horine, "At Last! Practical Farm Radio," *Radio News* 15 (February 1934): 462–63, 507; and "Rural Radio: The Editor—To You," *Radio News* 15 (January 1934): 389 (quotation).

7. *Variety*, September 22, 1931, 60; April 5, 1932, 58; April 26, 1932, 50; and August 16, 1932, 42. Also "Lum and Abner: Attack of the Clones," four-part series, *JEDJ* 19 (October 2002): 9–12; 19 (December 2002): 7–9; 19 (April 2003): 4–6; and 20 (August 2003): 7–8.

8. Katharine S. Melvin, "Lula Vollmer," in *Dictionary of North Carolina Biography*, ed. William S. Powell (Chapel Hill: University of North

Carolina Press, 1996), 6:100–101; *Cleveland Plain Dealer*, January 16, 1933, 8; and January 21, 1933, 17; and *Variety*, March 18, 1931, 76 (quotation). On Vollmer's plays, see Michael D. Coon, "From *Sun-Up* to *Moonshine and Honeysuckle*: The Theater of Lula Vollmer" (master's thesis, Texas A&M University–Commerce, 1999).

9. Douglas, *Listening In*, 136–37; Paul F. Lazarsfeld, *Radio and the Printed Page: An Introduction to the Study of Radio and Its Role in the Communication of Ideas* (New York: Duell, Sloan and Pearce, 1940), 22 (first quotation); Richard James Hurley, "Movie and Radio—Friend and Foe," *English Journal* 26 (March 1937): 210 (second quotation); Margaret Heaton, "The Foreground of the American Scene," *English Journal* 27 (April 1938): 339 (third quotation); Harrison B. Summers, comp., *A Thirty-Year History of Programs Carried on National Radio Networks in the United States, 1926–1956* (Columbus: Ohio State University Press, 1958), 54, 62, 69, 77, 86.

10. Susan Smulyan, *Selling Radio: The Commercialization of American Broadcasting, 1920–1934* (Washington, D.C.: Smithsonian Institution Press, 1994).

11. For an interesting primer on the importance of the gemeinschaft notion, see Steven Brint, "Gemeinschaft Revisited: A Critique and Reconstruction of the Community Concept," *Sociological Theory* 19 (March 2001): 1–23.

12. David B. Danbom, *Born in the Country: A History of Rural America* (Baltimore: Johns Hopkins University Press, 1995), chaps. 8 and 9; William L. Bowers, *The Country Life Movement in America, 1900–1920* (Port Washington, N.Y.: Kennikat Press, 1974); Kline, *Consumers in the Country*; Janet Galligani Casey, "'This Is Your Magazine': Domesticity, Agrarianism, and *The Farmer's Wife*," *American Periodicals* 14, no. 2 (2004): 179–211; Samuel A. McReynolds, "Eugenics and Rural Development: The Vermont Commission on Country Life's Program for the Future," *Agricultural History* 71 (Summer 1997): 300–329; and Louis H. Palmer III, "Pathologized Subjects: Southern Gothic, White Trash, and the Discourse of 'Race' in the 1930's" (doctoral dissertation, Syracuse University, 1998).

13. Lauck to Lee Coggins, June 25, 1973, Chet Lauck Collection, Archives and Special Collections, Ottenheimer Library, University of Arkansas at Little Rock (hereafter Lauck Collection) (quotation); "Biography on Lum and Abner," April 22, 1946, Lauck Collection; and *Mena Weekly Star*, January 15, 1931, 1. Lauck recalled walking two miles to school each day in Alleene in 1908. Lauck to S. D. Cook, February 24, 1972, Lauck Collection. For context, see George W. Balogh, *Entrepreneurs in*

the Lumber Industry: Arkansas, 1881–1963 (New York: Garland Publishing, 1995).

14. "Biography on Lum and Abner," April 22, 1946 (quotation); "Chester H. Lauck" (typewritten, undated two-page biography); Lauck to Alvin S. Moody, January 17, 1967; Lauck to A. J. Taylor, May 29, 1958; Lauck to Ernie Deane, January 31, 1974; and Lauck to Thelma Keith Streeter, April 23, 1973—all in Lauck Collection. Also "Lum and Abner," *Magazine of Sigma Chi,* October 1935, 23–25; Bill Lewis, "Chet Lauck Keeps Trying to Retire," *Little Rock Arkansas Gazette,* May 10, 1970, 5E, clipping in Lauck Collection; Betty Wood, "Laucks Look at Golden Years of Hollywood," *Little Rock Arkansas Democrat,* February 6, 1977, clipping in Lauck Collection; and *Mena Weekly Star,* December 18, 1930, 2.

15. *Mena Weekly Star,* March 5, 1931, 1, 7; and March 12, 1931, 1 (quotation).

16. *Mena Weekly Star,* April 23, 1931, 3; April 30, 1931, 3; May 7, 1931, 1; May 14, 1931, 1; May 28, 1931, 3, 5; June 25, 1931, 3; and July 9, 1931, 3. Also see David B. Kesterson, "A Visit with Radio Humorist Chester Lauck (Lum Edwards)," *Studies in American Humor* 3 (January 1977): 146 (quotations); and Ray Poindexter, *Arkansas Airwaves* (North Little Rock, Ark.: privately printed, 1974), 104–6. The *Mena Weekly Star,* December 24, 1931, 1, describes KTHS as "the 10,000 watt community broadcaster operated by the Chamber of Commerce for the purpose of boosting Hot Springs and the state of Arkansas."

17. *Variety,* July 21, 1931, 57 (first quotation); and *Mena Weekly Star,* May 14, 1931, 1 (second quotation). For later examples of Lauck and Goff exploiting the comic potential of visiting the city, see the scripts from March 7–16, 1932, describing a trip to Kansas City (McCoy collection), and the scripts from February 10–14, 1936, describing a visit to New York City, in *The Lum and Abner Scripts: February 1936* (Birmingham, Ala.: National Lum and Abner Society, 1994).

18. *Chicago Daily News,* August 30, 1935, clipping in Lauck Collection (first quotation); *Mena Weekly Star,* July 23, 1931, 1; and August 6, 1931, 5; and "Lum (Chester Lauck) Remembers Lum and Abner," *Inner-View Magazine,* August 1978, clipping in Lauck Collection (second and third quotations). On the openness of radio to new talent via auditions, see Samuel Kaufman, "Radio's Road to Fame," *Radio News* 15 (July 1933): 7–9, 54. On Lauck and Goff's audition, see also *Chicago Daily Tribune,* July 7, 1935, W4. On their initial broadcasts, they offered a spoon from Quaker as a free gift to listeners, a usual Quaker gambit, and a company-record seventeen thousand responses flooded in. See *Mena Weekly Star,* September 3, 1931, 5.

19. On this stage of their progress, see *Mena Weekly Star*, July 23, 1931, 1; August 13, 1931, 3; August 6, 1931, 5; August 20, 1931, 4; October 1, 1931, 1, 3; November 5, 1931, 3; November 12, 1931, 3; December 31, 1931, 3; February 18, 1932, 5; April 7, 1932, 1; April 28, 1932, 2; June 23, 1932, 3; July 28, 1932, 3, and December 1, 1932, 3. Also *Dallas Morning News*, September 26, 1931, 5; September 27, 1931, sec. 3, 8; September 28, 1931, 5 (first quotation); October 10, 1931, 4; October 13, 1931, 5; October 19, 1931, 5; December 25, 1931, 5; January 19, 1932, 5; and September 8, 1932, 11; and *Chicago Daily News*, January 12, 1932, 27 (second quotation). On their appeal to their listeners, see the script for June 2, 1932, in the McCoy collection. Also see *JEDJ* 17 (June 2001): 5–9; 18 (October 2001): 4–7; 18 (February 2002): 10–11; 19 (August 2002): 4–6; and 19 (December 2002): 4–5. On Gene Carroll and Glenn Rowell, see Wertheim, *Radio Comedy*, 11–12; and "Carroll, Gene," in *The Dictionary of Cleveland Biography*, ed. David D. Van Tassel and John J. Grabowski (Bloomington: Indiana University Press, 1996), 82. The WTAM connection may have arisen because Gene and Glenn also broadcast from there at times and were extremely popular in Cleveland, but this is only speculation. John F. Royal, the program director for NBC, had also spent earlier phases of his career as manager at WTAM, and perhaps he steered the *Lum and Abner* program there. Ironically, during their time in Cleveland, Lauck and Goff's program was on the rise while the Gene and Glenn act began to wane. *Cleveland Plain Dealer*, July 4, 1933, 17. Lauck and Goff advertised Gene and Glenn's Christmas special on *Lum and Abner* in their afternoon script for December 2, 1932, in the McCoy collection. See also "Lum (Chester Lauck) Remembers Lum and Abner," *Inner-View Magazine*, August 1978, clipping in Lauck Collection. On WBAP and WFAA, see Richard Schroeder, *Texas Signs On: The Early Days of Radio and Television* (College Station: Texas A&M University Press, 1998), 63–70; and *Dallas Morning News*, December 17, 1931, 3. On radio in Chicago, see Derek W. Vaillant, "Sounds of Whiteness: Local Radio, Racial Formation, and Public Culture in Chicago, 1921–1935," *American Quarterly* 54 (March 2002): 25–66; Lester R. Weinrott, "Chicago Radio: The Glory Days," *Chicago History* 3 (1974): 14–22; and Mary E. Cygan, "A 'New Art' for Polonia: Polish American Radio Comedy during the 1930s," *Polish American Studies* 45 (Autumn 1988): 5–21.

20. *Cleveland Plain Dealer*, November 24, 1932, 23, November 25, 1932, 8; December 12, 1932, 8; February 14, 1933, 15; and August 10, 1933, 12 (quotation). Also Barnouw, *History of Broadcasting*, 1:251, 271. On the production of two shows per day from November 24 until

at least December 19, 1932, see the relevant scripts in the McCoy collection. The rumors of a sponsor in February 1933 may have resulted from a hoax that falsely raised hopes at WTAM. An article on *Lum and Abner* from later in 1933 (likely written for a publication of their then-sponsor, the regional Ford dealerships) discusses a man who claimed to represent a cosmetics company wanting to sponsor a show in Cleveland. The fake representative signed *Lum and Abner* in early 1933, only to have the hoax revealed to the demoralized act when the man was arrested for passing bad checks. See unidentified article reprinted in *JEDJ* 20 (October 2003): 8–9.

21. *Variety*, July 4, 1933, 36; and July 11, 1933, 39; and *Cleveland Plain Dealer*, May 5, 1933, 12; May 6, 1933, 10; May 19, 1933, 8; May 20, 1933, 8; June 1, 1933, 13; June 4, 1933, A15; June 22, 1933, 12; June 23, 1933, 17 (quotation); June 29, 1933, 17; July 3, 1933, 12; July 4, 1933, 17; July 5, 1933, 7; July 13, 1933, 14; and July 21, 1933, 13. *Variety* reported that the contract with the Ford dealers would mean "a total income to NBC of around $850,000." *Variety*, July 11, 1933, 39. Directly inspired by *Lum and Abner*'s success for eastern Ford dealers, the Ford dealers of Oklahoma and Texas worked with NBC to create a three-station radio network (WFAA in Dallas, KVOO in Tulsa, and WKY in Oklahoma City) for at least a brief time beginning on September 6, 1933, in order to broadcast *The Feel of the Ford Revue*, which originated at WFAA. See "Southwest Ford Dealers Use 3-Station Hookup in New Radio Campaign," *Broadcasting* 5 (September 15, 1933): 13; and Schroeder, *Texas Signs On*, 115.

22. "History of Lum and Abner" (single typed page, undated), Lauck Collection (quotation); and *Cleveland Plain Dealer*, July 2, 1933, A11; July 5, 1933, 9; July 8, 1933, 2; July 15, 1933, 10; and July 16, 1933, A3. In Cleveland, automobile sales in August 1933 were the best for any August since 1929 and were up 175 percent from the previous August. *Cleveland Plain Dealer*, September 1, 1933, 1.

23. One report in August noted that "the Lum and Abner show went over the wires twice to catch stations in the southwest." It is not clear how widely the program extended beyond the Northeast and Midwest, but according to this report its reach at times included stations in the Southwest. *Cleveland Plain Dealer*, August 26, 1933, 5. It almost certainly reached most of the South as well.

24. *Variety*, July 11, 1933, 42; *Radio News* 15 (October 1933): 228; Lewis Y. Hagy, "Homely Wisdom," *Radio Guide* 2 (October 1–7, 1933): 5; *Washington Post*, October 10, 1933, 14; October 11, 1933, 22; October 12, 1933, 22; October 13, 1933, 22; October 14, 1933, 12; and Oc-

tober 16, 1933, 20; and *New York Times*, November 19, 1933, X11. For the script of the Washington, D.C., episode, see *JEDJ* 20 (October 2003): 4–7. See also *Pine Ridge News*, November 1933, reprinted in *JEDJ* 20 (December 2003): 11, from the Broadcast Pioneers Library of American Broadcasting (University of Maryland, College Park). For additional early national publicity, see "Lum and Abner," *Radioland* 1 (February 1934): 50. See also *Cleveland Plain Dealer*, November 13, 1933, 13; November 21, 1933, 17; and November 23, 1933, 6.

25. *Pine Ridge News*, November 1933, reprinted in *JEDJ* 20 (December 2003): 11.

26. *Cleveland Plain Dealer*, December 2, 1933, 13; December 19, 1933, 20; December 22, 1933, 17; and January 31, 1934, 15; and *Radio News* 15 (March 1934): 549. The Ford dealers sponsored the show because they considered the advertising approach of Henry Ford and the Ford Motor Company to be too conservative. When Henry Ford decided to go ahead with sponsorship of a national broadcast in 1934, the Ford dealers no longer needed to have their own program. See "Ford Resumes Advertising," *Advertising and Selling* 21 (May 11, 1933): 38; and "Ford Dealers Help Henry," *Advertising and Selling* 21 (August 31, 1933): 32.

27. "Lum and Abner," in John Dunning, *On the Air: The Encyclopedia of Old-Time Radio* (New York: Oxford University Press, 1998), 412–15; "Lum and Abner and Their Sponsors: Part 3 of a Series," *JEDJ* 6 (June 1990): 3–4; Bob Goddard, "Good Ol' Boy from Good Old Days," May 2, 1977, labeled *St. Louis Globe-Democrat*, clipping in Lauck Collection; "History of Lum and Abner," Lauck Collection (quotation); and *Chicago Daily News*, August 30, 1935, clipping in Lauck Collection. On the history of WCCO, see Charles F. Sarjeant, ed., *The First Forty: The Story of WCCO Radio* (Minneapolis: T. S. Denison and Company, 1964), 66–79. Lauck and Goff left Cleveland for Minneapolis on March 27, 1934. See *Cleveland Plain Dealer*, March 27, 1934, 11. Both WCCO and WTAM could be heard as far south as Dallas. See *Dallas Morning News*, September 19, 1931, 4. Another source confirms that the Horlick Company benefited from its association with *Lum and Abner*. A drugstore owner in Ohio reported in 1936 that the sale of Horlick's product had increased 80 percent when photographs of Lum and Abner were featured in the store window as part of a larger display. *Broadcasting Merchandise* 4 (June 1936): 107. While on Mutual, Lauck and Goff also recorded and distributed their program to other unaffiliated stations for later broadcast in other parts of the country. Subsequently, on NBC Blue they could be heard on WJZ in New York, WLW in Cincinnati, WBZ in Boston, WBZA in Springfield, WSYR in Syracuse, WGAR in Cleveland,

WENR in Chicago, KPO in San Francisco, KFI in Los Angeles, KGW in Portland, and KOMO in Seattle. See *Lum and Abner's 1936 Family Almanac and Helpful Hints* ([Racine, Wis.: Horlick's Malted Milk Corporation, 1935]), 3.

28. *Little Rock Arkansas Gazette*, June 16, 1978, 1B, 3B (quotation); Kesterson, "Visit with Radio Humorist Chester Lauck," 147; *Cleveland Plain Dealer*, February 25, 1933, 10. Arthur Allen and Parker Fennelly, the performers in *The Stebbins Boys*, did a number of other rural-oriented series during the 1930s, all set in New England but drawing on national ideas of rural life (underscoring again that *Lum and Abner* addressed national themes using a southern setting). The series included *Uncle Abe and David*, *The Simpson Boys of Sprucehead Bay*, *Four Corners USA*, and *Gibbs and Feeney, General Delivery*. In addition to *The Stebbins Boys*, there was another precedent for a comic series about storekeepers. Jim and Marian Jordan found lasting fame through their hit series *Fibber McGee and Molly* beginning in 1935. From March 1931 until August 1935, however, they played a tremendous variety of characters in *Smackout—The Crossroads of the Air*. Set in a rural hamlet, the story revolved around the operation of a store that was always "smack out" of everything. The show was broadcast from Chicago via WMAQ (on NBC beginning in November 1931); Lauck and Goff almost certainly knew of it. Later, Marian Jordan would make at least one appearance on *Lum and Abner*. See Dunning, *On the Air*, 622; Charles Stumpf and Tom Price, *Heavenly Days! The Story of Fibber McGee and Molly* (Waynesville, N.C.: World of Yesterday, 1987), 22–33; Hilmes, *Radio Voices*, 105–8; and *Cleveland Plain Dealer*, August 4, 1933, 15. *Lum and Abner* and most other programs ran contests as ways to increase fan involvement and loyalty. Another memorable contest during Ford's sponsorship was to name a baby circus elephant that had ended up with the two old fellows.

29. See Ely, *Adventures of Amos 'n' Andy*; Douglas, *Listening In*; and Wertheim, *Radio Comedy*. For brief histories and sample scripts of some of the most popular radio comedies of the 1930s and 1940s, see Jack Gaver and Dave Stanley, *There's Laughter in the Air! Radio's Top Comedians and Their Best Shows* (New York: Greenberg Publisher, 1945).

30. McFadden, "'Anything Goes,'" chap. 6; and Douglas, *Listening In*, chap. 5, 103–4 (quotations).

31. Scripts for May 9, 1934, and December 13, 1934, in *Lum and Abner Scripts: 1934* (Birmingham, Ala.: National Lum and Abner Society, 1993).

32. *Cleveland Plain Dealer*, February 18, 1933, 12; February 25,

INTRODUCTION / 55

1933, 10; March 6, 1933, 10; March 11, 1933, 12; March 16, 1933, 13; March 18, 1933, 12; and March 20, 1933, 10 (quotation). On at least one occasion the sociable may have been set at the county fair in Pine Ridge. *Cleveland Plain Dealer*, August 30, 1933, 12. In rural areas in the early twentieth century, local telephone networks (so-called party lines) were used for the community-wide broadcast of sermons, musical performances, announcements, and the playing of phonograph records. See Kline, *Consumers in the Country*, 42–48.

33. *Variety*, July 11, 1933, 42. The broadcast of one sociable, from July 28, 1933, survives in the NBC Radio Collection at the Library of Congress.

34. *Cleveland Plain Dealer*, March 6, 1933, 10 (first quotation); Robert S. Lynd and Helen Merrell Lynd, *Middletown in Transition: A Study in Cultural Conflicts* (New York: Harcourt Brace, 1937), 264 (second quotation).

35. Malone, *Country Music, U.S.A.*, 33–34, 68–75; James F. Evans, *Prairie Farmer and WLS: The Burridge D. Butler Years* (Urbana: University of Illinois Press, 1969), 151–231; McCusker, "'Dear Radio Friend'"; George C. Biggar, "The WLS National Barn Dance Story: The Early Years," in *Exploring Roots Music: Twenty Years of the* JEMF Quarterly, ed. Nolan Porterfield (Lanham, Md.: Scarecrow Press, 2004), 34–44; Charles Wolfe, "The Triumph of the Hills: Country Radio, 1920–50," in *Country: The Music and the Musicians from the Beginnings to the '90s*, ed. Paul Kingsbury, Alan Axelrod, and Susan Costello, 2nd ed. (New York: Abbeville Press, 1994), 40–63; Derek Vaillant, "'Your Voice Came In Last Night . . . But I Thought It Sounded a Little Scared': Rural Radio Listening and 'Talking Back' during the Progressive Era in Wisconsin, 1920–1932," in Hilmes and Loviglio, *Radio Reader*, 63–64; MacDonald, *Don't Touch That Dial*, 114–15; Louis M. "Grandpa" Jones with Charles K. Wolfe, *Everybody's Grandpa: Fifty Years behind the Mike* (Knoxville: University of Tennessee Press, 1984), 31; Louis M. Kyriakoudes, *The Social Origins of the Urban South: Race, Gender, and Migration in Nashville and Middle Tennessee, 1890–1930* (Chapel Hill: University of North Carolina Press, 2003), introduction and chap. 1; Chad Berry, *Southern Migrants, Northern Exiles* (Urbana: University of Illinois Press, 2000), 156–59; and Smulyan, *Selling Radio*, 23–26. On the broader changes in programming, see MacDonald, *Don't Touch That Dial*, 30–40, 47–50; Wertheim, *Radio Comedy*, chaps. 5 and 6; and Douglas, *Listening In*, chap. 5.

36. *Variety*, July 11, 1933, 42 (first quotation); *JEDJ* 19 (December 2002): 5 (second quotation); MacDonald, *Don't Touch That Dial*, 101

(third quotation); and *Cleveland Plain Dealer*, August 8, 1933, 16; September 6, 1933, 15; September 22, 1933, 21; October 22, 1933, 15; November 23, 1933, 6; December 9, 1933, 6; December 16, 1933, 6; and December 29, 1933, 19. A native of tiny Starke, Florida (near the Georgia border), Canova was "a female answer to Bob Burns." Dunning, *On the Air*, 377. On Canova, see also James Robert Parish and William T. Leonard, *The Funsters* (New Rochelle, N.Y.: Arlington House Publishers, 1979), 155–62.

37. Jones, *Everybody's Grandpa*, 41.

38. *Pine Ridge News* 1 (November 1933). *Lum and Abner* released several issues of this four-page newspaper as fan premiums (as well as the previously cited issue that targeted only the Ford dealers sponsoring the series). In addition to details about the Indianapolis show, this issue included staged photos of the pair in Pine Ridge, which were actually taken in the village of Peninsula, Ohio. Tabloid newspapers were one of several popular forms of fan premiums, along with booklets, product samples, photographs, contest prizes, and various novelties. See the NBC newsletter promoting radio advertising, *Broadcast Merchandising* 3 (June–July 1935). See also Timothy A. Patterson, "Hillbilly Music among the Flatlanders: Early Midwestern Radio Barn Dances," *Journal of Country Music* 6 (Spring 1975): 12–18; and Wayne W. Daniel, "The National Barn Dance on Network Radio: The 1930s," *Journal of Country Music* 9, no. 3 (1983): 47–62.

39. The exodus of blacks to the North has received more attention than the northward movement of southern whites, but scholars have begun to tell the story of white migration. See James N. Gregory, *The Southern Diaspora: How the Great Migrations of Black and White Southerners Transformed America* (Chapel Hill: University of North Carolina Press, 2005); Jack Temple Kirby, "The Southern Exodus, 1910–1960: A Primer for Historians," *Journal of Southern History* 49 (November 1983): 585–600; Kirby, *Rural Worlds Lost: The American South, 1920–1960* (Baton Rouge: Louisiana State University Press, 1987), chaps. 8 and 9; J. Trent Alexander, "'They're Never Here More Than a Year': Return Migration in the Southern Exodus, 1940–1970," *Journal of Social History* 38 (Spring 2005): 653–71; and Berry, *Southern Migrants, Northern Exiles*, esp. chaps. 1–3. See also Erdmann Doane Beynon, "The Southern White Laborer Migrates to Michigan," *American Sociological Review* 3 (June 1938): 333–43; and McCusker, "'Dear Radio Friend.'" Of course, rural white southerners were also moving to southern cities during this time period, and their recent memories of time in the country made them a crucial part of the

radio audience for many rural-oriented programs. Kyriakoudes, *Social Origins of the Urban South*, chap. 1.

40. Loran David Osborn and Martin Henry Neumeyer, *The Community and Society: An Introduction to Sociology* (New York: American Book Company, 1933), chap. 2 (quotations, 23–24, 31); and Robert S. Lynd and Helen Merrell Lynd, *Middletown: A Study in Contemporary Culture* (New York: Harcourt Brace, 1929). For other examples of the booming literature on rural communities, see Carl C. Taylor, *Rural Sociology in Its Economic, Historical and Psychological Aspects*, rev. ed., (1926; repr., New York: Harper and Brothers, 1933); Edmund de S. Brunner and J. H. Kolb, *Rural Social Trends* (New York: McGraw-Hill, 1933); Newell Leroy Sims, *Elements of Rural Sociology* (New York: Thomas Y. Crowell, 1928); Mary Mims, *The Awakening Community* (New York: Macmillan, 1932); and the bulky three-volume set by Pitirim A. Sorokin, Carle C. Zimmerman, and Charles J. Galpin, *A Systematic Source Book in Rural Sociology* (Minneapolis: University of Minnesota Press, 1930–1932). For context, see Lowry Nelson, *Rural Sociology: Its Origin and Growth in the United States* (Minneapolis: University of Minnesota Press, 1969).

41. Dwight Sanderson, *The Rural Community: The Natural History of a Sociological Group* (Boston: Ginn and Company, 1932), chaps. 12–14 (quotation, 474–75).

42. Twelve Southerners, *I'll Take My Stand: The South and the Agrarian Tradition*, rev. ed. (1930; repr., Baton Rouge: Louisiana State University Press, 1977), xlvii. While the agrarians had concerns similar to those of sociologists, the Vanderbilt group opposed sociological remedies. On clashes between the agrarians and pioneering southern sociologist Howard W. Odum and his followers, see Fred Hobson, *Tell About the South: The Southern Rage to Explain* (Baton Rouge: Louisiana State University Press, 1983), chap. 3; Daniel Joseph Singal, *The War Within: From Victorian to Modernist Thought in the South, 1919–1945* (Chapel Hill: University of North Carolina Press, 1982), chaps. 5 and 7; and Richard H. King, *A Southern Renaissance: The Cultural Awakening of the American South, 1930–1955* (New York: Oxford University Press, 1980), chap. 3.

43. *Radio News* 15 (October 1933): 228 (first quotation); *New York Times*, November 19, 1933, X11 (second quotation); Elgar Brown, "Behind the Scenes with Lum and Abner," *Radio Guide* 6 (April 10, 1937): 4–5 (third quotation).

44. See scripts from January 18 through 22, 1932, in the McCoy collection.

45. See scripts from April 30 through June 2, 1932, in the McCoy col-

lection. On Abner's withdrawal, see scripts for August 9 and 11, 1932, in the McCoy collection.

46. Scripts for the afternoon show on November 28, 1932 (first quotation), and the morning program on December 6, 1932 (second quotation), McCoy collection.

47. Chester Lauck and Norris Goff, *Lum and Abner and Their Friends from Pine Ridge* (Mena, Ark.: Mena Star Company, [1932]). In publishing the book, Lauck and Goff were following the lead of Freeman Gosden and Charles Correll, who had similarly published a guide to *Amos 'n' Andy* entitled *All about Amos 'n' Andy and Their Creators Correll and Gosden* (New York: Rand McNally, 1929). A number of analysts of early radio have drawn from Benedict Anderson, *Imagined Communities: Reflections on the Origin and Spread of Nationalism* (1983; rev. ed., New York: Verso, 1991). They have used Anderson's theory to argue (with appropriate caveats) that radio, an accessible national medium, served a unifying function among (white) Americans during the Great Depression and World War II. See Alexander Russo, "A Darke(ened) Figure on the Airwaves: Race, Nation, and *The Green Hornet*," in Hilmes and Loviglio, *Radio Reader*, 257–76; Douglas, *Listening In*, 23–24; Jason Loviglio, "The Shadow Meets the Phantom Public," in *Fear Itself: Enemies Real and Imagined in American Culture*, ed. Nancy Lusignan Schultz (West Lafayette, Ind.: Purdue University Press, 1999), 313–30; and Hilmes, *Radio Voices*. *Lum and Abner*'s popularity and its positioning of Pine Ridge as a national ideal for a community could be analyzed along similar lines.

48. Lauck and Goff, *Lum and Abner and Their Friends from Pine Ridge*.

49. Benjamin Filene, *Romancing the Folk: Public Memory and American Roots Music* (Chapel Hill: University of North Carolina Press, 2000), 64–65 (quotation); Richard A. Peterson, *Creating Country Music: Fabricating Authenticity* (Chicago: University of Chicago Press, 1997), esp. chaps. 1 and 5. For broader context, see part 3 of Miles Orvell, *The Real Thing: Imitation and Authenticity in American Culture, 1880–1940* (Chapel Hill: University of North Carolina Press, 1989).

50. Lauck and Goff, *Lum and Abner and Their Friends from Pine Ridge*.

51. Lauck and Goff, *Lum and Abner and Their Friends from Pine Ridge*. On the controversy about open range and fence laws in the South (to which the description of Sister Simpson refers), see Shawn Everett Kantor and J. Morgan Kousser, "Common Sense or Commonwealth? The Fence Law and Institutional Change in the Postbellum South," *Journal of Southern History* 59 (May 1993): 201–42.

52. Lauck and Goff, *Lum and Abner and Their Friends from Pine Ridge*. On women's lives in the southern hills and mountains, see Melissa Walker, *All We Knew Was to Farm: Rural Women in the Upcountry South, 1919–1941* (Baltimore: Johns Hopkins University Press, 2000).

53. Brown, "Behind the Scenes with Lum and Abner," 5 (first and second quotations); and script for July 1, 1937, in *The Lum and Abner Scripts: July 1937* (Birmingham, Ala.: National Lum and Abner Society, 2003), 6 (third quotation). Played at times by Goff and at other times by guest star Jerry Hausner, Gandel was presented in a positive light. Given his strong working-class, northern accent, he was the closest example on *Lum and Abner* of the ethnic characters prevalent in other 1930s comedies. On ethnic characters, see Wertheim, *Radio Comedy*, 116–17; and Hilmes, *Radio Voices*, 106–7, 205–8.

54. Sanderson, *Rural Community*, 499–500 (first, second, and third quotations); Gunnar Myrdal, *An American Dilemma: The Negro Problem and Modern Democracy* (New York: Harper and Brothers, 1944), chaps. 43 and 44 (fourth quotation, 927). The assumption that the presence of blacks (and immigrants) was abnormal in a typical, functional community also marked the Lynds' study of Middletown. They sought a small city with "a small Negro and foreign-born population. In a difficult study of this sort it seemed a distinct advantage to deal with a homogeneous, native-born population, even though such a population is unusual in an American industrial city." Lynd and Lynd, *Middletown*, 8.

55. Historical Census Browser, University of Virginia, Geospatial and Statistical Data Center, http://fisher.lib.virginia.edu/collections/stats/histcensus/index.html; and *Mena Weekly Star*, February 25, 1932, 7. In 1937 Polk County's only black resident died. *Mena Weekly Star*, December 9, 1937, 1.

56. Script for January 25, 1932, McCoy collection; and Hagy, "Homely Wisdom," 5.

57. Anthony Harkins, *Hillbilly: A Cultural History of an American Icon* (New York: Oxford University Press, 2004), chaps. 1–3; Brooks Blevins, *Hill Folks: A History of Arkansas Ozarkers and Their Image* (Chapel Hill: University of North Carolina Press, 2002), esp. chaps. 1, 6, and 9; J. W. Williamson, *Hillbillyland: What the Movies Did to the Mountains and What the Mountains Did to the Movies* (Chapel Hill: University of North Carolina Press, 1995); Henry D. Shapiro, *Appalachia on Our Mind: The Southern Mountains and Mountaineers in the American Consciousness, 1870–1920* (Chapel Hill: University of North Carolina Press, 1978); Allen Batteau, *The Invention of Appalachia* (Tucson: University of Arizona Press, 1990); and *Chicago Daily News*, August 30,

1935, clipping in the Lauck Collection (quotation). For additional context (though the analysis virtually ignores radio), see Jack Temple Kirby,
Media-Made Dixie: The South in the American Imagination (1978; rev.
ed., Athens: University of Georgia Press, 1987). Residents of the Ouachita region certainly maintained the distinction between their area and
the Ozarks. In September 1940 Lauck and Goff premiered their first film,
Dreaming Out Loud, in their hometown of Mena. RKO promoted the
film using the slogan "Meet the Two WIZARDS of the OZarks," playing
with the 1939 film title *The Wizard of Oz*. The Mena paper altered the
film company's ads (and destroyed its weak pun) by changing *OZarks* to
Ouachitas. See ad from the *Mena Star*, September 5, 1940, reprinted in
JEDJ 7 (October 1990): 3–5.

58. Harkins, *Hillbilly*, chap. 4. See also M. Thomas Inge, "The Appalachian Backgrounds of Billy De Beck's Snuffy Smith," *Appalachian
Journal* 4 (Winter 1977): 120–32.

59. Script for July 8, 1937, in *Lum and Abner Scripts: July 1937*, 20.
Lauck and Goff open one of their final few episodes with a similar ploy
of Abner reading the Snuffy Smith cartoon and making fun of Snuffy's
hillbilly ways. Listen to the show for April 2, 1954.

60. Dunning, *On the Air*, 414.

61. See Blevins, *Hill Folks*, chaps. 6 and 9; Richard D. Starnes, *Creating the Land of the Sky: Tourism and Society in Western North Carolina*
(Tuscaloosa: University of Alabama Press, 2005); and an essay collection
edited by Richard D. Starnes, *Southern Journeys: Tourism, History, and
Culture in the Modern South* (Tuscaloosa: University of Alabama Press,
2003), which includes a particularly relevant chapter by Brooks Blevins,
"Hillbillies and the Holy Land: The Development of Tourism in the Arkansas Ozarks."

62. Harold Coogan, *Mena Centennial History, 1896–1996* (Murfrees-
boro, Ark.: Looking Glass Media, 1996), 24–29; William H. Cobb, *Radical Education in the Rural South: Commonwealth College, 1922–1940*
(Detroit: Wayne State University Press, 2000), 112, 234n40; and Tim
Hollis, "Mena, Arkansas, 1896–1996," *JEDJ* 13 (October 1996): 4–6.

63. *Lum and Abner*, broadcast of July 28, 1933, NBC Radio Collection, Library of Congress.

64. Script for September 12, 1933, reprinted in *JEDJ* 20 (August
2003): 4–6. This same script has Lum planning for his upcoming mar-
riage to Evalena Schultz by getting rid of his antique furniture in favor
of fashionable new pieces: "I dont want to be behind the times. I gotta
be modern you know." Like many of Lum and Abner's statements, this
exchange lightly spoofs modern fashions and economics while also plac-

ing Pine Ridge in the middle of them. The other publicly available script that survives from 1933 is the episode in which Lum and Evalena travel to Washington, D.C., to be married. See *JEDJ* 20 (October 2003): 4–7.

65. Scripts for July 16 and 30, 1934, in *Lum and Abner Scripts: 1934.*

66. Kenny A. Franks and Paul F. Lambert, *Early Louisiana and Arkansas Oil: A Photographic History, 1901–1946* (College Station: Texas A&M University Press, 1982), 106–59; Dudley J. Hughes, *Oil in the Deep South: A History of the Oil Business in Mississippi, Alabama, and Florida, 1859–1945* (Jackson: University Press of Mississippi, 1993); Glen Martel, "Oil and Gas in Southwest Arkansas," *Arkansas Historical Quarterly* 4 (Autumn 1945): 196–214; Coogan, *Mena Centennial History*, 3–4; Rupert B. Vance, *Human Geography of the South: A Study in Regional Resources and Human Adequacy* (Chapel Hill: University of North Carolina Press, 1932), 335–47.

67. Script for December 20, 1934, in *Lum and Abner Scripts: 1934;* and recorded episodes for January 4, 7, 8, and 9, 1935. This conclusion to the story of the oil boom could have been inspired by reality. During Lauck and Goff's stay in Cleveland, the *Cleveland Plain Dealer*, January 9, 1933, printed an Associated Press story from Blackwell, Oklahoma: "Blackwell is having a rapid succession of 'oil booms.' First came the 'poor man's field' which 'produced' gasoline at a depth of a few feet. Oil men said the gasoline apparently was seepage from a pipeline leak. Yesterday brought discovery of a petroleum pool in eighteen inches of sand at a depth of 23 feet. Some oil men expressed belief the oil . . . was forced up by water. . . . Dozens of persons rushed to the petroleum scene with post auguers [sic] and began boring frantically. One citizen started leasing all available lots in the vicinity." Lauck and Goff likely drew from newspapers at times; Goff "subscribed to many rural Arkansas papers because he liked to read the personal columns to keep in touch with his roots," according to his obituary. Eric Pace, "Norris Goff, Abner of 'Lum and Abner,' Is Dead at 72," *New York Times*, June 9, 1978, B14.

68. On the matrimonial bureau, listen to the episodes from January 18 until February 5, 1935; for flashlights (a plotline linked to a premium giveaway), listen to February 1 and 4, 1935; and for the silver mine, listen to July 22 to September 27, 1935.

69. On the rubber company, see scripts from January 27 to March 18, 1932 (quotation from the January 27 script), in the McCoy collection; and on the gold-mining endeavor, see the script from December 18, 1932, in the McCoy collection.

70. For more on the movie theater, listen to May 28 through July 15,

1935; and for the circus, listen to March 8 through April 23, 1935. On the boll weevil plotline, see plot summaries in *Lum and Abner's 1937 Family Almanac* ([Racine, Wis.: Horlick's Malted Milk Corporation, 1936]), 29. On film exhibition and its civic importance, see Kathryn H. Fuller, *At the Picture Show: Small-Town Audiences and the Creation of Movie Fan Culture* (Washington, D.C.: Smithsonian Institution Press, 1996), 110–14; and on Arkansas and Kentucky specifically, see Gregory A. Waller, "Robert Southard and the History of Traveling Film Exhibition," *Film Quarterly* 47 (Winter 2003–2004): 2–14. A great topic for cultural historians would be a full-length study of the fate of traveling carnivals and circuses during the Great Depression (perhaps with a focus on the South—e.g., "Cornbread and Circus"). The shows often wintered in the southern states to take advantage of the extended playing season there. As the show promoters faced hard times, they quite plausibly could have ended up facing foreclosure from a southern merchant, as in the *Lum and Abner* plot. See "'30 Was Dying Year for Carnies, '31 May Be Just One Long Funeral," *Variety*, January 14, 1931, 60. On the ways railroad circuses evoked economic and social change and the values of an industrial society, see Janet M. Davis, *The Circus Age: Culture and Society under the American Big Top* (Chapel Hill: University of North Carolina Press, 2002). Also see Greg Renoff, "'Wait for the Big Show!' The Circus in Georgia, 1865–1930," *Atlanta History* 46, no. 1 (2004): 4–23. On the relevant changes in agriculture in the South, see Gilbert C. Fite, *Cotton Fields No More: Southern Agriculture, 1865–1980* (Lexington: University Press of Kentucky, 1984), 192–94; and Pete Daniel, *Toxic Drift: Pesticides and Health in the Post–World War II South* (Baton Rouge: Louisiana State University Press, 2005).

71. *Mena Weekly Star*, December 26, 1935, 1; George Livingstone, "The Strange Prophecy of Lum and Abner," *Radio Guide* 5 (week ending March 28, 1936): 3, 18 (quotation).

72. *Mena Weekly Star*, March 12, 1936, 6; March 26, 1936, 2; April 23, 1936, 1 (first quotation), 4; and April 30, 1936, 1, 4; and *Little Rock Arkansas Gazette*, April 25, 1936, 16; April 26, 1936, 1, 14; and April 27, 1936, 1–2. The broadcast of the April 26, 1936, ceremony is available through the National Lum and Abner Society, Birmingham, Ala. The quotations from the ceremony are from my transcription of the broadcast. Also see Kathryn Moore Stucker, *Hello, This Is Lum and Abner: The Story of Lum and Abner's Jot 'Em Down Store in Pine Ridge, Arkansas* (Pine Ridge, Ark.: Lum and Abner Museum, 1992), chap. 1; and Tim Hollis, "Lum and Abner and Their Sponsors," part 4, *JEDJ* 7 (August 1990): 5–7. Waters was not the only southern town that tried

to use a celebrity-based name change for a civic boost. Berwyn, with a population of 227 in the Arbuckle Hills in Oklahoma, changed its name to Gene Autry in late 1941, after the radio and film star purchased a two-thousand-acre ranch nearby. Autry had grown up in other small towns in the same general region. CBS broadcast Autry's *Melody Ranch* show on location from the name-changing ceremony, which also attracted Governor Leon C. Phillips and a crowd of thirty-five thousand. The town was "hitching its destiny to the chaps of U.S. Cowboy Number 1." *Movie-Radio Guide*, December 13–19, 1941, 9–10.

73. *Arkansas: A Guide to the State Compiled by Workers of the Writers' Program of the Work Projects Administration in the State of Arkansas*, rev. ed. (1941; repr., New York: Hastings House, 1948), 339 (first quotation); *Mena Weekly Star*, January 23, 1936, 2; February 6, 1936, 5; March 5, 1936, 4; April 2, 1936, 1 (second quotation); September 30, 1937, 8 (third quotation).

74. Also present at the renaming ceremony was Cling Wilhite. He had served as the model for Grandpappy Spears in the 1932 booklet *Lum and Abner and Their Friends from Pine Ridge*. There he was described as being "peert [pert] as a catbird." In a script from December 17, 1934, Grandpappy Spears claims to be "jist piert as a cat bird." *Lum and Abner Scripts: 1934*. He makes similar comments in the scripts for January 24 and 30, 1936. See *Lum and Abner Scripts: January 1936* (Birmingham, Ala.: National Lum and Abner Society, 1994). Wilhite embraced these fictional descriptions. Asked by the announcer how he felt, the seventy-nine-year-old Wilhite responded, "I'm as peert as a catbird." Ed Lasker Goble, who was the model for the Cedric Weehunt character, also attended the Little Rock ceremony. In the late 1930s Goble joined the touring troupes from Mena to play the role of Cedric. Goble also formed a singing group called Cedric's Quartet, which made regional appearances. See *Mena Weekly Star*, July 22, 1937, 5; and November 25, 1937, 3.

75. Transcript of April 26, 1936, broadcast, National Lum and Abner Society, Birmingham, Ala.

76. *Mena Weekly Star*, April 30, 1936, 1, 4; January 21, 1937, 4 (second quotation); February 25, 1937, 3; and July 8, 1937, 6 (first quotation); *Little Rock Arkansas Gazette*, April 27, 1936, 1–2; Ernie Deane, "Pine Ridge Brings Memories of Lum 'n' Abner," *Little Rock Arkansas Gazette*, April 3, 1960; Stucker, *Hello, This Is Lum and Abner*, chap. 1; Donnie Pitchford and Tim Hollis, "'Dick's Gurl' Ethel: A Tribute," *JEDJ* 14 (October 1997). On the band and Lum's bid for the presidency, see *Lum and Abner's 1937 Family Almanac*, 31. While touring in Wisconsin, Huddleston and the band visited the facilities of *Lum and Abner*'s spon-

sor, Horlick's Malted Milk Corporation, in Racine, symbolically welding the tight links between commerce, entertainment, and civic advancement. *Mena Weekly Star*, April 29, 1937, 4.

77. Travis Y. Oliver, "Hell's Fire—Arkansas!" *Vanity Fair* 41 (September 1933): 14, 57. In contrast, a more positive contemporary view of the Ozark region, similar to that of Lauck and Goff, can be found in Charles Morrow Wilson, *Backwoods America* (Chapel Hill: University of North Carolina Press, 1935).

78. See *Map of the State Highway System of Arkansas* (Little Rock: State Highway Commission, October 1936; on display at the Lum and Abner Museum in Pine Ridge, Arkansas). Opie Read was a late nineteenth-century journalist who spread humorous stereotypes of Arkansas through tales in his *Arkansas Traveller* magazine, based in Chicago. See Blevins, *Hill Folks*, 130–31. Lauck and Goff took particular pride in their mention on the state map. Goff brought a copy of the map back to California after a hunting trip to Arkansas (and a visit with Huddleston and Cling Wilhite). See Brown, "Behind the Scenes with Lum and Abner," 5. In 1941 the University of Kentucky also tried to use radio to counter negative images of its home state. The university created *From the Kentucky Mountains*, a series presented over the Mutual Broadcasting System and "designed to counteract the exaggerated impression of Kentucky as a wild region of moonshiners, snake-worshipers, child marriages and feuds. Authentic traditional ballads are heard, typical writings of mountain authors are dramatized, and interesting mountain people often participate." *Movie-Radio Guide*, June 14–20, 1941, 13. In June 1933 the university had also started a program to enable even the most isolated communities in the mountains to have access to radios. Using donations, the university purchased radios and identified prominent local citizens in out-of-the-way areas to host "listening centers." Technicians from the university installed the sets and antennas. One supporter explained: "These centers are to be located in settlement schools, consolidated schools, stores, or any other place where people may 'gather in' and where a reliable director may be found. The director must tune in upon the University of Kentucky programs, which include discussions of agricultural, geological, and legal problems and talks on generally cultural subjects. He must furnish a simple report to the University radio studios. In this report he is to list the number of listeners together with comments and suggestions. He is also supposed to choose with discrimination programs at other times for his listeners and to encourage people to come to hear the broadcasts." The goal, in short, was to "bring enlightenment and stimulation to the mountain people in the remote dis-

tricts." In early 1937 the twenty-fifth such listening center was put in place. Frances Jewell McVey, "Backwoods Kentucky Listens In," *Forum and Century* 92 (July 1934): 51–53 (quotations); and "Listening Center: Radio Reaches Kentucky Mountaineers," *Newsweek* 9 (February 6, 1937): 23. On radio in the mountains, see also Jacob J. Podber, "Early Radio in Rural Appalachia: An Oral History," *Journal of Radio Studies* 8 (Winter 2001): 388–410.

79. *Mena Weekly Star*, April 30, 1936, 4.

80. "Hillbilly: A Local Bazookist Makes Good in Some Big Cities," *Newsweek* 6 (December 14, 1935): 29; "The Arkansas Traveler," *Time* 32 (October 31, 1938): 26; Elmer T. Peterson, "Bob Burns: Real Human Being," *Better Homes and Gardens* 17 (February 1939): 13, 54–56; *New York Times*, March 19, 1939, 136; and February 3, 1956, 21; Dunning *On the Air*, 89–91, 102–3; and Harkins, *Hillbilly*, 160–64. See also Gary Giddins, *Bing Crosby: A Pocketful of Dreams, The Early Years, 1903–1940* (Boston: Little, Brown and Company, 2001), chap. 20. Harkins, *Hillbilly*, also points out that Paul Henning, creator of *The Beverly Hillbillies* television program, listened religiously to Burns's monologues (188). Like Lauck and Goff, who knew this fellow Arkansan, Burns used his newfound wealth to keep his rural ties alive by buying land outside Hollywood. He purchased a four-hundred-acre farm in the San Fernando Valley, real estate that made him even wealthier after World War II. See "Bob Burns: The Modern Arkansas Traveler," *Movie-Radio Guide*, November 22–28, 1941, 40. On Burns, see also Wade Austin, "The Real Beverly Hillbillies," *Southern Quarterly* 19 (Spring–Summer 1981): 83–94.

81. *Where to Go, What to Do, When to See Van Buren and Crawford County, Arkansas* (Van Buren: Junior Chamber of Commerce, 1941). The pamphlet also notes about Burns: "As the city's most famous native son, he has been feted on two occasions since his rise to fame in 1935. The first one on Dec. 7, 1935, when he was en route to Hollywood to join Bing Crosby in the Kraft Music hall; and the second on Aug. 7, 1939, when Paramount Pictures held the world premiere of his picture, 'Our Leading Citizen' in Van Buren." See also Blevins, *Hill Folks*, 136, 262, 304n81.

82. Robert B. Walz to Lauck, October 19, 1969, Lauck Collection; and *Arkansas: A Guide to the State*, 253.

83. Bob Lancaster, "Bare Feet and Slow Trains," *Arkansas Times* (June 1987): 93–94. See also Foy Lisenby, "A Survey of Arkansas's Image Problem," *Arkansas Historical Quarterly* 30 (Spring 1971): 60–71; and Ben F. Johnson III, *Arkansas in Modern America, 1930–1999* (Fay-

etteville: University of Arkansas Press, 2000), 39–40. For the developing image and a discussion of the Arkansas Traveler routine, see the Arkansas section of the influential early twentieth-century travel guide by Clifton H. Johnson, *Highways and Byways of the Mississippi Valley* (New York: Macmillan Company, 1906), 107–23. Even the district governor of the Lions Club in Arkansas condemned Burns. See *Mena Weekly Star*, February 25, 1937, 3. Broadcasters had to be attentive to listeners' opinions. Particular groups of consumers sometimes boycotted sponsors of offensive programs. See Kathy M. Newman, *Radio Active: Advertising and Consumer Activism, 1935–1947* (Berkeley: University of California Press, 2004), esp. part 2.

84. "Lum and Abner," in Dunning, *On the Air*, 412–15; Leslie Eaton, "Pine Ridge Goes Hollywood," *Radio Star*, June 1937, reprinted in *JEDJ* 13 (June 1997): 4–7; "Final Star of Stars Standings," *Radio Guide* 6 (week ending July 17, 1937): 15; Lou Dumont, "Lum and Abner," *Hobbies* 85 (July 1980): 94–96 (clipping in Lauck Collection); and Stucker, *Hello, This Is Lum and Abner*, chap. 4. See also Hilmes, *Hollywood and Broadcasting*, 62–63; Orrin E. Dunlap Jr., "The Swing to California," *New York Times*, October 17, 1937, 190; and "Studios for Radio Networks Near Completion in Hollywood," *Christian Science Monitor*, February 15, 1938, 11. Their advertising agency, Lord and Thomas, also claimed in December 1935 that Lauck and Goff had been "recently voted the third most popular air team." See *Wall Street Journal*, December 16, 1935, 3.

85. Ironically, given their later work for wartime propaganda, Lauck and Goff included an isolationist message in their script of February 4, 1932 (McCoy collection). Dick Huddleston points out a newspaper article about the United States sending battleships to the general region of Japan's invasion of China. Lum remarks, "Well I do know. I never knowed hit was gittin that bad. If they want my notions, we'd better stay away from over ther. Let them Chinamens and Japanamans settle twixt therseves." They also commented on China and Japan in one of the first bits of national coverage the program received. See "Hits—Quips—Slips: Lum 'n' Abner," *Radio Digest* 28 (April 1932): 44–45.

86. "Amid the Native Corn," *Newsweek*, October 6, 1947, 52; "Where Are They Now?—Lum 'n' Abner," *Newsweek*, December 31, 1956, 10; "Changes of the Week," *Time*, June 27, 1955, 86; *Wall Street Journal*, March 1, 1962, 1; "Lum and Abner," in Dunning, *On the Air*, 412–15; Stucker, *Hello, This Is Lum and Abner*. Various material in the Lauck Collection documents the duo's television efforts and later lives. Articles in the *JEDJ* have exhaustively discussed their films. On the work in Yugo-

slavia in particular, see Tim Hollis, "Lum and Abner Go Abroad," *JEDJ* 12 (December 1995): 7–9. For examples of Lauck and Goff's support for war efforts and coverage of them at the height of their celebrity status, see Helen Weigel Brown, "Plenty of Room for Young Fry," *Better Homes and Gardens* 20 (August 1942): 36–37; "Twentieth-Century Colonial," *House Beautiful* 84 (January 1942): 16–19; *Movie-Radio Guide*, January 2–8, 1943, 2; April 12–18, 1941, 34; July 1943, 52; November 1–7, 1941, 8; November 8–14, 1941, 36; May 2–8, 1942, cover and 5 and [37]; August 16–22, 1941, 22; June 27–July 3, 1942, 32; August 15–21, 1942, cover and 6; and June 14–20, 1941, 23. Beyond war propaganda they sometimes added other public service messages to their scripts. For a health-related announcement, see "Lum and Abner, Radio Pair, to Talk of Doctors' Problems," *Hygeia* 17 (January 1939): 31. Lauck in particular remained active until the end of his life. His speeches for Conoco and in the years following his retirement expounded on the fiscal principles of a conservative southern Democrat. He worried about the mores of the younger generation and about socialism interfering with business. Even in retirement he was a partner in an advertising firm—like his character Lum, he was an entrepreneurial man at home on Main Street and in the Chamber of Commerce until he died. His worry about socialism could have emerged during his time in Mena. The overtly socialist Commonwealth College conducted classes on a campus near Mena from 1924 until 1940, when local people forced its closure. See Cobb, *Radical Education in the Rural South*.

A Note on the Scripts

Late in life Chester Lauck recalled fondly the way he and Norris Goff crafted the scripts for their program:

> We'd go in about 10:30 every morning, and we'd shoot the bull for a while, and then one of us would say, "Well, where did we leave the old boys last night?" We usually had a slim thread of a plot that linked one show to the next. I did all the typing; Tuffy would kind of stride around the room thinking out loud, and I'd be doing the same thing at the typewriter. Most of the scripts ended up being about a 50–50 deal. Tuffy was the wittier of the pair, he came up with most of the funny lines. I was probably a little bit more creative as far as thinking up general story lines. I'd feed him an idea, and he'd run with it, thinking up ways for Abner to completely misunderstand some new scheme that Lum had come up with. He never looked over my shoulder at what I was typing; he just trusted me to get it all down. We almost never got ahead; most of the shows were done the day they were broadcast. Oh, once in a while when we wanted to take a trip or something, we might get three or four days ahead on scripts. Boy, that was like money in the bank—it sure was nice, but it didn't happen very often. . . . Tuffy and I used to purposely write each script about three or four minutes short so we could include our little ad libs as we went along. Our

rule was, when we started one of those little ad lib flings, we'd put our finger on the script right where we left it. That way, we could pick up where we left off.[1]

Before each broadcast they would generally read through the script only once to work on their timing, and ordinarily even the network executives did not see the script in advance.

The scripts that follow sample Lauck and Goff's writing from two points early in the show's development (the broadcasts of these episodes apparently have not survived). The first set of ten scripts is from the pair's initial broadcasts upon returning to Chicago in January 1932, following the expiration of their contract with Quaker Oats to broadcast in Texas. They are reintroducing themselves to the NBC audience. Abner, the constable, faces a dilemma when Dick Huddleston's store is robbed and the likely culprit is an intimidating local tough.

The second set is from two years later (December 1933 and January 1934), when they are broadcasting for NBC, with the sponsorship of Ford dealers, from WTAM in Cleveland. In those nineteen scripts, Lauck and Goff weave more complex situations and nurture richer characterizations than they had been capable of earlier. Abner is running for sheriff, with Lum as his campaign manager; a little girl is kidnapped; the two old friends rekindle an even older feud; and the politics of county-seat corruption reach the boundaries of Pine Ridge.

Each set follows one story line from beginning to end. As an ongoing series, of course, the program had to have another plot under way before resolving the first. Before each episode, a network announcer would make a few remarks to remind listeners of what had happened the day before, and at the close of the show he would return with a few comments. The announcer's words survive in only one of these scripts.

All of the scripts that follow reflect the spontaneity of the writing process. Lauck and Goff never intended the scripts to be seen by anyone other than the actors; thus Lauck sometimes typed his way beyond the edge of the page, leaving partial words. The punctuation of the scripts was intended only to aid them in the timing of their delivery, so periods and capitalization are often idiosyncratic. The ellipses scattered throughout the dialogue are in the originals; Lauck used them to establish pauses in the delivery. The letter "L" in parentheses indicates that the speaker should laugh. On occasion the two authors drafted a few lines and marked through them before resuming the script. I have not included the discarded material. I have silently completed some partial words, and when necessary for clarity, I have corrected capitalization, punctuation, and obvious typographical errors. Even more rarely I have added a word; those additions are enclosed in brackets. As a result of the light editing, these scripts preserve the rudimentary literature that the two actors brought to life.

When read slowly and conversationally—or better yet, aloud—the gentle humor and complicated life of Pine Ridge can entertain again in these pages. Along the way we can learn much about radio; rural politics, social mores, and the ideal of community; and how Americans coped with the darkest years of the Great Depression. Now, let's see what's going on down in Pine Ridge. . . .

NOTE

1. Mike Trimble, "Years of Humor Seen through Tears," *Little Rock Arkansas Gazette,* June 16, 1978, B1 (quotation); "Lum and Abner," *Hygeia* 17 (January 1939): 31; and Chester Lauck to "Janie," Chet Lauck Collection (Archives and Special Collections, Ottenheimer Library, University of Arkansas at Little Rock). For a picture of the two at work on a script, see *Chicago Daily Tribune,* June 2, 1935, S6.

LUM AND ABNER SCRIPTS

January 1932

January 11, 1932

(Dog Barks)

Lum: Hello, hello.

(Dog Barks)

Lum: Git out from here. Howdy Abner. You better come git this critter fore I ruirn him.

Abner: Git away from ther Lead. Git up under the house ther sir. I wisht somebody'd learn him to stop banterin everything that comes on the place.

Lum: As many times as I've been over here that ornery critter dont seem to want me to come in the yard.

Abner: Well old Lead is a good slow track dog but thats all abody can say fer him. He aint got a bit of jedgement bout peepul comin on the place. He's jist as lible to try to stop me as not.

Lum: I'd git shud of him if he was mine. I drapped over to see why you never come to the office this mornin. I allowed you'd be down ther bright and early tryin to track down whoever it was that robbed Dick Huddleston's store.

Abner: Well I caint make no errests till we find out who done it.

Lum: Hits bein talked round amongst the folks in the cammunity that you aint doin right by your office. You aint goin to find out who done it by piddlin round yer place here.

Abner: Oh, I aint give up lookin fer him. There's one desperadio I'd love to track down fer Dicks allus did so much fer me. Looks like theys so much fer me to do here about the place today that I jist aint got off down ther but I been studyin a

75

right smart about it. I hope the woman all mornin here make hominy.

Lum: Whats the matter with her a doin it, she aint down are she?

Abner: No, but her strenth is failin her somethin wonderfully here of late. She's jist as willin as she can be but she jist caint stand up to hard work like she ust to looks like. I caint hardly stand to see her chop wood no more. I allus go off sommers to mysef while she's at it.

Lum: I'm shore sorry to hear it fer I've allus said it of Elizabeth that she could do more work than arry mule I ever seen take her one day and another the year round.

Abner: She was jist bound and determined to make hominy and so I jist stayed around to hope her pore that hot ash water fer I was afeard fer her to handle it by hersef.

Lum: Home made hominy. To my notions they aint nuthin finer abody can cook up. I jist love em.

Abner: Well I reckon I'm turned different from most but I never was much of a hand fer em, whilst I eat em, I dont take to em like the women fokes does. Come on back here to the pen Lum, I want to show you my meat hogs.

Lum: Yea, I want to see them. I've heard about em.

Abner: Oh, they're blooded stock. Poling chinys.

Lum: Is them the ones you got offen Caleb Weehunt?

Abner: Yea, I give Caleb a skinnin on that trade. I swopped him a turnin plow and four buckets of sorghum fer them four shotes. There they air.

Lum: Well, them are right piert lookin critters.

Abner: You ort to saw em when I first brung em over here. They'd been out on rangs and was plumb gant but agin I throwed the corn to em they pierten right up.

Lum: So thems Polimg Chinys. I grannies they're gittin a heap better lookin stock in through here now days. I can recollect back when they wern't nothin but Razorbacks. Abody counldnt fatten them at tall looked like.

Abner: No feedin them razorbacks corn is jist like throwin it away. Thays a heap of difference in hogs thataway. Look at them snouts how short and stubby they air.

Lum: Yea, you take one of them razorbacks, they can might nigh drink water outa a fruit jar. They're gist about half head.

Abner: I wouldnt have nuthin but blooded stock on my place no more.

Lum: Well now I'm proud to hear you talkin thataway fer I've saw the day when you had a dreadful hard time makin it through the winters. With these meat hogs and what corn you've got cribbed yonder you ort to have enough grease in yer smokehouse and enough corn to bread youns through the winter.

Abner: Yea, these hogs here is fat enough to butcher right now. I'd sorter laid off to butcher tomorrey if this cold snap hangs on.

Lum: Well now Abner while I aint no hand to meddle in other fokes bizness, but you'll be makin a terrible mistake when you do.

Abner: What's yer idys in sayin that Lum?

Lum: Why the signs. They're right square backards agin you. I was jist lookin at the alminac last night. They wont be right fer you to butcher fer another week.

Abner: Wellsir, I'm prod you told me. We aint got a alminac at our place and we're jist plum lost thout it. I caint never think to git one when we're in town ther.

Lum: Why, you ort to could tell that the moon aint right fer you to butcher. Hits on a decline. Hit was about like this when Ezra Seestrunks got after me to hep him butcher last fall. . . . . I told him he was makin a mistake. Told him ever bit of his meat would cook right in to grease but you know Ezra. . . . . . . Abody caint tell him nuthin.

Abner: Yea, stubbernest feller I ever knowed.

Lum: He went right on ahead and butchered and I hope him. . . . . and he give me a batch of sassidges fer me to take home . . . . and jist like I told him they went right straight to grease.

I patted out a few cakes as big as my hand and agin they got done they wern't no bigger'n a hicker nut.

Abner: Oh, abody caint go agin the signs in butcherin no more'n he can at plantin crops and sich as that.

Lum: Looky yonder's Dick Huddleston. Wonder what he's doin over here at your place?

Abner: Well, I bound you he's found out somethin bout who robbed his store. Come on back Dick. I want you to see my meat hogs.

Lum: Look at him grinnin. He's got some kinda develment up his sleeve.

Abner: How'd you know wher we was at Dick?

Dick: Why, I come by the house ther and yer women told me you was back here, lookin at the hogs. I told her I never knowed whether I could find you or not but she sorter splained to me that you two was on the *out*side of the pen.

Lum: (Laughs) I swan Dick you're the beatenest feller I ever seen at tryin to git somethin or nuther off on a body.

Dick: Thems nice lookin shotes ther Abner.

Abner: Yea, they do tollably well I reckon. You aint got no slant on who broke in to your store I dont reckon.

Dick: Naw, I aint. Thats what I come over to talk to you and Lum about. I been sorter checkin up to see what all they got and they got away with more'n I thought they did.

Lum: What all is missin Dick?

Dick: Well you see I takend invoice on the first and so I can tell purty clost to whats missin. I made out a list of it so's you can keep a eye peeled fer it, Abner.

Lum: Thats a right good idy Dick. Jist give Abner the list and me and him both'll look out fer it.

Dick: I aint got the list right here with me but they's several articles that I'd know in a minit if I seen anybody'a wearin. Course the groceries they taken'll be sorter hard to put yer finger on.

Lum: Yea, shore.

Dick: They was some right red fasinators I got fer the Christmas trade. I never sold none so if we can find any of them we'll have somethin to go on. They was some overhalls taken and some of them striped shirts.

Abner: I doggies, whoever stole that stuff is same as ketched right now. I got Pearl to do some out loud readin out of that *det*ective book last night and I got some idys on how to lay my hands on the scoundrel.

Lum: Now you dont want to do like you done when they robbed the post office over to Bellville and put everbody in the cammunity in that little jail you built.

Dick: No Abner, you want to be might keerful fer the folks around here is gettin sorter down on you anyhow.

Lum: Thats what I been tellin him Dick. Here I aint had but one case in my Jestice of the Peace court since Abner's been constable. If it wern't fer a few couples gittin spliced ever onst in a while my office wouldn't be payin nuthin.

Abner: Well, I caint make no sence outa you fellers talk. Here you are sayin I done wrong errestin everbody when I was tryin to ketch that Post Office robber and now yer jumpin on me on account I aint errested nobody fer robbin the store.

Lum: Well we aint tellin you not to errest nobody but we're jist tellin you to use some gumption about it. Why when you was lookin fer that Post Office robber you errested everthing that come down the big road and tried to lock em all up in that little jail. Men women and children.

Abner: I never errested no children no sech a thing.

Lum: Jist cause you never seen none is the reason.

Abner: Well I ketched him didn't I?

Lum: Oh, you was bound to git him the way you went at it. Jist lock up everbody in the county and you'll be shore to ketch the feller that robbed Dick's store too. But you caint do that.

Dick: Best thing fer us to do is to sorter lay low and keep our eyes open. Hit'll turn up sommers. Theys one thing shore, whoever done it knowed wher things was at ther in the store jist about as good as I do. Looked like they'd come down ther with a list and jist filled it out.

Lum: You better git Grandpappy Spears to hep you Abner. He was constable here fer so long——

Abner: Nossir, I aint goin to git him or nobdy else to hep me. That detecitive book says not to put no confydense in nobody. I aim to track down that robber by mysef.

Lum: Well, alright. I'm jist tellin you as Jestice of the Peace of Cloverleaf Township I want to see that crimynal brung to jestice.

Dick: I bleave you're jist bustin to try somebody in your Jestice court Lum.

Lum: Well yes while I need the fee I need the practise too.

Dick: Well, I got to be gittin back to the store. You fellers let me know if anything turns up.

Lum: Yea we will Dick.

Abner: Dont worry yersef a minit about it now Dick. I got a idy studdied up and I aim to have the scallawag that broke in your store fore night.

Dick: Alright Abner (fade) I know you'll do your best. Well youall come.

Lum: Yea, we will, you fokes come. (to Abner) Wellsir Abner ther goes as fine a feller as ever lived here in Pine Ridge Community.

Abner: Yea he shore is. Dick's allus doin fer somebody.

Lum: Yea he's a alright feller. We just got to ketch that robber.

Abner: If I jist had some blood hounds I could track whoever done that right down.

Lum: Yea, but them blood hounds runs into money when abody goes to buy em.

Abner: I doggies I bound you old Lead yonder'd might nigh track a feller down. I aint never put him on a trail yit that he never follered. Whilst I aint never tried him on humings, he's as good a varmit dog as ever set nose to a trail, If I do say it mysef.

Lum: Well, as the little boy says, abody never knows till he tries.

You could take him down ther to Dick's store and show him
them tracks and set him on the trail.

Abner: (Laughs) Wellsir I jist bleave I'll chance that.

Lum: What was that idy you told Dick you had studied up?

Abner: Well I never aimed to tell nobody but I know in reason
you aint goin to spread it none.

Lum: No I aint goin to say nuthin bout it.

Abner: Why I was figgerin on puttin on one of my detecitive
disguises after dinner and jist sorter detecitive around all
evenin and see what I can pick up.

Lum: Why everbody around here seen them disguises of yourn
when you put on that exybition down ther at the litary
extrasizes.

Abner: Yea, but they never seen this newun of mine.

Lum: Oh, you've got a newun have you?

Abner: Yea, I got a set of whiskers I made outa squirrell tail
that'll fool might nigh any of em. I put it on this mornin and
fooled the woman with it. (laughs) She was sayin yes-sir and
no-sir jist as nice as pie till I told her who I was.

Lum: I've lived clost nabors here with you too long fer you to
fool me though.

Abner: I doggies I'll gist show youns. I bound you I'll fool you
fore night. And another thing, you better be readin up on the
statutes fer Abner Peabody, the great detecitive, the man with
a thousand faces is goin after his man——fade

JANUARY 14, 1932

Lum: Howdy Dick.

Dick: Well, hello Lum how you today?

Lum: Oh, only tolably Dick only tolably. You aint got no mail fer
me ther dont reckon.

Dick: Yea, you got a post card from your gurl Maudy. She says
they're up now.

Lum: They air huh. Well I'm proud to hear it. Last hearin I had from her she said some of her yongins was took down sorter foundered therseves on that Christmas candy I sent em. Was that all she had to say?

Dick: No she said somethin another else I caint recollect now jist what it were. They's so many post cards comes in I caint keep it straight in my mind jist what all of em says. I'll git up and git it fer you dreckly.

Lum: Oh, they aint no hurry, I jist come by the store here to see if I couldn't git up a checker game.

Dick: Draw yersef up that nail keg. Git yersef thawed out good.

Lum: Have youns found out any more bout who it was broke in your store?

Dick: No I aint. Hit looks to me like now whoever done it made a clean gitaway.

Lum: I reckon Abner's out lookin fer the robber, he aint been down to the office all day.

Dick: Wellsir, when I come down to open up the store this mornin I thought I seen Abner. It wern't quite good day but I know hit [was] his old dog, Lead, with him. He had on the beatenest git up abody ever seen.

Lum: Well, I bound you hit was Abner alright, fer he said yistidy he was aimin to put on a new disguise he had and use old Lead fer a blood-hound.

Dick: I reckon that git-up he had on was a disguise. Wher'd he git the idy fer a constable to be wearin a disguise?

Lum: Oh, he's been havin his gurl Pearl do out loud readin to him out of that book on how to become a great detective. And he calls hissef Abner Sherlock Peabody now. Got the name from that detective in the book.

Dick: (Laughs) I swan to goodness, Abner can git some outlandish idys in his head.

Lum: To my notions, he'd git a heap futher if he'd git out and look fer that robber stead of tryin to make out he's a detective.

Dick: Why Old Grandpappy Spears when he was constable

he'd go right out and git em. Wern't no foolishness about him.

Lum: Yea, Grandpap was bout as good a constable as ever sarved Cloverleaf township. In his day he had the name of bein bout as handy with fararms as arry feller in these parts.

Dick: Yea, but I never takened much stock in that story he's allus tellin bout him shootin Jesse Jameses trigger finger off.

Lum: Well, agin abody gits up in years like Grandpappy, them things allus gits bigger ever time they tell it.

Dick: Well, I swan to goodness, settin here talkin bout Grandpappy and yonder he comes in the front door ther now.

Lum: Yessir shore is. Got his head all wropped up with that fasinator like he was lookin fer a cold wave.

Dick: Come on back to the far Grandpap.

Grpap: Howdy Lum. How're you Richard?

Dick: Oh, fairly middlin I reckon. How you feelin?

Grpap: Why, I'm spry as a right yong colt. In spite of my years. Fokes says I'm livin on borrowed time now. (laughs.)

Dick: Yea you dont look a day older'n you did forty year ago.

Lum: What yons got in them buckets ther Grandpap?

Dick: I can tell you them's eggs.

Grpap: Yea, thats what they air. The woman sent these down and Sister Simpson stopped me and ast me to fetch this bucket along.

Dick: How many you got ther?

Grpap: Why, the woman claims they's two dozen here, but yons better count em.

Dick: Why if she counted em they aint no use.

Grpap: Sister Simpson says they's twenty three here in her bucket.

Dick: Yea, she does that all the time she knows blamed well I'll count it even two dozen so's I wont have to bother my patience bout figger'n it up.

Lum: Looks like she's got more cotton seed in ther than she's got aggs.

Dick: I reckon she was afeard you was goin to fall down with em Grandpap.

Grpap: I told her they wern't no ust to have me carry haf a bale of cotton seed around jist to git them eggs down here, but abody dont git fer arguin with a woman. (laughs)

Dick: Alroght Grandpap, here's yer buckets. Did youns want credit fer them or do yons want to trade it out?

Grpap: Oh, I'll get some snuff and tobacker in a minit. I wanted to ast youns, Have youns got any trace of whoever it was broke in your store?

Dick: No we're still lookin fer em.

Grpap: Well, hit jist looks like Abner aint the right man fer constable. Why, I'd a had that robber ketched long fore now.

Lum: Now, Abner's doin all he cin. Abody caint jist walk right out and lay his hand on them fellers.

Dick: Oh, I think Abner'll ketch em, jist give him time.

Grpap: I recollect one time I went after Jesse James. In them days I could throw guns with the best of em, if I do say it mysef. Lets see that was back in in- Now let me think—

Dick: Back in '98, and you shot his trigger finger off.

Grpap: Well, I must of told you bout that Richard.

Dick: Yea, bout hunderd and fifty times is all.

Grpap: Oh I never done no sech athing, you're jist tryin to git somethin off on me now.

Lum: What did you do with him after you shot his finger off Grandpap.

Grpap: Oh, he come right over and shooken my hand and said hissef, I was the onlest feller that had ever did that.

Dick: You was the only one that ever shot that finger off was you?

Grpap: Yea, but you dont see me goin round namin it to everbody. If that was Abner that done that, he never would git done tellin it.

Dick: You and Abner dont hit off very well since he got to be constable do you Grandpap?

Grpap: Well, no we aint had no fallin out. I jist dont take to some of his carryin ons in the constable's office. The first thing he done was to build that calibuse down ther. That was rediculisest thing I ever seen. Why hit aint big enough fer a cat fight.

Dick: Lum, looky yonder, Look comin up the road.

Lum: Well what in the world is that?

Dick: Caint you make him out? Thats Abner in his disguise.

Lum: What in the name of common sence is that he's got on ther?

Dick: Thats that bath robe he got fer Christmas. He wore it around here fer a day or two thinkin hit was a overcoat till I told him better.

Lum: Now aint he a sight. Looks like he jist can git along.

Grpap: Hit aint no wonder look at the far arms he's packin. Ther's two shotguns and a highpower.

Dick: That looks like a sword he's got strapped on him ther.

Lum: Yea, thats what that is. Thats the one his old pappy had doin the war. Reckon what he thinks he looks like in that disguise?

Dick: Look at the whiskers. He's got all shapes and kinds on ther. I bet he's bob-tailed half the stock on his place to get them.

Lum: He told me yistidy he was goin to fool me. I'd know that walk of hissen as fer as I can see him.

Dick: I tell you what lets do. When he comes in, lets make out we dont know him. Now dont let on now.

Grpap: I dont want him to thank fer a minit he's got me fooled none.

Lum: Yea, Grandpap, We can have a lot of fun outen him. Make out we never seen him before.

Dick: Dont let on now here comes in. . . . .

Lum: I dont know wher I can keep from laughin or not.

Abner:——Evenin Gentlemen.

Lum: Howdy do sir.

Dick: Is they somethin fer you mister?

Abner: No I dont want to buy nuthin. I reckon you fellers dont know me do youns?

Lum: No, you've got me stranger. What might you call your name?

Abner: Why, . . uh . . my name . . oh . . uh . . Smith is my name.
Lum: I'm proud to make yer quaintance Mr. Smith. This here's
    Mr. Dick Huddleston and thats Mr. Milferd Spears right ther.
Abner: Proud to meet youns.
Dick: Smith, Smith. We ust to have some Smith's that lived here
    in Pine Ridge. Dont reckon they was any of your relations?
Abner: No, I aint never had no relations. I was the olest one in
    the family.
Lum: That looks a right smart like a sword you got on ther Mr.
    Smith.
Abner: Yea, thats the one my old pap—Yea, thats a sword.
Grpap: Is them guns youre packin ther loaded Mr. Smith?
Abner: Yesir them guns is loaded.
Grpap: Well they've got a sort of a law around here that caint
    nobody but ossifers pack loaded fararms thataway.
Abner: Well, I'm the const—You say they is?
Lum: Yea, theys a law agin it and we've got a constable here
    that'd throw you in jail in a minit if he knowed you was
    packin em.
Abner: He's a purty brave feller is he? (laughs)
Lum: Well, I dont know. He thinks he is but everybody knows
    he's skeered of his own shadder.
Dick: Yea, my store was robbed here the other night and jist
    between us I bleave he's the one that done it.
Abner: Now dad blame it caint nobody stand to my face and—
    You say you think he done it huh?
Lum: Yea, if Abner Peabody never done it, looks like he'd find
    the feller that did.
Abner: I've got some business with Dic—I mean Mr. Huddleston
    here would you two fellers mind to step up to the front of the
    store whilst I talk to him?
Lum: No, go right ahead Mr. Smith. Come on Grandpap. . . .
Dick: Alright Mr. Smith, what can I do fer you?
Abner: My name aint shore nuff Smith. Dont you know me Dick
    . . I'm Abner.

Dick: Abner? Abner who?

Abner: Abner Peabody. You know me Dick.

Dick: No stranger, you caint fool me, I've knowed Abner
Peabody fer years. You dont look a thing like him. He wears
chin whiskers but he aint got whiskers all over his face like
you've got.

Abner: Honest Dick, I'm Abner. These whiskers is jist stuck on
ther with molases. This is jist a disguise I put on so's I could
track down that robber that broke in your store.

Dick: Disguise? You mean to tell me that them whiskers aint
growed on ther?

Abner: Yea, I dont want to take em off fer I dont want Lum and
Grandpap to know who I am.

Dick: You're tryin to fool me. Why Abner Peabody is the
constable here in Pine Ridge.

Abner: Well, I'm the constable. Thats who I am Dick. Honest. I'll
cross my heart and body that I'm Abner. Wait a minit I'll take
off some of these whiskers sos you can see fer yersef. Now
looky ther.

Dick: Well I jist do declare. I never would of knowed you, I shore
wouldn't.

Abner: I fooled you didn't I. (laughs)

Dick: Well I reckon you did. Wells thats a good en on me.

Abner: Now listen Dick. I've found your robber. I know right
wher I can lay my hands on him.

Dick: How'd you find him?

Abner: Why, I takened old Lead and set him on the trail right
here at your back door wher the robber broke in and he
follered that trail plum out acrost Eagle Mountin and down
through Holly Bottom and he's back trailed and wound
round all day. Me with these new rubber boots on and rubbin
blisters on my feet but I stayed with it, and I've found yer
man.

Dick: Well thats good work Abner. It shore is. Where's he at?

Abner: Hit'll be the biggest surprise you ever had when I tell you

but you caint fool me and old lead . . . The feller that broke
in your store is right here in your store right this minit. . . . . .
. . . . .

JANUARY 15, 1932

Lum: (over telephone) Yessum, he locked Grandpappy up late
yestidy evenin. . . . . Why, Abner thinks he's the one that
robbed Dick Huddleston's store. . . . . Yessum. . . . . .
. . . Why of course he never. Hits the rediculist thing I ever
heard of. . . . . I dont know wher he got the idy. He's
been readin a book on how to become a great detective and
to my notions hits ruriend his reasonin. . . . . How's
that?. . . . . Why me and Grandpappy was down to
Dick's store late yistidy evenin and Abner come in ther with
one them disguises of hissen on and dreckly he called Dick
off and told him he'd found the man that broke in his store.
. . . . . . Yessum. and fore we knowed it he throwed a gun on
Grandpap and marched right over here and locked him up
in the calibuse. . . . . Well me and Dick thought he was
jist joshin. . . . . Mam?. . . . . . Oh yessum, he's still
locked up in ther, been ther ever since late yistidy evenin. . . .
. . .
Dick: Well hello Lum—Oh scuse me I never seen you talkin on
the telephone.
Lum: Jist a minit Sister Simson hold the receiver. (to Dick) Jist
hep yersef to a cheer ther Dick I'll git done talkin here in a
minit.
Dick: Go right ahead on, dont mind me.
Lum: Hello, . . . Now what was that you was sayin Sister
Simpson?. . . . . Oh, shore. Yessum, we're doin all we can
to git him let out but Abner's got the keys to the jail house
and he aint showed up yit this mornin. . . . . . Well you aint
the only one, might nigh everbody in Pine Ridge has called up
bout it this mornin. . . . . Alright, Sister simpson . . Not at

tall not at tall. Alright. (click) Well Dick, Abner aint showed up all mornin.

Dick: Wher's he at?

Lum: I've been tryin to ring his place but dont nobody answer the telephone over ther.

Dick: Well we've got do somethin bout Grandpap. Thats a down right shame Abner lockin that old man up thataway.

Lum: Why course it is.

Dick: They was a crowd down to the store this mornin jist raisin kane about it. If he aint let out of ther fore long I'm afeard they'll try to gang up on old Abner.

Lum: Reckon wherebouts he could be at?

Dick: I reckon he's jist stayin away from the office here cause he knows everbody'll be jumpin on him to make him turn Grandpappy loose.

Lum: Yea thats jist what the trouble is. He's about hid out sommers to wher nobody caint find him.

Dick: You're shore he's got the keys to the jail with him.

Lum: Yea, I looked all through his desk ther and they aint a thing in it ceptin some mail order catalogues.

Dick: What in the name of goodness has got in to Abner here of late?

Lum: Oh, readin that book on detecitivin, he's got the idy he's a great detective.

Dick: Why this aint like him at tall, I've allus thought a heap of Abner but I'm bout to git all I can stand on this deal.

Lum: You know Dick, I bleave Abner and Grandpap has had a little fallin out here of late. Maybe thats got somethin to do with it.

Dick: Well they may be at outs I dont know bout that but I dont bleave Abner would take it out on him thisaway. He's dead sartin that Grandpap done it but he dont give his reasons fer thinkin so.

Lum: We ort to go out ther and talk to Grandpap a little and sorter cheer him up.

Dick: Yea, we better do that.

Lum: He caint hardly talk above a whisper he's hollered and carried on so out ther.

Dick: He's been hollerin has he?

Lum: Yea, you never heard such carryins on. Poundin on them walls and kickin the door and hollerin. I could hear him plumb over ther to my place. He woke me up long in the night. I finally jist got up and dressed and brung him some comforts over to sleep on.

Dick: Wellsir ther's Abner shore as the world.

Lum: Well hits about time he was showin up.

Dick: Lets jist talk straight to him. We got to make him let Grandpap out.

Lum: We can talk to him but I dont know wher hit'll do any good or not. I argied and reasoned with him fer two hours last night but he's got his head set.

Abner: Hi fellers. How youall this mornin.

Lum: Howdy Abner.

Dick: Abner we want to talk to you and want you to listen to reason.

Abner: Alright name yer business.

Dick: We want you to go out ther and onlock that door and turn Grandpappy Spears loose.

Lum: Yea, now you've carried things fer enough. Too fer even.

Abner: They aint a bit of use in you fellers arguin. I'm the constable of this township and I've tracked down and ketched the one that broke into Dick's store. I've got him locked up and I'm aimin fer him to stay ther till his trial comes off.

Lum: Well if you're waitin on a trial, I can tell you right now what I aim to decide agin it comes up in my Jestice court . . . He aint guilty.

Dick: Course he aint guilty. Why you ort to know yersef as well as anybody that Grandpappy wouldn't do nuthin like that. He's lived right here in this settlement fer more'n sixty year.

Ever since the Cival war, and I never knowed of him gittin
into no kind of trouble.

Lum: Why, he was constable fer years here till last fall when he
resigned to let you have the office.

Abner: Oh, I hate it jist as bad as you fellers do but law is law.
I'm jist doin my duty. If hit'd a been one of you fellers hit
would of been the same. (((((telephone))))) I swore to uphold
the laws of the country—

Lum: Wait a minit thats our ring. Go ahead and answer it Abner.

Abner: You answer it Lum hits most likley somebody else wantin
to jump on me bout errestin Grandpap. They got to callin up
last night gittin me out of bed way up till after nine o'clock so
I jist set the receiver offen the hook so's the bell couldn't ring.

Lum: Hello, This is Eddards and Peabody's Law and Constable
office. Lum Eddards, Jestice of the Peace doin the talkin. . . .
. . . . Who?. . . . . Oh How are you Aint Charity? (to Abner)
Hit's Grandpapy's woman. . . . . Yessum he's here.
Do youns want to talk to him?. . . . . . . Well jist hold the
receiver. . . . . (to Abner) Aint Charity wants to talk to
you Abner.

Abner: Why'nd you tell her I wasn't here.

Lum: Oh, I couldn't tell her that.

Abner: Well tell her I'm too busy to talk to her.

Dick: Go on Abner and talk to her.

Abner: No I aint agoin to do it I tell you.

Lum: Hello, Why uh . . Abner uh says he caint talk to you right
now. . . . . Are they anything I could do fer you?. . . . . . . Uh
huh. . . . . . Well me and Dick both has been talkin to him
bout it Aint Charity. . . . . Well he says he dont aim to
turn him loose. . . . . Why course not. Everbody
knows he never done it?. . . . . . . Yea. . . . . Well now
dont you worry none fer we'll git him outa ther someway . .
(to Abner) Abner you ort to be shamed of yersef this pore old
woman is cryin her eyes out, jist plum heart broke. . . . .

Abner: I caint hep it. Law is law.

Lum: How's that Aint Charity?. . . . . Uh huh. Well
I dont bleave I'd do that. I'll talk to him somemore and if he
dont change his mind, you can do that as a last resort. . . . . .
yea, ... Well now dont you worry yersef. . . . . . Oh, thats
alright. I'm proud to do fer you if I can. Alright. (click) Now
Abner, you're bout to git yersef into it shore nuff.

Abner: What you mean Lum? What did she say?

Lum: She said if you never let Grandpap loose, She's goin to call
up the County Jedge and tell him all about it.

Dick: He's the one that appinted you to the office Abner. Now if
she gits him in behind it, he'll jist about take the constable's
office away from youns.

Lum: I want to know what ever give you the idy that Grandpap
done that in the first place.

Abner: Well I'll jist tell you. I got up early yistidy mornin and
me and Watson struck out lookin fer the feller that broke in
Dick's store.

Dick: Yea, I think I seen you round the store down ther jist as I
was goin down to open up.

Abner: Well we was pickin up the trail ther wher the robber
broke in and I set Watson on it.

Lum: Now wait a minit who's Watson?

Abner: Oh thats a new name I got fer old Lead my dog.

Lum: Wher'd you git sich a name as that?

Abner: Well in that Detecitive book Pearl's been readin to me, the
feller that heps Sherlock Homes is named that.

Lum: You've got a idy you're goin to be a great detecitive like
that feller Homes aint you?

Abner: Well they aint nuthin to keep me from it are they.

Dick: Go ahead and tell us how come you to arrest Grandpap.

Abner: Well me and Watson got on the trail and sir we follered
it plum accrost Eagle Mountain and down through Holly
Bottoms and then he back tracked and wound around then
circled back up through Grandpap's meader and right up to
his back door.

Lum: Well he wasn't on no trail. He was jist huntin I reckon. He
  bout smelled vittals cookin ther at Grandpaps place and went
  up ther after some grub.
Dick: Wait a minit now, That hound of yours might of been
  trackin Grandpappy. You say you picked up the trail ther at
  the back door of my store?
Abner: Yea, thats wher we started in.
Dick: Grandpap was down ther Monday I bleave it was and got
  me to hand him some cateridges out the back door ther. He
  said he was goin over on Eagle Mountain squirrel huntin.
Abner: Well now he claims that he went squirrelin the other day
  and went them same rounds I taken. I jist figgered hit was a
  excuse he'd studdied up.
Lum: If them's yer reasons fer doin it Abner. You may as well
  turn him loose fer if you dont they's goin to be trouble
  shore.
Dick: Yea, Now hit was my store that got robbed and Lum's the
  Jestice of the Pease and we're both astin you turn him loose.
  Why even if Grandpap had of done it I wouldn't want to set
  the law on him.
Abner: Alright, alright. If nuthin else aint goin to do you, I'll turn
  him out. You fellers can out argue arry woman I ever seen.
Lum: Thats the time Abner, I knowed you'd see reason. Lets go
  right on out and onlock the door.
Dick: Pore old feller I bet he'll be glad to git outa ther.
Lum: Now Abner, Grandpappy's been frothin at the mouth on
  account of he's so mad at you. Me and Dick'll sorter smooth
  things over fer you so's he wont hold it agin you.
Dick: I dont hear no noise in ther. He must be asleep.
Lum: I reckon he is. He never slept none last night to mount to
  nuthin and he wouldn't let nobody else sleep neither. Git the
  door onlocked Abner.
Dick: Hey Grandpap . . Come on to the door. Abner's goin to let
  you out.
Lum: Go ahead caint you find the keys?

Abner: Wellsir fellers I caint find the blame things. I've looked in ever pocket and I caint find em nowher. I doggies I must of lost em———

Lum: Hold on there. Why they aint nobody in ther. Grandpapy's got out. And the door's locked.

Abner: Well I doggies. He's gone. He's got out. Jist as shore as the world.

JANUARY 18, 1932

Lum: Well, I'm plumb tuckered out. I'm glad to git to set down.

Dick: That was right smart of a jaunt we taken. I bout made up my mind Grandpap aint out in them mountings nowher.

Lum: Better chunk up the far ther Abner. Hit may be gone out, They's some splinters ther in that box back of the stove.

Abner: Whats the matter with you chunkin it up, you aint growed to that cheer aready air you?

Lum: Go ahead Abner. I'm done set now. I couldn't git up fer nuthin.

Dick: I dont know wher to start in lookin but we've got to find Grandpap. Hits a cinch he aint in them mountains.

Lum: Ezra Seestrunks and Caleb Weehunt and a bunch of them fellers is lookin over ther in the saw-tooth mountains today. They might run on to him.

Dick: I dont know, hits got me worried till I aint at mysef.

Lum: Hits the strangest thing I ever heard of. Jist peers like the ground has jist swollered him up.

Abner: I caint see fer the life of me how he ever got outa that jail house. The door is still locked and they aint a hole in that jail nowher he could of clum out of.

Lum: Oh, hit'd jist astonish abody how he got out and wher he went.

Dick: I dont know how he got out but he aint in ther thats a cinch.

Lum: He's jist doin like anybody else would that had broke jail, he's jist layin out sommers. I felt dead fer right that we'd find him in that old minin shanty on old Briar Creek.

Dick: I swan Abner, I git mad at you ever time I think about it. That pore old man eighty seven year old and havin to hide out thisaway.

Abner: He dont have to hide. He's a free man if he jist knowed it.

Dick: Yea, but you ort to knowed better'n to errest him in the first place. A ten year old youngin would of had more gumption about em than do that.

Lum: The one I feel sorryful fer is Grandpappy's pore old woman settin over ther cryin her eyes out. The circuit rider was tellin me yistidy at service that Aint Charity had hysterics all day Saturday.

Abner: I'm gittin tired of you fellers jumpin on me bout that. I told youns how sorryful I was. I thought I was dead fer rights or I never would of errested him. I've did all I could. I've might nigh walked my legs off the last three days alookin fer him.

Lum: Oh, you're doin all you can now. Wher you done wrong was ever errestin him.

Abner: I know it. I aint sayin but what I was in the wrong. But hits too late now. Why everbody in the cammunity is down on me. They aint nobody on speekin terms with me. Even the woman treats me like I was a stranger round the house.

Lum: I bleave if I was you, I'd call up Aint Charity on the telephone and try to comfort her.

Abner: Well, I dont know, she's pisen mad at me. I'm jist afeard hit'll agg on trouble.

Dick: Yea, thats the thing to do Abner. I bleave she'll think a heap more of you fer it.

Lum: Jist tell her that you know now that you made a mistake to errest him and you're doin everthing you kin to find him and tell him he aint under errest no more.

Abner: I'm willin to do anything I kin to put things at rights. Whats their ring?

Dick: Lets see. A long and two shorts I think. Talk as cheerin as you can to her. Tell her they's two or three searchin parties out lookin fer Grandpap.

Lum: ((((Telephone)))) Yea, tell her not to worry none.

Abner: Hello, Hello. Is that you Aint Charity?. . . . . . Well this her's Abner . . . Abner Peabody. . . . Hello, hello . . Hel——— (to Lum) She's hung up the receiver right in my year.

Lum: Well, I knowed she was mad. What did she say?

Abner: She never said nuthin. When I told her who I was she hung up the receiver like hit was burnin her hand.

Lum: Wait a minit let me call her up.

Abner: If you want my notions on it, (((((Telephone)))))) yer goin to make bad matters worser.

Lum: Hit wont hurt nuthin to try to comfort he—Hello . . . Aint Charity this is Lum Edards talkin. . . . . Yea . . Yessum, Abner was goin to tell you how sorryful he is——Well he knows he done wrong by errestin Grandpappy. . . . . Course thats already been did now but he's been lookin night and day fer him to tell him he's a free man now. . . . . Yessum. . . . Well now I wouldn't worry none about it fer he'll turn up sommers. He's about hid out sommers thinkin they're still after him fer robbin Dick's store. . . . . Me and Dick and Abner jist got back from a round over Old Piney Mountain and down Briar Creek. . . . . No we never seen no track of him, but they's some more fellers out lookin fer him, some of em'll shorely find him.

Dick: That aint very cheery news you're givin her Lum.

Lum: Jist a minit Aint Charity. (to Dick) How's that Dick?

Dick: I say, you're sposed to be cheerin her up. I bleave Abner's right, you're makin matters worse.

Lum: Well, she's cryin and takin on so here. I caint think of nuthin cheerful to say.

Abner: Tell her a funny yarn or somethin or other.

Lum: She aint in no humor fer no monkey business. Hello. Now dont take on thataway Aint Charity fer hit aint goin to hep

none, everbody's doin all they know how to find Grandpap. .
. . . . . No he aint lost why you could blindfold him and turn
him loose forty mile from here in arry direction and he'd find
his way back. He knows every pig and cow trail in the whole
county.
Dick: No he may be hidin out but I know he aint lost.
Lum: We'll call you jist as soon as we learn anything. Now dont
worry. Everthing'll be alright. . . . . . Uh huh . . . Yessum. . . .
. . Not at tall. Alright. (click)
Abner: Did she say anything bout me Lum?
Lum: Oh, course she's mad. Abody caint blame her fer that, then
she's worried along with it.
Dick: I was jist lookin out the winder here. Ther's old Lead your
dog Abner, He trailed Grandpap out over Eagle Mountain
when you was lookin fer the robber reckon he couldn't trail
him again?
Abner: No, I've sided old Watson aint much hep to me in
detecitivin. I tried to git him to pick up the trail ther Saturday.
Tried him three or four times and evertime he lead me right
over to Oscar Field's place.
Lum: Over to Oscar Field's. Reckon Grandpappy could of went
over ther?
Abner: No they wern't nobody on the place. Oscar's been gone
fer a week. You know they been visitin some of his wife's
relations over round Menar sommers.
Dick: Him and his fokes is back though. I seen Oscar this
mornin.
(Dog Barks)
Lum: What in the world is old Lead barkin at out ther. . . . . . .
Why thats Oscar Fields he's got cornered out ther . . . Here
Lead. Cut out that foolishness. Abner you better step ther to
the door and call that dog off fore he takes a leg offa Oscar.
Abner: Git fer home ther Watson . . Well howdy Oscar. Come on
in. Why'n you pick up a rock to that ornery critter.
Oscar: Well hits a good thing fer you he never bit me.

Dick: Howdy Oscar. You been visitin aint you?

Oscar: Yea, been gone all week. I been hearin bout your store gittin broke in.

Dick: Yea, Someone broke in it last Monday night.

Oscar: Aint they found who done it yit?

Dick: No, we aint. Abner here had Grandpappy Spears locked up thinkin he done it and when he went to turn him loose, he was gone.

Lum: Yea, and aint nobody saw him since Friday.

Abner: You see Oscar he thinks I'm still after him and he's hidin sommers.

Oscar: Well if he broke outa jail and is hidin, hit sounds like you had the right feller alright dont it?

Abner: Well, I dont know. Thats what I thought at first but I done changed my mind.

Lum: Why course he never done it. You ort to know Grandpappy wouldn't do nuthin like that.

Abner: No, I dont think he done it. None of us does.

Lum: Anybody with jist ordinary reasonin ort to know that.

Oscar: What do you know bout it Lum Edards. You aint the constable here, why dont you keep your mouth outa this.

Lum: Why I was jist givin you my views on it.

Oscar: Well we dont care bout hearin em. If Grandpap never robbed that store what you do you reckon he'd be hidin out thisaway fer.

Dick: Now listen Oscar, we been workin on this case all week and here you come in this mornin and you're tryin to tell us all about it.

Lum: Yea, come round here hoppin all over me bout nuthin. One of these days I'm goin to git all I can stand and- and—

Oscar: And What? Why I could break you in two fore you knowed what had hold of youns.

Abner: Well the great I am looky yonder comes Grandpappy. Jist shores the world.

Lum: Hit shore is. Well I swan to goodness.

Dick: Yessir. Why he dont look a bit wore out. Walkin jist as spry as ever.

Lum: *Hello ther Grandp*appy. Glad to see you back.

Abner: How you feelin Grandpap?

Lum: Come right on in.

Abner: I doggies Grandpap, I dont bleave I ever was as proud to see anybody——

Grpap: Dad blame you Abner Peabody I dont want to have a thing to do with you.

Abner: Now, I'm jist as sorryfu———

Lum: Jist let that go now Abner.

Dick: Where in the world have you been. Everbody in Cloverleaf township has been lookin fer you fer three days.

Grpap: Yea, I been seein em go by and loud thats what they was doin. I jist allowed they was tryin to ketch me and put me back in that jail house.

Dick: Why, no we went out ther to turn you out of jail last Friday and you'd already got out.

Grpap: Has the old woman been oneasy bout me?

Dick: Yea, she's worried hersef might nigh down about you. I better call her and tell her your back.

Grpap: Jist wait a minit I'm goin on over ther dreckly. Wher'd Oscar Fields git off to?

Dick: He was standin right here a minit ago. He must of went out the back door. Why?

Grpap: Why, you better ketch him. He's the one that robbed your store Dick. I been up ther in his barn loft ever since I got outa that Jail. I found all that stuff thats missin outa yer store up ther in his loft while ago and————

JANUARY 19, 1932

Abner: Soon as you git done readin the weekly paper ther, I'll banter you to a game of checkers.

Lum: We got to cut out that playin checkers here in the office.

Fokes round here's lible to make a complaint that we aint
tendin to the duties of our offices.
Abner: Why, I dont see nuthin wrong in it as long as we aint got
nuthin to do.
Lum: Nuthin to do? Why you've got aplenty to do if you'd jist git
up from ther and do it.
Abner: What you drivin at?
Lum: You know what I mean—Errestin Oscar Fields fer breakin
in Dick Huddlestons store. You ort to had him in jail first
thing this mornin.
Abner: I dont aim to lock him up till I know fer shore he's the
one that done it. I got everbody down on me over lockin
Grandpappy up and I dont aim to make no more mistakes.
Lum: Well he's the one that done it alright.
Abner: Yea, I bleave he is too, but bleavin and knowin is two
diffrent things.
Lum: Didn't Grandpappy tell us that he seen all them things thats
missin out of Dick's store up ther in Oscar's loft?
Abner: Yea, but I never seen em.
Lum: Did youns go over ther to look fer em?
Abner: No I aint went on account of I know hit'll make Oscar
pisen mad if I go meddlin round his barn out ther.
Lum: I know what the trouble is . . You're jist afeard of Oscar—
——
Abner: No I aint no sich a thing.
Lum: You've allus been afeard of him. You know blamed well
he's the one that stole that stuff and hit's your duty as
constable to fetch him over here and lock him up.
Abner: Now Lum dad burn it, I dont want you to git the idy that
I'm afeard of Oscar, fer I aint. I jist want to be sartin he done
it fore ever I errest him.
Lum: Well you aint goin to find out nuthin by stayin round the
office here and playin checkers. You ort to ask Grandpappy
some more bout that.
Abner: Trouble of it is, Grandpappy's mad at me fer lockin

him up to wher he wont talk to me. I caint git nuthin outa him.

Lum: Why'nt you call him up and talk to him on the telephone maybe he's cooled off some by this time.

Abner: Nossir. I tried to tell him yistidy how sorryful I was bout the wrong I done him but he wouldn't even talk to me. Said he never wanted to have a thing to do with me.

Lum: Oh, he was mad then but I bound you he's alright now.

Abner: Nopesir, I can be jist as stubburn as he can. If they's any talkin done he'll have to be the first un to speak.

Lum: I grannies, you two old roosters stays mad at one another more'n half the time.

Abner: Well caint nobody git along with Grandpappy.

Lum: You got to recollect Grandpappy's gittin up close on to Ninety year old. I recollect he was a growed man when I was jist a kid of a boy round here.

Abner: Yea, and the older he gits the harder he is to git along with.

Lum: I bleave I'll call him up and git him down here. You can set here and I'll ast him a lot of questions bout why he thinks Oscar done it and you can listen.

Abner: Go a head on and do as you like about it but I'm tellin you right now, I dont aim to take nuthin offen him.

Lum: What is his ring? Two shorts and a long. (TELEPHONE)

Abner: I bet he wont come if he knows I'm down here.

Lum: Hello . . . Is this Spears's place? . . . . . I reckon you was mighty proud Grandpappy's back. I want to talk to him Aint Charity. . . . . Alright.

Abner: Is he ther Lum?

Lum: Yea, she's callin him to the telephone . . (Laughs) I grannies, I hear Evalenar talkin to somebody.

Abner: What's she sayin?

Lum: Be quiet a minit and I'll tell you. . . . . I heard her say her and Jake Means has had a bust up. . . . . She said somethin another bout me ther I couldn't make out what it was. I jist heard her call my name———

Abner: Maybe she's talki——

Lum: Be quiet. . . . . . . Oh, Hello, (to Abner) Hits Grandpappy.
This is Lum Edards. . . . . yea. What youns doin. . . . .
uh huh. . . . . Well I'm sorry I woke you up. . . . . Oh,
nuthin in pertickler. Could you come over to the office fer a
few minits?. . . . . . . Well, me and Abner is workin on that
case tryin to find out who it was robbed Dick's store. . . . . . .
. . Yea, I know you did, thats what we wanted to talk about. .
. . . . Yea, he's here. . . . . . Now Grandpappy they aint
no use to feel thataway, he's jist as sorry as he can be. . . . . . .
. . . Yea, he says hissef he done wrong and he's willin to shake
hands and be friends if you'll fergit about it. . . . . .

Abner: I aint neither Lum Edards. I aint goin to shake hands with
him no sich a thing.

Lum: Yea, well come right on over then Grandpap. . . . . Alright
(click)

Abner: Did he say he would come over?

Lum: Yea, he'll be here dreckly. I wonder what that was Evalener
was sayin bout me?. . . . . . So her and Jake Means has had a
bust up? Well I knowed she'd git tired of him.

Abner: Who was it she was talkin to Lum?

Lum: I aint fer shore but hit sounded a right smart like hit was
the widder Abernathy. So her and Jake aint hittin it off.

Abner: You act like you're sorter tickled over it Lum.

Lum: I reckon I ort to be shamed of mysef but to be right honest
I am glad to hear it.

Abner: Lum Edards you caint fool me, you're still in love with
that woman.

Lum: No I dont bleave I'd go so fer as to say that whilst I
will admit, she's about as fine a little woman as I ever
knowed.

Abner: She's a good looker alright I'll say that fer her.

Lum: Oh yea, trim as a two year old colt. And smart as a whip.
Everbody says she's teached the best term of school here this
year we've ever had in Cloverleaf deestrict.

Abner: Ther you go. You'll be sparkin her again the first thing we know.

Lum: No I aint. I saw I was through with women and I meant it.

Abner: Reckon what she was sayin bout you ther when you heard her call your name?

Lum: I dont know I couldn't hear fer you talkin. Bleave I'll jist pick up the receiver and see iff she's still talkin.

Abner: If Dick was to come in here and ketch you evesdrappin, you never would hear the last of it.

Lum: Hesh up Abner, I caint hear and you talkin thataway. . . . . They're still talkin. . . . . . . Be right still. . . . . Well, I heard her say she'd like to go over to Ezra Seestrunks to Singin tomorrey night but she aint got no way to git over ther.

Abner: Why dont you call her up and ast her to let you carry her over ther?

Lum: Wait a minit, she's hangin up I bleave. Well. (click)

Abner: Air you goin to call her up?

Lum: No, I tell you Abner. New Years day they was a crowd of us down to Dick's store and everbody was givin their New Years resolutions and I give mine sayin I wasn't goin to have nuthin to do with women.

Abner: Why, I wouldn't let that stand in my way fer I bound you most all of them fellers has already fell down and broke thers nohow.

Lum: Oh, I know but if Dick was to hear bout me callin Evalener up, he'd josh the life outen me. When he starts in they aint no stoppin him.

Abner: Well, now's yer chance with Evalener. Sister Simpson was tellin my old woman jist the other day that Evalener talked bout you all the time.

Lum: Did she say that shore nuff?

Abner: Course she did. I knowed mysef she was struck on you. I been takin notice at her castin sheep eyes at you in meetin.

Lum: I might jist call her up and talk to her jist a little. I dont reckon that'd hurt nuthin.

Abner: Go ahead on and call her up. I want to hear youns.

Lum: Dont you tell no body bout me callin her up.

(TELEPHONE)

Abner: I aint goin to say nuthin bout it.

Lum: What if she wont talk to me? . Hello, Sister Simpson is Evalener ther? Tell Evalener I'd like to talk to her if it wont discomfort her none. . . . . . . Oh this is Lum, Lum Edards. . . . . Alright . . .

Abner: I doggies she'll be tickled half to death.

Lum: I dont know—Hello, What youns doin. . . . . . . Uh huh. . . . . Was you sprized at me callin you?. . . . . uh huh,. . . . . No I aint been mad, you was the one that——yea but——No I never neither. What started it was, you sayin you'd druther ride in that automobile of Jake Meanses than that surry of mine. . . . . You have. . . . . . . Well you can shore ride in it some more. . . . . Oh anytime you say. . . . . Alright whats doin tomorrey night. . . . . Well I aint much of a hand at singin but I'll be proud to carry you over ther.

Abner: Lum, you better hurry up here comes Grandpappy Spears.

Lum: Yea, well, Uh huh Yea, Well theys a man comin in the office to see me on some business, I'm going to have to stop right now. . . . Alright Goodbye.

Abner: Howdy Grandpappy. Come on in.

Grpap: Hidy Lum. What was it you was wantin of me?

Lum: Hello ther. I jist wanted you tell Abner here bout seein all that stuff over ther in Oscar's loft and all.

Grpap: Well, I dont minds to tell you but I aint tellin Abner nuthin. He's the constable and hit his business to find out them things fer hissef.

Abner: I wouldn't bleave nuthin you said nohow.

Lum: Here, here, Now you two old roosters has got to cut this foolishness out. Both of youns orter be ashamed of yerseves. Now lets see you shake hands and fergit about all this trouble you been havin.

Abner: I wouldn't shake hands with him at tall.

Grpap: I know you wouldn't I wouldn't let you. Acusin me of robbin Dick Huddleston's store and lockin me up in that calibuse of yourn out ther all night. I wouldn't let you tetch me.

Lum: I swan, you two is a sight. Here you air livin clost nabors to one another fer all these years. I know down in your hearts you love one another. Why dont you recollect Grandpappy a few years back when you was bed rid with the fevers and Abner come over ther and worked out your crops fer you? And Abner, Grandpappy and Aint Charity has might nigh raised your gurl Pearl.

Abner: Yea, thats so they have. She thinks as much of them as she does her own mammy.

Lum: Why you've hope one another thataway. Set up with one another when you was down. Jist fergit about all of this and shake hands.

Grpap: Well I'll shake hands if Abner will.

Abner: I'm sorry fer what I've did. Thers my hand on it.

Grpap: Hits alright Abner. Does look like though anybody'd a had more sence than to errest me fer robbin Dick's store lessen he was a ediot.

Abner: Dad Blame you. Caint nobody stand to my face and call me no idiot.—Aint no use to try to git along with you.

Grpap: Thats what I call'd you anyway.

January 20, 1932

[The script for January 20, 1932, has a handwritten note attached to it. It reads as follows: "pages 1, 2, & 3 of carbon missing— original in office file." Of course, the other copy can no longer be located, so this script begins a bit after the show's halfway point.]

Lum: I bleave you're jist afeard of him Abner.

Abner: No I aint neither. I aint afeard of nuthin or nobody but I know Oscar and I know he goin to make trouble agin I start to errest him.

Lum: Yea, he's lible to make trouble but he caint resist a officer.

Abner: He aint sposed to but I bound you he will.

Lum: Well if he does, you can errest him fer that too. Thats agin the law.

Abner: I tell you Lum, I smell trouble in it. I dont see why he caint go head and let hissef be errested like anybody else would. I dont know what to do hardly.

Lum: Well you better be doin somethin bout it fer fokes round Pine Ridge is beginnin to talk bout it. They want to know why you dont go head and errest Oscar.

Abner: Yea, I know it.

Lum: You got all the evvydence you need to prove he's the one that robbed Dick's store.

Abner: Yea, they aint no way round it he done it alright. I jist caint brang mysef to do it some way.

Lum: You might git the high sherrif in ther at Menar to come in and lock him up fer you.

Abner: No I dont want to do that, they might git the idy I'm afeard of him and try to take my constable's office away from me.

Lum: I'm rarin to try him in my Jestice court jist as quick as you git him locked up.

Abner: I wisht they was some way fer me to git him over ther in the jail thout him knowin it and jist shet the door and lock it fore he knowed it.

Lum: Might toll him over ther with a year of corn like abody does a hog. (L)

Abner: Shore nuff now Lum, hep me study up some way to git him locked up.

Lum: Well now. He's skeerd to death of that dog of yourn, Old Lead.

Abner: Yea, What about it?

Lum: You might git him over round the office and set old Lead on him then holler fer him to hide in the jail house. Then you could slip out ther and lock the door.

Abner: I'm afeard that wont work. Old Lead's so triflin lazy he's lible to quit runnin him fore he got in the jail and then Oscar want to jump on me fer sickin him on him.

Lum: Well lets see. Couldn't set a steel trap fer him could you?

Abner: Nossir, I dont want to do that. That would make him mad shore nuff.

Lum: He's right smart of a carpenter, you might git him to go down ther and do some repairin on the jail house and while he aint lookin jist lock the door and ther he is.

Abner: I bleave thats a good idy you got studdied up ther now Lum.

Lum: Wait a minit though, No, that wont work. no. That wont be OK.

Abner: What's the matter it wont?

Lum: Why if he was doin some carpenter work in ther, ther he'd be in ther with his hammer and saw. Hit wouldn't take him no time at tall to git out.

Abner: Yea, thats so alright.

Lum: He's goin to be a hard one to git over ther anyway abody takes it. I know in reason he's heard that Grandpappy told youns bout findin all stuff that was stole out of Dick's store up ther in his loft.

Abner: I aint saw Oscar since Grandpap told us bout it. I hope he's left the country.

Lum: Well hit would be a good sheddance, if he left and never come back.

Abner: I wish somebody had of did that, that wouldn't of been so much bother to errest. If hit'd been Old Grandpap that done it I'd a had him long ago.

Lum: Yea, but you caint order them robbers to your own likins.

Abner: Lum, I bleave you could git Oscar down ther to the jail fer some reason or ruther for me. He wouldn't be lookin fer you to try to lock him up.

Lum: I dont know Abner, that aint none of my look out and If I
was havin my ruthers, I'd a heap ruther not have nuthin to do
with it.

Abner: Well, I mean all you'd have to do would be to git him
down here. I'll look after lockin the door and all. He couldn't
blame it on you.

Lum: Trouble of that is hit aint diginfied. The Jestice of the Peace
aint sposed to have nuthin to do with the errestin.

Abner: I hate mightily to ast another favorance of you Lum.
You've allus did so much fer me looks like. I dont know what
I'd do if I never had you to lean agin when I git in a tight
thisaway.

Lum: Well OK I'll hep you if I can. You git to talkin thataway, I
caint git around you.

Abner: I doggies, I knowed you would. I knowed you would.—
———

[A handwritten line through the script seemingly indicates that the
actual broadcast ended here; however the script continues. Perhaps
Lauck and Goff rehearsed the script before airtime and needed to
stop here to stay within the allotted time.]

Lum: To my notions bout the best way to git Oscar down ther is
to make out you want him to look at the jail house fer some
reason or ruther. I can telephone him up and ast him to come
down and see if he can help us figger out how Grandpappy
got out of it the other day.

Abner: Yea, he's been tryin to let on that Grandpap done that
robbin so he'll be right in fer comin down I bound you.

Lum: Hits too late to start in on it this evenin but we ort to git a
right airly start in the mornin.

Abner: Hit wont take no time at tall Lum. Lets telepone him up
right now. I'm tard of fokes jumpin on me fer not havin him
locked up.

Lum: Caint do it now Abner. Here I am all dressed up to go after
Evalener.

Abner: Well I doggies. I'm goin down right now and tell Dick I'll have Oscar Fields in the calibuse fore tomorrow night.

January 21, 1932

Abner: Well Lum I was jist about to give you up ever gittin down this mornin.

Lum: Air you tryin to set ther and bawl the Jestice of the Peace out?

Abner: No now Lum I never meant it thataway. I jist wonderin what was keepin you. Most generally you're down here by good day light.

Lum: Well, facts is I overslept mysef this mornin . . Too much Party last night I reckon.

Abner: Did the party hold late?

Lum: Yea they never broke up till might nigh ten oclock. Used to, I could stay up thataway ofa night without bothern me any to speak of but here of late agin I go past my bed time I aint fittin fer nuthin all the next day looks like.

Abner: Well, I've allus said abody caint stay out all hours of the night and feel like nuthin the next day.

Lum: I never riz till round haf past six this mornin. Jist laid ther in bed sorter no count feelin.

Abner: Yea, you'll plum rurn yer milk cows lettin em go past milkin time thataway.

Lum: Oh, I aint got no regrets over it. I dont bleave I ever had sich a good time in one evenin.

Abner: What all did youns do?

Lum: Oh, we'd sing awhile then carry on a batch of foolishness. Agin the singin was over we got to playin games.

Abner: I dont like to pester you bout it Lum but hits bout time you was callin Oscar Fields up if yer aimin to git him down here this mornin aint it.

Lum: Yea, I'd might night let that slip my mind.

Abner: I aint fergot it. I was down to Dick's store this mornin after the mail and everbody in ther was jumpin on me bout not errestin Oscar Fields.

Lum: Lets see how was it we's aimin to git him in that jail thout him knowin it?

Abner: Dont you know you said you'd call him up and git him to come off down here to hep us figger out how Grandpappy got out of jail when I had him locked up.

Lum: Well now Abner, I wouldn't do this fer nobody else in the world but you. I jist a little skittish about it I'm afeard we're gittin into somethin we'll both have our regrets over.

Abner: No now, you git him down here and git him to go out ther in the jail and while he's in ther I shet the door right quick and lock it.

Lum: Alright I'm goin to call him now but if hit dont work, recollect I told you hit wouldnt.

Abner: His ring is a long and a short and a long. (Telephone) I know he's at home fer I seen him out back of his place while ago.

Lum: If he's to home hit wont take him no tim—Hello, hello . . . Is this Fields' place?. . . . . . Is Oscar about the place? . . . . . Uh huh. . . . . Well would yons mind to call him to the telephone?. . . . . . . Alright . . (to Abner) He's out back sommers.

Abner: What if he wont come over here?

Lum: Oh, I can handle Oscar alright. Agin I git through talkin to him he'll break his neck gittin over here. You know he's been tryin to make ever body think Grandpappy Spears done that robbin and I'll jist make out like we think so too.

Abner: Jist let on like I aint over here cause he wouldn't come at tall if he knowed it.

Lum: Yea, I'll take him right on out to the jail soon as he gits here and you can hide under the desk here.

Abner: You better not say nuthin bout that jail business to him over the telephone or he wont——

Lum: Wait a minit. HELLO, Is that you Oscar?. . . . . . What

youns doin?..... Oh, this is Lum Edards talkin ... Yea.
...... Why I jist called you up to talk to you a little bout
Grandpappy Spears robbin Dick Huddleston's store........
Yea, I think so too....... I bleave Abner had the right feller
when he had Grandpapp locked up ... Yea...... I never
have figgered out how he got out of jail. ...
Abner: I know how he got out Lum.
Lum: Wait a minit Oscar, hold the receiver. Hesh up Abner I'm jist
leadin him on now. I was jist fixin to ast him to come over here.
Abner: Yea, but Grandpappy told me this mornin how he got
out. I fergot and left the keys in the door after I locked him
up and he give em back to me and I come by and onlocked
the door this mornin.
Lum: I aint keerin how he got out. I'm jist lettin on I do. Hello
Oscar. . . . Hows that?..... Oh that was a law customer I
was talkin to. He was wantin some legal advise bout a matter.
.... Why I was jist sayin a minit ago, I caint figger fer the
life of me how Grandpapp got out of that jail. The door was
locked and I caint find a hole in ther nowher.
Abner: Why Lum Edards I jist got through tellin you.
Lum: I was jist wonderin Oscar if I could git you to come over
here and hep me figger out how he got out. You're a sort of a
carpenter and know more bout them things than I do.....
Well I've tried to git Abner to figger it out but he aint takin
no intrust in ketchin the robber looks like........ You will?
Could you come right on over?.... Alright Oscar. ... Yea,
alright. ... Dont let on to nobody what we're doin. . .
alright. (click) There you air worked as smooth as plowin
bottom land.
Abner: He's acomin is he?
Lum: Yea, said he'd be over here dreckly.
Abner: That was as slick a batch of talkin as I ever heard Lum.
Lum: Thats what you call pycology I was usin on him. Thats
somrthin else I learnt outa that book on how to develop yer
personality.

Abner: I aimed to ast you some more about that book of yourn Lum.

Lum: What is it you want to know bout it?

Abner: I was tryin to tell the woman bout it last night and I couldn't recollect jist what it was you said abody's personality is.

Lum: Oh, you mean you want me to explain what personality is.

Abner: Yea, what it is and wher hits at.

Lum: Well, yer personality is a, hits sorter hard to explain. Everbody's got em, some of em has got more'n others has. You know when you. . . . Well take a feller that. . . . . you've saw some fokes that jist peered to, to, . . I swan Abner you're the hardest feller to explain anything to I ever seen.

Abner: I caint make no sence out of no sich of talk as that.

Lum: Hits a right smart like yer concious is. You know what yer concious is?

Abner: No I caint say that I do. Wher's it at?

Lum: Why hit aint nowhers in pertickler hits all over you. Inside of yons.

Abner: Wait a minit, whichen was it you say is inside of yons, yer personality or yer concious.

Lum: Yer concious is. When you do sometin yer shamed of, thats yer concious a shamein you.

Abner: When you do sometin or ruther your proud of is that yer personality?

Lum: No yer personality—you dont feel hit.

Abner: Well you got me so mixed up I dont know nuthin bout nuthin. I bound you I couldn't find my way home right now.

Lum: The thing fer you to do is to take that book and git Pearl to read it to you.

Abner: Yea, jist as quick as you git done with it I want to borrey it.

Lum: Your jist plumb welcome to it. That chapter ther on how to be the life of the party hope me more'n arry thing yit. Why last night I jist had em bustin ther sides at me. Evalener said herself that I jist never seemed like the same feller.

Abner: I wisht I could of saw you. Did they find out bout you
    developin yer personality?

Lum: No and I dont want you to say nuthin to nobody bout me
    havin that book neither. Jake Means is lible to order him one
    and start developin hissen.

Abner: Aint you even goin to tell Evalener?

Lum: Course not, I'd a heap ruther might nigh anybody in the
    community'd no bout it then her.

Abner: How did she like them new expressions you was tellin me
    bout yistidy?

Lum: Oh fore the party was over last night I had might nigh
    everbody ther sayin OK and Oh Yea. Even the womin fokes.

Abner: Well I do know. I want to learn them mysef.

Lum: Drivin home last night in the surry Evalener sorter lent her
    head over on my shoulder and looked up at me. I couldn't
    hardly keep from smackin her one right in the mouth.

Abner: Why'nt you do it? I'd like to saw the expression on her
    face I bound you she'd a been sprized.

Lum: I dont know I jist couldn't brang mysef to do it someway or
    ruther. I dont want her to git at outs with me again. She said
    she was sorry bou—

Abner: Yonder comes Oscar Fields. Where bouts can I hide at.

Lum: Jist crawl up under the desk ther. I'll git Oscar on out to the
    jail house jist as quick as I can.

Abner: (Under Desk) This is awful hard on my rhumatics under
    here. I caint double up under here long.

Lum: I'll carry him right on out to the calibuse.

Abner: Let me know when he come——

Lum: Be quiet here he is now. Hello ther Oscar.

Oscar: Howdy Lum.

Lum: Draw up a cheer ther Oscar.

Oscar: Wherbouts is Peabody at?

Lum: He aints showed up yit this mornin. I reckon he's doin
    some chores about his place over ther.

Oscar: He's a great constable. Had the feller that robbed Dick's store then let him git away.

Lum: Thats what I wanted to talk to you about Oscar. I caint figger out how Grandpap got out of ther. I want you to look at it.

Oscar: Yea, let me look at that jail. I aint as easy fooled as some. More'n likely they's a loose board out ther sommers.

Lum: Well they may be but if they are I never seen it.

Oscar: I want to hep all I can fer I want to see the guy that stole that stuff off of Dick, put in jail and kept ther.

Lum: Hit's the strangest thing that ever happened since I been Jestice of the Peace.

Oscar: Hit might be that he had somebody on the outside a hepin him.

Lum: No I dont bleave he did Oscar. I bleave they's a way of openin that door from the inside but I caint find it. Jist go on in ther.

Oscar: This back winder here looks like it might of been meddled with. Come on in here Lum. Looky ther. See ther looks like somebody's been prizen on them bars.

Lum: Yea, shore does.

Oscar: Ther's the constable now. Come on out here Peabody. I think we've found wher old man Spears got outa here.

Abner: Yea, but you aint agoin to git outa ther Oscar Fields.

Oscar: What are you doin ther? What are you doin, tryin to lock that door.

Abner: I doggies I got you now. Your the feller that robbed Dick Huddleston's store. Yer under errest.

Oscar: Why, you little runt, I'll tie you in a knot if you dont let me outa here. Jist wait till I git out of here.

Abner: (Laugh) Yea, but you aint goin to git out of there.

Lum: Why, Abner you blamed ediot, you got me locked up here too. Onlock that door————onlock that door————

JANUARY 22, 1932

Abner: Mornin Lum. Here's some vittals the woman cooked up fer yer breakfast.

Lum: I aint wantin nuthin to eat I want out of here. What yons standin way back ther fer?

Abner: Wherebouts is Oscar at?

Lum: He's layin over ther in the corner asleep. Onlock this door right quick and let me out fore he wakes up.

Abner: Air you shore he's asleep now?

Lum: Yea, he ranted and raved all night and jist awhile ago drapped off to sleep.

Abner: Be right easy now Lum and be ready to slip out the door agin I git er onlocked.

Lum: Well hurry up, hurry up, git that door open.

Abner: Now, ther you are. Now let me lock it back up.

Lum: Yea, you better be shore he caint git out fer he spent haf the night tellin me bout what all he was goin to do to youns agin he got out.

Abner: Well I dont keer what he says. I aim to keep him ther till he cools off.

Lum: I orter to give you a good lickin mysef fer lockin me up ther with him.

Abner: Now Lum you know I'm jist as sorryful as I can be. I never aimed to do it.

Lum: Well why didn't you onlock the door and let me out yistidy evenin. The very idy of havin the Jestice of the Peace locked up in a jail.

Abner: I know I done wrong but they wern't no way round it. If I'd a onlocked the door to let you out I knowed blame well Oscar would of got out too.

Lum: Worst part about it I had a pintment with Evalener last night. I know she was settin over ther mad as a hornet on account of I didnt show up.

Abner: Well why'nd you tell me bout and I could of telephoned her up fer youns.

Lum: Tell you? Why didn't you hear me hollern over ther at your place last night?

Abner: Yea, I heard you hollern but jist allowed you was wantin me to turn you out and I knowed I couldn't do it.

Lum: You ort to of come down here and found out what I was wantin.

Abner: Now Lum I told youns how sorryful I was.

Lum: Well I learned one thing. I dont ever aim to try to hep you no more. Looks like you can git a feller into more trouble than anybody.

Abner: I shore want to thank you fer what you've did fer me. If hit hadn't of been fer you I never would of got Oscar errested.

Lum: I got to git in the office here and telephone Evalener and explain to her why I never showed up last night. I know in reason she's goin to be pisen mad.

Abner: Jist lay all the blame on me if you want to Lum.

Lum: Dont you worry, I'm goin to.

Abner: I'll jist fetch those vittals on in the office here. Chances you'll git hongry nuff to eat dreckly.

Lum: Well I'm hongry nuff but I aint got time to eat now. Jist lay it down ther on the desk.

Abner: I'll kinle up a far here.

Lum: Yea, I'm might nigh friz. That jail house out ther is cold as bein down in a well.

Abner: I doggies, that reminds me. I aimed to brang you down some civers last night and I jist plumb let hit slip my mind till right now.

Lum: This is a fine time fer you to be thinkin bout it. Is that Dick Huddleston comin yonder.

Abner: Yea, yea, thats Dick. Reckon what he's awantin. I called him up and told him last night that I had Oscar locked up.

Lum: Did you tell him you had me in ther with him?

Abner: Why no I never. I knowed I'd have a hard time explainin
 to him how come me to lock you up too.
Lum: Well you ort to of told him. He'd a come down here and
 got me out.
Abner: Yea, and he'd about let Oscar git out to while he was a
 doin it.
Lum: Well long as you aint told him, dont say nuthin to him bout
 it fer I never would hear the last of it.
Abner: Well I wont make no mention of it to nobody.
Lum: Come in Dick.
Dick: Good Mornin Lum. How you Abner?
Abner: Jist only tolably Dick.
Dick: Lum you look sorter peaked this mornin.
Lum: Yea, I never got much sleep last night, I'm sorter wore out.
Dick: Out sparkin the school marm agin I reckon. (laughs)
 You're too old to be stayin up to all hours of the night
 thataway.
Lum: No I wern't neither.
Dick: What you got yer breakfast down here fer? The Jestice
 of the Peace business so rushin you have to have yer meals
 sarved at yer office?
Abner: No my woman sent that grub down here fer Lum——
Lum: Hesh up Abner.
Dick: So you've got Oscar locked up have you?
Lum: Yea, he's out ther asleep.
Dick: Did you have much trouble when you errested [him]
 Abner?
Abner: No hit wern't no trouble. They aint none of em gits too
 bad fer me.
Lum: Yea wait till he gits outa ther he'll make you hard to ketch.
Dick: I think I'll go out ther and have a talk with him. I want to
 see if I caint git him to tell me wher all that stuff's at he taken
 outa the store. You better go long with me hadn't you Abner?
Abner: No I aint a goin out ther.
Dick: Well let me have your key.

Abner: Nosir, You can jist talk to him through the winder. I aint runnin no chances of him gittin outa ther.

Dick: Alright I'll talk to him through the winder then——

Lum: I hope Oscar dont tell him bout me bein in ther too. While Dicks out ther I better call up Evalener.

Abner: Yea you better (TELEPHONE) ketch her fore she leaves fer the school house.

Lum: I'm almost afeard to talk to her I know she going to be— HELLO . . I was tryin to ring Sister Simpson's place. . . . . . I wisht you would. Ring em fer me. . . . . .

Abner: Who was that you was talkin to Lum?

Lum: Oh it was Caleb Weehunt's woman, She's allus got to put her say in and wants to know who yer ringin.

Abner: Yea, she must set ther with the receiver stropped to er year.

Lum: Hello. Is that you Evalener. . . . . . I reckon you know who this is. . . . . . Yea, thats who. What youns doin?. . . . . Whats the matter you dont sound like yer feelin good today. . . . . . Well whats the matter then?. . . . . . . Well now thats what I was callin you up to explain to you. . . . . Yea but I want toxsplain to you why I never showed up last night. . . . . Well you ort to give me a chance to tell yo——. . . Well it wern't my fault. . . . . . . Now listen Evalener. . . . . Why I couldn't call you they wern't no place I could git to a telephone. You see Abner got me to——No I never neither I spent last night in jail. . . . . . Yea in jail. . . . . . Why I never did nuthin. . . . . Well let me tell you how come me in ther . . . Hallo, Hallo Hallo. . . . I grannies, she's hung up the receiver on me. Now see what you've did Abner.

Abner: Why I never done nothin. She's the one that hung up the receiver.

Lum: Yea, but you're the one that got [her] at outs with me. Here I was gittin along so good with her too.

Abner: If hit'll do any good, I'll call her up mysef fer you. I'll jist tell her the straight of it.

Lum: I dont know what to do hardly. Evertime we git
   straightened out with one another somethin allus turns up to
   split us up again.
Abner: Any way I can hep I'll jist be proud to do it.
Lum: You've caused enough trouble thout makin it any worser.
   I'll figger out some way to git her back in a good humor.
   Maybe hit tells in that book what to do in sich cases as this.
Abner: What book you talkin bout?
Lum: That'n I been readin on how to develope yer personality.
Abner: Does hit tell sich as that in ther?
Lum: Tells everthing bout how to git along with women.
Abner: I doggies, thats what I ort to had forty years ago. Here
   comes Dick.
Lum: Draw yersef up a cheer ther Dick.
Dick: Wher'd you say you was last night Lum? (laughing)
Lum: I never said. Why?
Dick: Oscar was tellin me you spent the night out ther with him
   last night.
Lum: I might of knowed he go tellin it round.
Dick: Well thats mighty nice of the Jestice of the Peace to come down
   and spend the night with the prisoners to keep em company.
Lum: Now Dick hit was bad nuff spendin the night in ther thout
   you joshin the life outen me bout it.
Abner: Hit was my fault Dick. I went to lock Oscar up and I
   frgot Lum was in ther and locked him up too. Oscar got to
   makin his brags about what all he was aimin to do to me to
   wher I was afeard to onlock the door to let Lum out.
Lum: I never got out till jist fore you come over here awhile ago.
Dick: Why, I want to speak to you two bout Oscar.
Lum: What about him?
Dick: I had a heart to heart talk to him jist now and in spite of all
   his orneyness and short comins, I caint keep from feelin jist a
   little sorry fer him.
Abner: Well I dont feel sorry fer him? Did he admit to stealin that
   stuff outa yer store?

Dick: Yea, I told him we had done found it up ther in his barn loft and he seen we had him dead fer rights. He couldn't do nuthin else but admit to it.

Lum: Well I dont feel sorry fer him but I do feel sorry fer his woman and them youngins of hissen.

Dick: Yea, thats what got me to studyin bout it. I went over ther this mornin to look at that stuff and I told his woman what had happened. She never even knowed wher Oscar was at last night. She got to beggin me not to send him to the penententury and all that. Got to cryin and all I tell you fellers hit got next to me.

Lum: Yea, she's a good woman. She shore is. Sendin Oscar to the pen is goin to hurt her and them youngin a heap worser than hit will Oscar.

Dick: Well now I bleave old Oscar is sorry bout it. He told me while ago that he'd bring all of that stuff back. He said they'd ett some of the groceries and he'd used some terbacker but outside of that the stuff was all ther.

Abner: You reckon his woman knowed wher them groceries come from.

Dick: No I ast her and him both about that. She jist sposed he'd bought em down ther . . . What do youall think about turnin old Oscar loose. I dont bleave he'll give you are me neither one no more bother. He offers to pay fer the stuff he's used. That is he'll give me a note till gatherin time.

Lum: Why, I fer one dont want to see them youngins and that woman of hissen suffer fer somethin he done. If I was havin my ruthers I'd a heap ruther see him turned loose mysef.

Dick: What do you think bout it Abner?

Abner: Well, I hate to turn him loose after havin sich a hard time gittin him locked up but if you two's fer turnin him out I aint goin to stand in yer light.

Dick: Good fer you. Lets go out and let him out—

Lum: Yea, you got the keys ther aint you Abner?

Abner: If hits jist the same to you fellers I wish you'd take the

keys and onlock the door fer him and wait till I git in my own
yard fore you do it. I'll holler when I'm ready————————

JANUARY 24, 1932

Abner: Well Lum if youns aint goin to talk to me or play checkers
or nuthin else, I bleave I'll poke on back to the place.
Lum: I jist aint in the humor fer no checker game.
Abner: Well whats the matter of you? All you've did all mornin is
jist set ther and look out the winder.
Lum: I told you they wern't nuthin the matter with me.
Abner: You aint been at yersef fer the last two days. You got a
long face ther like you'd jist heard jedgement was comin this
afternoon.
Lum: Oh, hits Evalener. The way she's been actin.
Abner: Whats she done now?
Lum: She's still at outs with me bout not showin up over ther
after her last Friday night.
Abner: Why dont you jist explain to her bout you gittin locked
up ther in the jail by mistake?
Lum: She wont give me a chanst to tell her. I've teleponed her
up two or three times and bout the time I git to explainin it
she hangs up the receiver. All I got to tell her was that I was
in jail and she dont give me time to tell her how come me in
ther.
Abner: Looks like you'd see her and tell her all about it.
Lum: They aint no chanst to see her to talk to her. That Jake
Means is hangin round her all the time. Aint a bit of tellin
what he's told her.
Abner: Is he keepin company with her agin?
Lum: Yea, they was out to meetin together yestidy. Settin up ther
in the choir singin outa the same hymnal. I aint gotta bit a
use fer that Jake Means nohow.
Abner: Jake pears to be a great hand with the womin fokes.
Lum: If hadn't been fer you lockin me up in that dad blamed

jail, I'd a showed him how courtin ort to be did. I never got more'n haf through that book on how to Develop yer Personality.

Abner: Does hit say in ther what to do when abody's sweetheart gits mad at him fer gittin locked up in jail?

Lum: Course not. Abody aint sposed to git hissef locked up in jail accidental.

Abner: Everbody to ther own notions but If I was you I wouldn't worry my patience over Evalener. Jist looks like her and you caint git along notime without gittin at outs with one another.

Lum: I aint at outs at her. I will say she aint did me right by not lettin me explain about bein in jail.

Abner: I bleave she's jist keepin company with Jake Means jist to make you jelous.

Lum: Reckon she is shore nuff?

Abner: Thems jist my notions on it. Thats what Sister Simpson told the woman.

Lum: Well, if thats whats she's tryin to do she spends more time at makin me jelous than she does keepin company with me.

Abner: I bleave she sorter likes to ride in that automobile of Jake's.

Lum: Yea, I seen him carryin her past here this mornin in it carryin her over to the school house.

Abner: Oh, he carries her backards and forards might nigh ever day in it.

Lum: If she jist knowed it, she'd be a heap more safer ridin in my surry.

Abner: You ort to git you a automobile Lum. I bound you she'd drap old Jake like he was a hot pertater.

Lum: Well I dont know hardly. I've studdied about it a right smart. The pesky things is so complincated I'm jist afeard I never would learn to handle it.

Abner: Why they aint no trouble to ketch on to.

Lum: How come it you aint drive yourn none then?

Abner: Well the woman and Pearl's afeard to ride with me since I run over that heifer of Ezra Seestrunks and I dont keer nuthin bout drivin round by mysef.

Lum: If you dont aim to drive it you ort to git shud of it. Got it settin out ther in yer yard thataway takin the weather, hit wont be no count fer nuthin first thing you know.

Abner: Oh, I wouldn't take nuthin fer it. That was sumpthin I allus wanted was a automobile.

Lum: Yea, but if you dont aim to use it none, whats the good in havin it?

Abner: Well, Elizabeth and Pearl gits so much comfort outa jist havin one sos the others round here thats got em caint put on a batch of airs in front of em.

Lum: They jist enjoy knowin they got it huh?

Abner: Yea, The woman has made her and Pearl both one of them dusters and they give one another some googles fer Christmus outa the egg money and hits down right suprisin the dreadful mount of pleasure them two gits outa jist goin out ther and settin in it and makin out they're goin ridin.

Lum: Well I do know.

Abner: They set there by the hour wavin at everbody that goes by.

Lum: I'd love to have one but I've jist allus been afeard to try my hand at runnin one mysef. Whilst I aint afeard to ride with Dick in hissen.

Abner: If youns want to try on that'n of mine, you're jist plumb welcome to use it any time. They wouldn't be no need of you buyin one as long as I got that'n settin over ther.

Lum: I was jist thinkin, I might git Dick to show me how to handle it. I already know a right smart about mechanics, jist naturally turned to em I reckon.

Abner: First thing abody's got to lern is how to guide the blame thing.

Lum: Reckon how hit'd be to hitch that young span of mules of yourn to it and sorter pull it around at first till I could git my sef located.

Abner: You mean not start up the engine at tall?

Lum: Yea, If you'd drive the mules, I could set up ther and hold on to the guidin apparatus till I catch on how it's did.

Abner: Best thing to do would be to pull it down ther in that meader back of my place. They wont be no danger of youns runin in to nuthin thataway.

Lum: Here I am talkin bout learnin how to drive a automobile and I aint got no way of knowin if Evalener'll ride with me after I learn how.

Abner: You might telephone her up and ast her.

Lum: They aint no use fer me to try to call her up she wont talk to me.

Abner: I doggies Lum, Whats the matter of me callin her fer you.

Lum: Only trouble I'm afeard you'll git things in worse shape than they air already.

Abner: I can explain to her bout how come me to git you locked up in jail with Oscar. I'll tell her it was all my fault.

Lum: Maybe it would be a good idy fer you to call. Go head and while youre talking to her, ast her about ridin in a automobile with me.

Abner: How can I ast her? What'll I say?

Lum: Well lets see. You want to jist lead up to it sorter gradual like. You know, ast her how she likes ridin in automo-biles and work around till you can find out if she would ride with me if she gotten a chanst.

Abner: Lets see she's stayin ther with Sister Simpson. Whats ther ring?

Lum: Three shorts and a long. I'll ring em fer you.
(TELEPHONE)

Abner: I doggies, I'm as narvous as I can be.

Lum: Now cam yersef, You're shakin all over. You're lible to say somethin wrong and spile everthing.

Abner: Hallo, hallo. Is this Sister Simpson's place?. . . . Is the school marm handy ther? . . . I want to talk to her fer a minit. . . . . Alright.

Lum: She's ther is she?

Abner: Yea, she's comin to the, HELLO, Evalener?. . . . This
here's Abner Peabody. . . . . . yessum. Why I was jist callin
youns up to explain to you how come it was that Lum got
locked up in the jail, the other night. . . . .
Lum: Now right ther is as fer as I could ever git. Thats her hangin
up place.
Abner: Well jist hold the receiver a minit. She says she dont keer
nuthin bout hearin bout it.
Lum: Go head on and tell her anyhow fore she hangs up.
Abner: Hello, You see Evalener, I got him locked up ther with
Oscar Fields and I was afeard to onlock the door to let him
out on account of Oscar might of got loose.
Lum: Dont fergit to ast her bout ridin in the automobile with me.
Abner: Wait a minit hold the receiver Evalener. (to Lum) Hows
that Lum?
Lum: Go ahead and ast her bout ridin with me in the automobile.
Abner: Oh, yea, I was bout to fergit about that. Hello. Evalener.
Lum wanted me to ast. . . .
Lum: Dont tell her I said nuthin.
Abner: Why, yessum he's settin right here. . . . .
Lum: Dont tell her I'm here she'll think I put you up to callin her
up.
Abner: He got me to call you sid you allus hung up on him.
Lum: Wait a minit Abner you're makin things worser all the time.
Give me that receiver. . . . . . . Hello Evalener. . . . . This
is Lum talkin now. . . . . Well he's the one that
wanted to call you up. . . . . No I wasn't afeard to call
you but I knowed you wouldn't give me a chanst to explain
bout bein locked up in jail. . . . . Well I dont see how
hits disgracen you when it was jist a accident. . . . Hello
(click Receiver) Hello. Jist what I thought. She's hung up the
receiver on me again.
Abner: Call her back up right quick.
Lum: Nosir, I'm done with her. I grannies caint no woman treat
a Edards thataway. If she's got the idy in her head I'm goin

to run after her, she's got another think a comin. I'll git some woman that can preciate me.

Abner: Who you aim to git?

Lum: Thats jist the trouble. They aint no single womin round here abody'd have ceptin her.

Abner: You ort to do like Levi Singleton done. Order yersef one outa the mail catalogue.

Lum: You mean git one from one of them Matrimonal Bureaus?

Abner: Yea, whatever it is you call them places. That woman of Levi's is a right good looker.

Lum: Now wait a minit that aint sich a bad idy. I might write in to em and git the name of one of em and git to writtin backards and forards with her. First thang you know Evalener'd hear bout me gittin all them letters and she'd set up and take notice I bound you.

Abner: I doggies if I was you I'd shore do that. I reckon Levi's still got the name of that company.

Lum: Hits up ther in Kansas City sommers, I'll see Levi and git the perticklers of it. No I better not let Levi know what I'm up to fer he's lible to spread it round over the community.

Abner: How you goin to find out the name of that place lesson you ast him?

Lum: I was jist tryin to figger out some way.

Abner: I reckon Dick Huddleston would know fer [he] allus writes all of Levi's letters fer him.

Lum: Trouble with Dick, if I was to ast him, he'd bout josh the life outa me bout it. I never would hear the last of it.

Abner: Yea, if Dick ever found out bout you writin into that company, he'd pester you to death.

Lum: Reckon couldn't you git the name of that company and the address fer me. Dick wouldn't think nuthin bout you astin him.

Abner: Yea, I got to go down ther after the mail dreckly and I'll ast him then.

Lum: I'll jist wait fer you here at the office. I grannies I'm goin to write em a letter this very day. I'll show Evalener a thing or two. Go on down after yer mail now Abner. I want to hurry up and git started on it.

Abner: What'll I tell Dick?

Lum: Tell him to give you the names of all the matrymonal places he knows of. (Laughs) I grannies, I'll have womin fokes writin me letters from all over the country.————

JANUARY 25, 1932

Abner: Aint you got that letter writ? You been writin on it might nigh all mornin.

Lum: Well hits a heap bigger job than abody might think tryin to answer all the questions these fokes want to know.

Abner: What all do they ast you ther?

Lum: Hit'd be a heap easier to tell you what they dont ast. Hits a reglar application blank. They want to know how old you air, and how much money you got and if you been married before and all sich as that.

Abner: Reckon what they want to know all them things fer?

Lum: Oh, I reckon some of them womin this matrimonial bureau has got on ther list is terrible pertickler. They's bout a thousand questions here I got to answer.

Abner: Read some of em out loud maybe I can hep you.

Lum: First thing they want here is a recent photograft of me. I aint had a pitcher struck in twenty year I dont reckon.

Abner: Why dont you send in one of them they taken of me and you when I ketched that robber?

Lum: Nosir I wouldn't send thatn to nobody. That photographer ketched me jist as I was gappin. Had my mouth open as wide as a gallon bucket.

Abner: Yea, but that was a right good likeness of me.

Lum: Well now which one of [us] is it thats writing to this booreau?

Abner: I jist allowed hit might do some good to have you standin ther by me and me with my policeman's suit on.

Lum: They'd think I was bein errested fer somethin or ruther. I recollect when the newspaper printed that story bout you ketchin that robber and had that pitcher in it, They had it readin Constable Peabody ketches robber and a heap of fokes thought I was the robber.

Abner: Well you was bound and determined to be in the pitcher.

Lum: Wonder if Dick's still got that picture takin apparatus of hissen?

Abner: Yea, I reckon he has. Why dont you git him to take a pitcher of youns?

Lum: Well if I could git him to do it thout him ketchin on to what I want with it. If he ever finds out I'm writin in to a matrymonal booreau, I know I'd never hear the last of it.

Abner: Now Lum, jist to be right honest about it I bleave he ketched on to it when I was down ther yistidy evenin.

Lum: I told you not to tell him who you was gittin that applincation blank fer.

Abner: Well I never told him. He started in to guyin me soon as I ast him bout it. Wanted to know if I was aimin to git shud of my woman and all that. You know how he is.

Lum: What did you tell him.

Abner: Why I jist told him I was wantin to git it fer another feller. But I never told him who it was.

Lum: How come you think he figger hit was me a wantin it?

Abner: Well he ast me. But I told him right off that you told me not tell him who it was.

Lum: I swan Abner, tellin you somethin to keep is jist like tellin it over the party line.

Abner: You needn't worry yersef I dont aim to tell nobody bout it.

Lum: Reckon wher he got this application blank?

Abner: He said when he was writin in fer Levi Singleton, they sent along a extra un. He said that'd save you writin in fer one yersef.

Lum: Well if he said that, he's bound to know who it was wantin it. I may as well go ahead on and tell him now. I bleave I'll

telephone him up and see if I can git him to take my pitcher
fer me.

Abner: Yea, may as well tell him. I dont see how he guessed who
it was yistidy. I wouldn't be a mite sprised if he dont know
right now.

Lum: Well he'd find it out any how quick as the letters start
comin in here fer me.

Abner: Yea, you better let him in on it fer if you dont and he
finds out about it, you'll have to stay away from his store
down ther. He'd tell it right in front of the biggest crowd he
can find.

Lum: I'll telephone him up and tell him to come over here.
(TELEPHONE)

Abner: Be shore and tell him to brang that pitcher takin outfit.

Lum: Yea, I will thats the mainest reason I want him to come—
Hello, Hello. Is that you Dick?. . . . This is Lum Edards. . . . . .
. . . . . Yea, I got it. I told Abner not to tell you who it was fer.

Abner: I never told him.

Lum: Well he told me you guessed who it was fer. . . . . . . Yea,
but Dick I'd a heap ruther not to talk to you over the party
line. . . . . . . I was jist wonderin if you still had that pitcher
takin outfit. . . . yea. . . . . . Well you know they want you
to send in a pitcher of yersef and I aint had arrin struck in
the last twenty year outside of thatn they taken of me and
Abner when he ketched that robber awhile back. . . . .
. . . Yea, recon could I git you to fetch it over here and take
one of me?. . . . . . uh huh. . . . . Do which? . . filims?. . . .
Whats them?. . . . . Oh, well aint you got none there
at the store?. . . . . . How much air they?. . . . . . . Uh huh.
Well I got to have a pitcher looks like. . . . . Alright Dick.
I'll wait fer you right here at the office. . . . . . Now dont say
nuthin to nobody bout all this Dick. I'll explain it to you
when you git over here. . . . . . . alright Dick. . . . . Thank you
fer yer kindness towards me . . Alright. (click) Said he'd be
right over. Comin over in his automobile.

Abner: He is? I doggies Lum you orter have yer pitcher struck settin up ther in it.

Lum: Yea, I can set up ther like I'm a drivin it. They wont know but what hit blongs to me.

Abner: You ort to have a seegar in yer mouth too. That'll make you look prominence.

Lum: Thats so, wisht I'da thot to had Dick fetch me one over from the store.

Abner: Well I can whittle you one outa of a stick to wher hit'll look jist like a seegar in the pitcher.

Lum: Yea, go ahead on. Theys some kindlin over ther in the wood box back of the stove. . . . Wait a minit I got a better idy. Wonder if abody couldn't slip one of them braces outa the legs of that cheer settin ther?

Abner: Yea, hit'll come out. We can take and slip it back in ther when you git done with it. Let me see if I caint jist slip it out.

Lum: I ort to have that new necktie I got the other day.

Abner: They aint nuthin the matter with thaten you got on ther. They aint a hole in it nowher. . . . Now here you air (laughs) Thers yer seegar.

Lum: Hits a little long. Looks bout like a fifteen center.

Abner: Run it back in yer mouth a little futher. Now that looks better.

Lum: That glue ther on the end of it dont taste very good. I reckon we'll have to cut it off a little.

Abner: Let me have it and I'll stick one end of it in the far ther so's hit'll look like you been smokin it.

Lum: When Dick comes over I'll git him to drive his automobile right up in front of the office so's my Jestice of the Peace sign'll show in the pitcher. Wisht I had a sign tellin bout me bein president of the school board too.

Abner: I was jist studyin Lum. If you're a mind to, I can set up in the front seat and make out I'm a drivin the automobile and you can set in the back seat like you was one of them rich fellers that has a man hired jist to drive you round.

Lum: Now that aint sich a bad idy. I could [be] jist fixin to git in
like you had come down to the office to take me home.
Abner: I doggies, them womin'll shore set up and take notice agin
they git that pitcher.
Lum: I ort to borrey Grandpappy Spearses walkin stick, and be
leanin on it sorter. I've saw pitchers of em thataway. Well I
better git to work on these questions or I never will git done.
Abner: Whats the nextun you got ther?
Lum: Lets see wherbouts I was at. Here it is right chere.
Abner: Read em out lod Lum.
Lum: Well here's that'n bout my age I aint answered yit.
Abner: How old do you aim to tell em you air Lum?
Lum: I dont know hardly. I bleave I'll jist tell I'm forty five. Aint
no use to tell em how much more'n that I am.
Abner: Yea, but agin they see that pitcher of you they'll know
blame well you aint tellin em the straight of it.
Lum: Well I dont look no older than that.
Abner: Yea you do too Lum. Why yer mustache is as gray as a
rat.
Lum: Well they'll jist figger hit turned gray ahead of time.
Abner: Put down ther what you want to but you better put down
somethin. You'll be a week writin on that thing the way
you're goin.
Lum: Forty five . . . Now here's one thats a hard en. What
natinality?
Abner: Read thaten again.
Lum: What nationality? Meanin I reckon If you're a indian or
irshman or german or what.
Abner: You aint nuthin air you?
Lum: Nope, I'm jist a Arkansawer. I reckon though I ort to put
somethin down ther to make it look right.
Abner: Put down ther that yer a chinese.
Lum: I dont look like no chinese. I'll jist say I'm a Arkansawer.
Now lets see. Next un here is Race.
Abner: Race?

Lum: Yea, jist plain race. R A C E question mark.

Abner: What kind a race they talkin bout foot racin or horse racin?

Lum: I dont know I'm jist goin to set down "no" here.

Abner: Read anothern.

Lum: Here's one I can answer says Disposition. I'm puttin down gentle.

Abner: Wait till they see you riled. Why I've saw you mad enough to bite.

Lum: Occupation? Lets see I ort to know the meanin of that.

Abner: I dont knows I ever heard of that. Sounds a right smart like location.

Lum: No this is got somethin to do with the kind of business abody's in.

Abner: Well jist set down ther that you farm principally.

Lum: Yea, but I got to say somethin bout me bein Jestice of the Peace and president of the school board and a deacon in the church.

Abner: You better wait and ast Dick if thats the right meanin fer that word. Hit jist dont sound right to me.

Lum: Looks like they jist tried therseves tryin to see how many big words they could use. I'll jist jump thaten too.

Abner: Looks to me like you jump more of em than you answer.

Lum: I'll git Dick to hep with them I caint answer.

Abner: Thers Dick drivin up out in front ther now.

Lum: You show him how to set his automobile out ther, I gotta git mysef ready fer that pitcher.

Abner: He's done stopped now.

Lum: Tell him to come on in and git hissef thawed out.

Dick: Howdy Abner. Well, hello ther Romeo.

Lum: Now Dick, I knowed you'd start that foolishness of yourn.

Dick: Rich widower, Jestice of the Peace, wants wife. That ort to catch em.

Lum: Now Dick I aint lookin fer no wife.

Dick: Well what you writin into a matrimonal Bureau fer then?

Lum: Well you see me and Evalener aint gittin along so well, she's keepin company with Jake Means agin now so I jist figured to write into this bureau so's I'd start gittin a batch of letters from womin.

Dick: What do you want with the letters?

Lum: Well you see agin Evalener heres bout me gittin all them letters she'll bust outa the traces to git me to sparkin her again————

Chester "Chet" Lauck (lower left) and Norris "Tuffy" Goff (lower right), shown in costume in 1931 as Lum (upper left) and Abner (upper right), began their radio careers at station KTHS in Hot Springs, Arkansas.

(Above) The hamlet of Waters, Arkansas, shown in 1935, served as the model for the fictional Pine Ridge. In 1936 residents of Waters successfully petitioned to change the name of their post office to Pine Ridge. The change was marked by a nationally broadcast ceremony in Little Rock. *(Below)* Dick Huddleston's store in Waters, Arkansas, recorded in this 1932 photograph, was an often-used setting in the early years of the program.

Dick Huddleston, pictured in 1932, hosted hundreds of visitors to Pine Ridge during the 1930s and made goodwill tours promoting *Lum and Abner* and tourism in Arkansas.

For a 1932 promotional book titled *Lum and Abner and Their Friends from Pine Ridge,* Lauck and Goff had Mena, Arkansas, photographer Oscar Plaster take photographs of various people and buildings in Waters. They then used those images to illustrate the characters and buildings mentioned on the show. They disguised the Waters post office, shown here, as Lum and Abner's office.

Waters resident Cling Wilhite was the model for the character Grandpappy Spears in *Lum and Abner and Their Friends from Pine Ridge.*

Women rarely had speaking roles on the program, but a number of women characters were mentioned often. In promotional photos taken in Waters, local resident Nancy Chambers served as Lauck and Goff's illustration of the character Evalena Schultz, the Pine Ridge schoolteacher and Lum's love interest.

Lauck and Goff got their first national exposure over the NBC network.

In 1933, while broadcasting from WTAM in Cleveland, Lauck and Goff made a series of publicity shots in character for use in a tabloid that they distributed as a listener premium. The photographs were taken in the village of Peninsula, Ohio.

Ed Lasker Goble, modeling here as the lovable but slow-witted Cedric Weehunt for *Lum and Abner and Their Friends from Pine Ridge,* later played the role of Cedric in touring troupes and created a musical group called Cedric's Quartet.

Lauck and Goff added the Jot 'Em Down Store to their program in early 1933, making Lum and Abner on-air competitors of storeowner Dick Huddleston. In the hamlet of Waters, a second store also operated across the road from Dick Huddleston's establishment. The A. A. McKinzie store building, shown here, and Dick Huddleston's store building were later combined and now house the Lum and Abner Museum in Pine Ridge.

Norris Goff, shown here, gave voice not only to Abner but also to Dick Huddleston, Squire Skimp, and other characters. Chester Lauck provided the voices for Lum, Grandpappy Spears, and Cedric Weehunt.

(*Above*) Chester Lauck, a talented cartoonist, drew the two characters for the 1932 book *Lum and Abner and Their Friends from Pine Ridge*. (*Below*) This cartoon by Lauck closed *Lum and Abner and Their Friends from Pine Ridge*. Note the characters' dignity even in the midst of a farming chore, a far cry from more prevalent stereotypical depictions of hillbillies during the 1930s.

THE END

LUM AND ABNER SCRIPTS
December 1933 and January 1934

December 7, 1933

Lum: No Abner you'll find out that they's a heap more to politics than jist nouncin yersef fer office.

Abner: Yea I [am] beginnin to find that out. I never went to all this bother with mysef when I was runnin fer constable.

Lum: Well you was the only one in the race then. You've got some real competition now.

Abner: Got some what?

Lum: Competition. Some opposition in other words.

Abner: Why jist Butch Dolan's runnin agin me.

Lum: Well he's competition aint he?

Abner: Yea but they aint but one of him.

Lum: I know it.

Abner: Well you said I had some competition. If they aint but one you ort to said uh competition.

Lum: Alright you've got uh competition then.

Abner: Well thats better.

Lum: If you'd spend more time tryin to hep me with yer campaign stid of startin arguments you'd gitt along a heap better.

Abner: Well what is it you want me to do.

Lum: Well I was jist fixin to give you some pinters on what you ort and ort not to do.

Abner: Go head. go head.

Lum: Now in the first place you want to speak to everbody. Call em by their give names if you know it, and shake hands with everbody you can. Ask em bout all their relations and brag on em.

Abner: Yea.

Lum: Are you puttin them things down like I told you.

Abner: Yea dont go so fast.

Lum: When you go to church Sunday. You want to stand around and speak to everbody when they drive up. If they're drivin a car step over and open the door fer em and hep the wimmen fokes out.

Abner: What if they're drivin a team and wagon?

Lum: Why thats all the better, You git to tie their team fer em thataway. Thats a sure fire vote gitter. Might even brag on their team a little. Tell em what a fine lookin span of mules they've got.

Abner: If they're drivin horses I dont want to say that huh?

Lum: No.

Abner: I didn't think I would.

Lum: Then the thing to do is hep the wimmen fokes down outa the wagon or buggy or whatever they're drivin and if they've got a baby with em hits a lot better. You want to insist on holdin the baby and then talk about what a beautiful child it is.

Abner: Brag on all the babies huh?

Lum: Yea if the mother's holdin it say how much it looks like her.

Abner: And if the father's holdin it you want me to say it looks like him huh?

Lum: Thats the idy exactly. And if they're both standin ther say it looks like both of em.

Abner: Thats sorter the way Hal Norwood the torney General does when he runs fer office aint it.

Lum: Yea (L) They aint a child in this state that Hal Norwood aint held in his arms at one time or another.

Abner: Yea and he's a good handshaker too.

Lum: Well Governor Futrell is give up to bein one of the best handshaker's in the state.

Abner: Yea (L) put them two off to therseves and I doggies they'd shake hands till they was give plum out.

Lum: Nother thing now you want to carry a lot of seegars round in yer pocket. Hand them out.

Abner: Well I want to git some gooderns. I never will fergit
smokin a seegar that feller Fred Duke give me in ther at the
county seat last year. He was runnin fer mayor and musta
thought I lived ther. Handed me a seegar that liked to choked
me.

Lum: Oh yea we gotta be keerful bout that you can loose votes
might easy handin out cheap ones thataway . . . We'll buy
some gooderns. Git you some two fer a nickle ones . . That
ort to git the votes.

Abner: Yea that'll git the mens votes but they's lots of wimmen
that dont smoke seegars.

Lum: Yea you ort to have sompin to give them. Might carry a
little sen sen and some chewin gum round with you. But the
best way to git the wimmens votes is to tell the slim ones
they're gittin fatter and tell the fat ones they're fallin off to
wher you dont hardly know em.

Abner: Yea but what if I dont even know em. Never seen em
before.

Lum: Well now right ther is another good stunt. When you meet
a woman and her growed daughter. You want to allus ast em
which one is the daughter. Thats flatterin.

Abner: I see right now hit aint goin to do fer me to take
Lizzybeth round with me on my campaign.

Lum: Now that gits down to the table etikuet.

Abner: Gits down to what?

Lum: Table manners. How to eat.

Abner: Well thats one thing I do know how to do is eat.

Lum: Yea you know how but you dont know how to eat proper.

Abner: How to eat what?

Lum: What do you mean What?

Abner: That stuff you said I never knowed how to eat.

Lum: Proper Abner. Eatin with table manners. Fer Example.
When you pour your coffee out in yer saucer to drink. You
mustn't blow on it to cool it. Either take yer napkin and fan
it or let it set ther till it cools itsef off.

Abner: Reckon why they've got rules agin a feller blowin it thataway.

Lum: Oh I dont know. . Feard you'll blow too hard and slosh it over on the clean table cloth I reckon. Styles changes in eatin same as they do in anything else.

Abner: Well looks like whoever studdies up them styles tries to make eatin as oncomfortable as they can.

Lum: Oh they've got it down now to wher abody caint enjoy a meal to save his life. You caint even lean yer elbow agin the table now. Regardless of how much you've ett.

Abner: Well I do know.

Lum: Another thing while I think about it. Dont never raise up out of yer chair to reach fer nuthin, if you caint reach the bread or pertaters or sompin like that barehanded, take yer fork and spear it.

Abner: Well now ther startin sompin ther thats plum dangerous. Somebody's lible to git a hand speared.

Lum: Well you want to watch yer chances. Dont want to criple nobody. Nother thing Abner dont never try to eat your peas with a knife. They'll roll off ever time.

Abner: Well whats a body goin to eat em with.

Lum: Well the knife's alright but you want to mix the peas up with yer mashed pertaters sos they wont roll so bad.

Abner: I doggies what will they think of next——

Lum: Wait a minit. Here comes Dan Davis.

Abner: Yea.

Lum: I grannies that jist reminds me. I promised I'd come over ther and hep him deecorate the show room ther in the Pine Ridge Motor Company to display the new Ford fer 1934.

Abner: Well we aint goin to show it till Satidy are we?

Lum: No but we got to git the place all fixed up. Dan said the new cars would be here today or tomorrow. I got to figger up some excuse why I aint been over to hep.

Abner: Tell him we been so busy with the campaign—

Lum: HIDY DAN. .

Abner: WELL DANNEL COME ON BACK AND SET.
Dan: (fading in) SAY YOU SHOULD COME OVER AND SEE
   THE NEW FORDS.
Abner: ARE THEY HERE AREADY?
Dan: Yea they just brought them out while ago. We have a
   Standard coupe and a four door sedan to display Saturday.
Abner: Well.
Lum: HOW THEY LOOK DAN?
Abner: Yea have they changed em up much?
Dan: Oh say, we thought this nineteen thirty three model was
   the last word in an automobile. But they've made some
   improvements on this 34 model that takes your breath.
   Eighty five horse power under that hood.
Abner: Fer the land sakes.
Dan: And it has a new system of carberation that increases
   gasoline mileage two and a half more miles to the gallon.
Lum: Well thems tetchnicalities.What I want to know is what
   does it look like Dan?
Abner: Yea does it look as good as that 1933 of mine.
Dan: Say this is by far the most beautiful car that Ford has ever
   built. It has everything. More powerful, faster, smoother. .
   More economical. It's the crowning achievement of Ford's
   thirty years of successful Automobile building——
Abner: I doggies Dan. What you tryin to do sell me and Lum
   another car.
Dan: No (L) but I just want you to come over and look at it.
   You'll be just as enthusastic as I am when you see it. Just wait
   till the public sees it Saturday. . It'll be the talk of the whole
   country—
Abner: I doggies Lum, lets jist lock the store and run over ther
   and see it fer a few minits.
Lum: Well I reckon we can. Business is sorter quiet.
Abner: Well git yer hat. Lets go.
Lum: Well come on. Come on. (fading)
Abner: I'm comin.

Dan: (faded) And the inside finish. Say Mr. Edwards you wont believe that a car selling for the price of the Ford——

Abner: WAIT A MINIT LUM HERE COMES DICK HUDDLESTON.

Lum: (faded) YEA I RECKON HE WANTS TO SEE US ABOUT SOMPIN. I tell you Dan we'll wait and see what Dick wants and we'll be on over ther dreckly.

Abner: Yea we'll get done with him jist quick as we can and be right on over ther.

Dan: (fading out) Alright I'll go ahead and you come as soon as you can——

Dick: (Faded) Well Hidy Dan. How're you today?

Dan: (faded) (L) Oh fine. Just wait till Saturday and you'll see why I'm feelin so good.

Abner: COME ON BACK DICK.

Lum: Yea. WE WAS JIST FIXIN TO LEAVE WHEN WE SEEN YOU COMIN UP.

Dick: (fading in) Well I just run over to bring Abner this letter. Come special delivery. Here Abner.

Abner: Much obliged I'll see who hits from.

Lum: Set Down Dick Set Down.

Dick: No I caint stay. I've got to git back and git ready to go in to the County Seat fer the Possum Club Banquet tonight.

Lum: Well we're goin to. Aint no rush hit dont start till eight oclock.

Dick: Well I've got to go by Brack Whisenant's to git a shave.

Lum: Well you've got more nerve than I have. A mans jist takin his life in his hands to lay down in that barber chair and let that feller git over him with a razor.

Dick: Oh (L) Bracks alright. Quiet sort of feller never says much.

Lum: Why he draws yer head back over that head rest till yer adams apple looks like the breast bone of a turkey gobler and then he jist wells to take a hack saw to shave you with. Wouldn't hurt no worse.

Dick: Well I cant wait to git ther to the banquet. They're figgerin on havin a big time. They're having quiet a race fer president this year.

Lum: Wells hits about time they was makin a change. Petefish has helt the office now fer nearly twenty year.

Dick: I bleave Gene Twiford'll run him a close race this year.

Lum: I reckon. Duke Frederick and Uncle Tom Jones Mrs Stratton and Henry Coffman'll be ther . . . And Albert Robertson.

Dick: Yea yea they'll all be ther.

Lum: Wait a minit here. Whats the matter with you Abner?

Abner: I jist dont bleave I'll go to the Possum Club Banquet tonight.

Lum: Whats the matter of you. You look like you'd saw a ghost.

Abner: I doggies fellers this is the end. . I'm through . . . This is a letter here from Butch Dolan and he says he's givin me my last warnin. If I dont withdraw from the sheriff's race before tomorrow noon . . He'll put me outa the race in his own way . . . and I doggies I know what that is——

DECEMBER 12, 1933

Lum: Nossir thats what you need Abner is publicity.

Abner: What you mean publicity?

Lum: Why gittin yer name in the paper and gittin everbody to talkin bout you.

Abner: Why everbody I've saw yit says their goin to vote fer me.

Lum: Yea but you gist been talkin to the fokes round Pine Ridge here. Natural their fer you bein a local man and all. You got to recollect this is a county office you're runnin fer and the voters all over the county will decide it. Lots of em aint even heard of you.

Abner: Oh well I aim to stump speech the county forever the lection comes off.

Lum: Yea but you goin to have to do more'n that. You've got to git everbody to talking bout you. Make a hero out of yersef.

Abner: Well Butch Dolan aint makin no hero out of hisef.

Lum: No but he's got his name on everthing you pick up. Look at that big advertisement we read in the county paper yistidy.

Abner: Well why caint we put some advertisements in the paper too.

Lum: Why we could if we had the money.

Abner: Well we've got money. I give you a thousand dollars to start with fer the campaign fund.

Lum: Yea but that wouldn't last no time agin you start buyin full page ads in the newspapers and bill boards and sich as that. You know how much we've spent aready?

Abner: No I dont know. Fifteen or twenty dollars I'd say off hand.

Lum: Nossir I was jist lookin over the books fore you come in. We've spent $300.

Abner: Three hunderd dollars? What fer?

Lum: Well I caint figger out wher all of it went. All I can account fer here is two hunderd and fifty dollars. Cordin to that hit makes me fifty dollars short.

Abner: Well I dont even see wher we could have spent two hunderd and fifty dollars.

Lum: Well I'll go over the books here and show you. I've got ever thing down I can think of.

Abner: Books? Are you keepin a set of books on the campaign fund?

Lum: Why course I am. Abody's got to keep books on sich as that same as he does in a store or any other kind of business.

Abner: He has huh?

Lum: Why course. Have yer debits and credits and all them things. Now if you'll listen, pay tention I'll read you what all we've spent outa the campaign fund.

Abner: Yea go head and read it out.

Lum: Now in the first place we started out with a thousand dollars. Ther it is up ther at the top.

Abner: I doggies thats a string of o's aint it.

Lum: Yea. That goes on the credit side. Now these down here on this side is all expences . . . First item here is seegars. 2.50. And havin pitchers made 4.00.

Abner: Did he charge four dollars fer takin that pitcher?

Lum: Why yea he had to come way out here from the county seat and all. He wanted to charge six dollars and I taked him down to four. Ther's two dollars I saved you so I put it over here with the thousand.

Abner: What you puttin it over ther fer?

Lum: Well thats a profit two dollars we made so natural we put it on the credit side of the ledger. You've heard that old Edards sayin, A dollar saved is a dollar made.

Abner: Yea but—

Lum: Well hit works jist the same on two dollars as it does on one. Now the next item here is them signs we had printed. They come to ninety six dollars.

Abner: Ninety six dollars jist fer them?

Lum: Thats what they come to.

Abner: I dont know nuthin bout them things but looks like thats a outlandish price to pay fer em.

Lum: Why I made you four dollars right ther. See ther ther it is over ther in column amongst the credits.

Abner: Is all that column there money you've made fer me?

Lum: Yea but now wait till we git down to the othern.

Abner: How'd you make that four dollars ther?

Lum: Well I told you I talked em down four dollars on the printin. You see they wanted fifty dollars fer two thousand of them signs and he said he'd make me four thousand fer ninety six dollars. I takend him up on that right quick fore he seen what a mistake he made in his figgers.

Abner: Did he make a mistake?

Lum: Why yea anybody with jist ordinarry reasonin would know that if two thousand signs come to fifty dollars, four thousand signs would run to a hunderd dollars even up. Now thers wher hit pays to have a manager that knows business and is quick in figgers.

Abner: I swan Lum you beat all I ever seen. Abody's got to git up turible early in the mornin to git ahead of you aint he?

Lum: Well I dont like to make no brags on my own doins I will say this you couldn't of got a better manager.

Abner: Did that printin feller ketch on to beatin hisef outa four dollars?

Lum: No No. I got us both off to talkin bout another subject right quick, and he never give it no mind. I was shamed of mysef after I left. My concious allus bothers me after beatin a feller thataway. I think the next time I'm in town I'll drop in ther and jist hand him four dollars. You know ill got gains never done nobody a might of good . . Thats a old Edards sayin.

Abner: Well what I want to know is how much have we got left in the campaign fund.

Lum: Well I'm gittin down to that. You caint jist jump right out in the middle of it. Thats the trouble with most everbody, agin they go to keep books. They git in too big a hurry to find out how much they've got and they caint tell how nor wher they got it. If they have got it.

Abner: Well go head. What else have we spent?

Lum: Lets see next item here is hat, four dollars.

Abner: Hat? Why I aint bought no hat . .

Lum: I know you aint.

Abner: Is that the one we was goin to throw in the ring.

Lum: The one we was goin to throw in the ring?

Abner: Yea you said when I got in the sheriffs race I'd have to throw my hat in the ring.

Lum: No this is a hat I bout fer mysef.

Abner: Well what you doin chargin it to the campaign fund?

Lum: Well you never wanted your manager goin round meetin fokes in a old wore out hat did you.

Abner: No I reckon not. but if you never throwed that olden of youres away I'd love to have it fer mysef, if you dont minds. Thisin of mine is——

Lum: Why I dont mind at all. Glad to hep you. Hit ort to be alright fer you. Little big but you can stuff some paper in it to wher hit'll fit alright.

Abner: Yea I'm glad to git it.

Lum: Well now lets see the next item here is them callin cards you had printed they come to twenty dollars.

Abner: Why I never had no cards printed. If they SENT SOME CARDS OUT HERE AND SAID I ORDERED EM THEY CA——

Lum: I had the cards printed mysef . . They're callin cards fer me to use fer you . . . Here's one you can have. LUM EDARDS JESTICE OF THE PEACE AND PRESIDENT OF THE SCHOOL BOARD . . Then see down here I've got down here at the bottom in little letters I've got campaign manager fer Abner Peabody.

Abner: Yea thats fine. I never seen *my* name at first.

Lum: Now the next item here is . . Oh needin mind about thaten though. Now the next—

Abner: Well what was thaten.

Lum: Oh hit dont make no difference, we'll jist go on to the next un.

Abner: Well take yer hand offen the book. Let me see.

Lum: Alright look.

Abner: Seegars. $2.50.

Lum: Yea, them's vote gitters. Them seegars is.

Abner: Well I allowed you was goin to vote fer me anyway.

Lum: Huh?

Abner: Well you're the only one that ever smokes em. I aint saw you since I started runnin fer sheriff that you aint had a seegar in yer mouth.

Lum: Well you dont spect me to do all this brain work thout sompin to smoke do you? I've give out some of em anyway. I takend some over to Evalener's papa last Sunday.

Abner: Oh well I never knowed that.

Lum: Thats allright. I'll jist fergit about it. Now the next item here is book-keepin books fer book keepin. Thats the ones I'm usin here to keep track of yer campaign fund in.

Abner: How much did they come to?

Lum: I bought them fer fifteen dollars.

Abner: Thats a little steep aint it?

Lum: Steep? . Now ther's preciation fer you. I've made you more money on that deal than arry one I've made yit . . . The feller tried to sell me a set of books that cost thirty dollars and I bought these. Thers fifteen dollars I saved you . . See ther I've got it right down here on the credit side. Fifteen more dollars I made you.

Abner: Well what I want to know is HOW MUCH MONEY HAVE WE GOT ON HAND NOW.

Lum: Well I caint tell you. The books is the wrong kind. I caint git em in balance.

Abner: Aint in what?

Lum: Aint in balance. The debits and the credits dont figger up with what we got on hand.

Abner: I still dont [know] what you mean.

Lum: Well in little bitty words. The whole thing biled down is. The campaign fund is short.

Abner: Short?

Lum: Yea. Over here in this column is the thousand dollars we started with. And all this money I've saved you on different deals added in makes the credits side figger a thousand and fifty dollars.

Abner: Why Lum I never give you but a thousand dollars to start out with.

Lum: Yea but that fifty dollars I saved you blongs to you too. We got to add it in. Now thats a thousand and fifty dollars I've had to spend and we've spent two hunderd and fifty dollars. Lets see how that figgers.

Abner: Yea, count that up and see how much we ort to have.

Lum: Naught from a naught leaves a naught and five from five leaves——

Abner: Well why dont you jist count the money you've got left.

Lum: I've already done that but we ort to have cordin to the books eight hunderd dollars and we aint.

Abner: How much have we got?

Lum: We aint got but seven hunderd and fifty dollars. We're fifty dollars short sommers.

Abner: Same amount you made *fer* me on what you saved on the different deals aint it.

Lum: Yea but you needn't worry bout it fer I aim to make up ever dime of it.

Abner: No you aint goin to do no sich a thing I know if they are some gone it aint no fault of yourn.

Lum: Nope you ort to have eight hunderd dollars cordin to my own figgers and I grannies I know they're right. I jist owe you fifty dollars. I'll git it tomorrow too.

Abner: Oh they (((((TELEPHONE)))) aint no hurry bout it.—

Lum: Wait a minit . . I'll answer it. Hit's more'n likely Evalener wantin to talk to me. . . . HELLO. . . . . HIDY DICK. YEA HE'S HERE. . . . HUH?. . . . . . . YEA I'LL TELL HIM WHAT IS IT?. . . . . . . WELL FER THE LAND SAKE. . . . YOU DONT MEAN IT . . . BIG HEADLINES IN THE PAPER HUH?. . . . . . . YOU MEAN BANKER MULLINS LITTLE GIRL? . . . WELL OF ALL THINGS. YEA I'LL TELL HIM TO BE ON THE LOOK OUT . . MUCH OBLIGED FER CALLIN . . (CLICK) I GRANNIES ABNER I WAS TALKIN TO YOU WHILE AGO BOUT MAKIN A HERO OUT OF YERSEF AND HERE'S THE CHANCE OF A LIFE TIME. DICK SAYS THE COUNTY PAPER HAS GOT HEADLINES IN IT TODAY SAYIN THAT BANKER MULLINS LITTLE GIRL HAS BEEN KIDNAPPED AND THEY BLEAVE THEY'RE HEADED OUT THIS DRECTION. .

Abner: I DOGGIES IF THEY COME OUT THIS WAY I'LL KETCH EM.

Lum: ABNER IF YOU CAN KETCH THEM AND RETURN THAT LITTLE GIRL TO HER MAMA AND PAPA YOU CAN BE LECTED SHERIFF OF THIS COUNTY SO EASY IT WONT———

DECEMBER 13, 1933

Lum: Well let him go ahead, he's already spent more money'n he'll make outa the sheriff's office.

Abner: Yea but that aint goin to do me no good.

Lum: Well Abner they aint no use fer us to try to advertise yer campaign as much as Butch Dolan is hissen. We jist aint got the money to do with.

Abner: Reckon wher he's gittin all the money he's spendin on this campaign.

Lum: I dont know but he's shore spendin it. I seen somebody out here passin round hand bills this mornin.

Abner: Why hits a sight. If I keep on seein his name round on everthing I'm feard I'm lible to go to the polls and fergit and vote fer him mysef.

Lum: Well now if you'd git busy and do what I told you, git out here and ketch the honery critters that kidnapped that little girl in at the county seat yesterday, hit wouldn't make no difference how much advertisin Butch Dolan does, you could win the sheriff's race in a walk.

Abner: Well I'm a workin on it. I want to find that little girl and take her back to her mammy and papa regardless of wher hit'll hep me or not.

Lum: Oh yea course you do. But you aint goin to ketch em settin round the store here Abner.

Abner: Well I went out this mornin and done some detecitive work on it.

Lum: Detecitive work?

Abner: Yea I put on my train robber disguise and went over to Ezry Seestrunks house.

Lum: Train robber disguise. Why these aint train robbers.

Abner: I know it but I aint got no kidnapper ketchin disguise.

Lum: Well what was you doin over at Ezry's. You ondoubtedly dont think Ezry had anything to do with it.

Abner: Oh no no. The reason I went over ther, he lives on the main road to the county seat and I jist wanted to ast him if he'd saw any strange cars go by yistidy.

Lum: Well that was a good idy. What'd he say?

Abner: Why he ast me what I was doin dressed up thataway.

Lum: Oh (L) He recognised you huh?

Abner: Huh? Oh no no Wasn't a bit of hep to me. Hadn't saw a car.

Lum: I mean he knowed who you was.

Abner: Oh yea he knowed who I was or he wouldn't of asked me what I was doin dressed up thataway fer.

Lum: Well here comes Cedric back. Now we can git them groceries delivered to Sister Simpson.

Abner: We better git em over ther. She called me up while ago and I thought lightnin had struck the wires. You coulda fried a egg on the telephone.

Lum: WHERBOUTS YOU BEEN CEDRIC.

Abner: YEA HITS ABOUT TIME YOU WAS GITTIN BACK.

Cedric: (faded in). . . . I WENT BY THE POST OFFICE DOWN AT DICK HUDDLESTON'S STORE AND GOT THE MAIL FER YOUNS.

Abner: Well take them groceries settin ther on the counter and git em over to Sister Simpson jist as quick as you can fore she throws another fit.

Lum: Here let me have the mail Cedric . . . Wher's the rest of it.

Cedric: Thats all they was. Jist the county paper.

Abner: See if they've got that article in ther about me you give the reporter the other day Lum.

Abner: Yea thats what I'm lookin fer.

Abner: Go on now Cedric git them groceries over ther and hurry right straight back. GIT YER HAND OUTA THAT SHOW CASE TOO.

Lum: Well here's some more bout that kidnappin. Headlines says. ABDUCTORS DEMAND TWENTY FIVE THOUSAND DOLLARS FOR RELEASE OF LITTLE MARY MULLINS.

Abner: Twenty five thousand.

Lum: Sheriff Dolan says no clues have been found as yet that might lead to the recovery of local Banker's daughter.

Abner: Well I aint sprised at that. He's too busy goin round sli[n]gin mud about me.

Lum: Little Mary Mullins is well and is being properly cared for according to the note received by her father this morning from her abductors. The note also demanded twenty five thousand dollars ransom for her release. Mr. Mullins stated that he would spend several times that amount if necessary to recover his child. A posse was being organized early this morning to assist the sheriff's office in hopes of finding some clue as to the childs wherabouts. The only information thus far brought to light is that Mrs. E. D. Whalen neighbor of the Mullins family states that she saw a large yellow sedan draw up in front of the Mullins home yesterday about noon and two men enter the yard. George Wilkerson a farmer living on Route eight advises that he saw a car of this same discription pass his home yesterday afternoon headed in the direction of Cherry Hill and Pine Ridge.

Abner: Well I do know.

Lum: Yeller sedan . . Peers to me I've saw a big yeller sedan sommers . . Who is it thats got a automobile like that.

Abner: I dont know. Theys lots of em I reckon.

Lum: Well now thers sommpin fer you to start workin on. Find out who all owns yeller sedans and keep liminatin and liminatin em till you bile it down, you'll more'n likely find the right one.

Abner: The first thing I'm goin to do is——

Lum: Wait a minit. LOOKY HERE. I GRANNIES HERE'S THAT STORY I GIVE THE NEWSPAPER reeporter bout you.

Abner: They finally got it in ther did they?

Lum: Yea . . Looky ther . . Look at them headlines. Lum Edards to manage Peabody's campaign for Sheriff . . . This ort to do you a awful lot of good Abner.

Abner: Yea all that write up about me and the nice thing about it is hit aint costin us nuthin.

Lum: Not a cent. Hit aint jist everbody that could git the newspapers to print a big story bout you tellin all your qualifycations fer sheriff. I jist hope they got it in here like I give it to the reeporter.

Abner: Yea read it outloud. I'm curious to see what all you said about me.

Lum: PROMINENT Pine Ridge Jestice of the Peace is assisting Abner Peabody who is seeking the office of [sheriff of] Polk County in the January election. Mr. Edwards is confident that he will lead Mr. Peabody to victory. Mr. Edards who is Jestice of the Peace and President of the school board in Pine Ridge has been very active in that community for several years. Judge Edards is president of the—

Abner: Judge Edards?

Lum: Yea I figgered that'd hep you some in yer campaign if he called me that. Lets see wher was I at? Yea . . Jedge Edards is president of the Pine Ridge Motor Company, president of the Jot Em Down Store and a large land owner in the eastern part of the county.

Abner: Large land owner?

Lum: Yea I dont know wher he got that idy.

Abner: (L) Why you aint got but forty acres. I've got sixty mysef.

Lum: Judge Edards states that he believes in the future of this section and has invested his fortune in Polk County Real estate.

Abner: Oh.

Lum: Judge Edards states that he is a native of Polk County. Born on the Headwaters of the Ouachita River and educated himself by reading at night by the light of a fire place and splitting rails in the day time. He studied law after he had reached the age of twenty one. He is a bachelor but—

Abner: A what?

Lum: A bachelor. I aint married.

Abner: I know you're not.

Lum: Well thats what that means.

Abner: Oh.

Lum: He is a bachelor but says he does not intend to remain so if the right woman comes into his life.

Abner: Well wher's that story you wrote about me Lum?

Lum: Why this is it I'm readin.

Abner: Go head.

Lum: Judge Edards states that he expects someday to become governor of the state and in due course of time will divulge his plans for upbuilding the state.—What are you doin . . Leave the paper alone Abner.

Abner: Well I was jist lookin fer sompin.

Lum: Why you ort to be interested in what all I said about you here in this article. What are you lookin fer anyway?

Abner: Oh nuthin I was jist tryin to see if I could find that pitcher they come out here and took of me and you.

Lum: Well we can look fer it agin I git done readin this. Whats the rush anyway?

Abner: Oh I jist wanted to see if they had me in it.

Lum: Course they have. Me and you was standin ther together wasn't we?

Abner: Yea but if the pitcher's anything like this article I wouldn't be a bit sprised if they never left me plum out of it.

Lum: Why they couldn't, Dont you know we was handcuffed together sos they could say under the pitcher that Lum Edards and Abner Peabody is hooked up together in the sheriff's race.

Abner: Yea thats right.

Lum: What do you keep talkin bout leavin you out fer.

Abner: Well you aint said nuthin tall bout me there hardly.

Lum: Oh yes I did . . Jist listen. Right here the next thing is about you.

Abner: Oh well scuse me. I never knowed it.

Lum: See here. Judge Edards urges the voters of Polk County to support Abner Peabody in the insuing election because his

reputation as a Political leader is at stake. I grannies that ort
to git you some votes—

Abner: Turn the page here Lum I bleave I see that pitcher of us.

Lum: I swan to goodness Abner I caint read and you pawin over
the paper tryin to turn the——

Abner: Look and see if that aint it on the next page ther.

Lum: (rattles paper) Wher. YEA YEA (L) THER IT IS. LOOK AT
THAT AINT THAT A GOODERN. LOOK AT ME THER I
GRANNIES. Look extinguished dont I?

Abner: Well look at me though I must of turned my head or
sompin. Dont favor me at tall.

Lum: Yea but look at me though. Best pitcher I ever had took
. . . Look at them eyes (L) Put mysef in mind of a college
prefessor. or sompin.

Abner: Well read the readin under ther see what hit says.

Lum: Yea (L) Hooked up together fer sheriff I reckon. Thats
what I told him to put. See if he got it right. . . . Hit says . .
uh . . Says . . I grannies. Hold on here . . . I wisht you'd look
at that. I'll sue that paper fer slanders if hits the last thing I
ever do . .

Abner: What is it, whats the matter?

Lum: Now if that aint a fine howdy do . . . I'm goin to burn this
paper.

Abner: Well dont burn it yit. Let me see whats on it.

Lum: Well here look. Says. CONSTABLE PEABODY OF PINE
RIDGE SHOWN HANDCUFFED TO A DESPERATE
CRIMMINAL HE CAPTURED A FEW MONTHS AGO.
Now if that aint a nuf. . . .

DECEMBER 14, 1933

Lum: (to Evalena) Well wait a minit Evalener. Let me git a
pencil and paper and set some of them things down . . (sings
FADE)—Hello . . Huh? . . . Oh that was me singing (L) Yea
I heard it on the radio . . they sung it awful purty too . . .

Alright now name over some of them things you want. . . .
Wrist watch huh?. . . . . . Prefumery. . . . . . New Ford My
goodness Evalener I'm feard that'd be too much of a load fer
Santy Claus (L) He's more'n likely drivin one of them this
year hisef. (L) Facts I know he is . . . What else was it you
was wantin hon—er Evalener. . . . String of pearls . . . Uh
huh. . . . What kind of a fur coat?. . . . . Uh huh . . . What
else now? . . . Well aint they some little things you want too?.
. . . . Wouldn't have nuthin sept them things you've named
over huh?. . . . Well I'll tell Santy Claus bout it but I'm afeard
you're goin a little strong fer him this year. I understand his
business aint been very good. . . . . Who me? . . . (L) Oh I
dont know I hadn't studdied much about it . . . Anything
at tall. . . Neckties and handkerchiefs I reckon thats all I
ever git I may as well wish fer em—Wait a minit I see Dick
Huddleston comin up out front. I'll make out a list and brang
em over with me tonight. Alright honey. alright . . Huh Yea I
put em all down . . . GOOD BYE . . (CLICK) HIDY DICK.
COME IN. COME IN.
Dick: (FADED) HOW YOU LUM.
Lum: Oh first rate I reckon Dick.
Dick: Wher's Abner?
Lum: Why he's out seithin he can find any clews on that
kidnappin.
Dick: Well thats what I wanted to talk to him about. You know
yesterday's paper said that there was a big yellow car used in
the kidnappin.
Lum: Yea I read that.
Dick: Well Sister Simpson was down at the store awhile ago and
she said that Mose Moots wife told her that she saw a big
yellow sedan right here in Pine Ridge late in the afternoon the
day the kidnappin was done.
Lum: Well you know the paper said they headed in this
direction.
Dick: Abner's workin on it is he?

Lum: Yea he's been out the biggest part of the day.

Dick: Well all of us ort to do all we can to find her if she is out in this part of the country. I know the little girl's mother must be grievin herself to death.

Lum: Oh yea bound to be, bound to be. Like I told Abner I dont bleave they's anything lower downer or oneryer than to take a innocent child like that and take advantage of the love they is betwixt parents and their children to git their hands on a few dollars.

Dick: Oh its inhuman.

Lum: Oh hits a cowardly thing to do and wouldn't nobody but the lowest yellerest type of crimminal ever git mixed up in no sich as that.

Dick: Wellsir I've got a huntch some way or ruther that these fellers are goin to be caught.

Lum: Well I dont know I've got my doubts about it. With that Butch Dolan in ther as sheriff of the county I aint got no confidence in him. He does a lot of mouth talk about what all he's goin to do but you never hear of him ketchin nobody.

Dick: No theys been some purty mean things done in this county since he's been in office and if he's ever caught any of em yet I dont know when it was.

Lum: Thats one of the mainest reasons I want to see Abner elected. Git that feller outa ther.

Dick: Well I bleave he's got a good chance too Lum. I'm glad to see him start doin a little more advertisin.

Lum: Oh he's goin to start out the first of the week and make a batch of speeches all over the county.

Dick: Was them signs Cedric come down to the store and got today?

Lum: Yea you said they was from the printin office in ther at the county seat didn't you.

Dick: Yea the mail carrier left em ther this mornin.

Lum: Well I knew in reason thats what they was fer we had a batch of em ordered. I reckon Cedric has been nailin em up all afternoon. I told him to put em up all over town today and tomorrow he could go out on the roads and nail em long on trees and barns and all. I heard him nailin some on the side of the store here whal ago.

Dick: Yea you're going to have to advertise an awful lot. Butch Dolan has got the whole county plastered with that ugly mug of his.

Lum: Oh he's been spendin money like water. I bet he's already spent ten thousand dollars on this campaign.

Dick: I wonder wher he's gittin all the money to spend thataway.

Lum: I dont know. Me and Abner was talkin bout that yistidy. They's sompin turible strange about it if you want my notions on it.—Well here comes Cedric. I reckon he's all through.

Dick: Oh yea Hit wouldn't take him long to nail up all you'd want here in town.

Lum: Cedric's good hep you know it?

Dick: Oh yea aint afraid of work.

Lum: WELL CEDRIC DID YOU GIT THE SIGNS UP?

Cedric: Yessir I nailed em up on everthing I could find to nail em on.

Lum: Well thats fine.

Dick: Put up a lot of em did you Cedric?

Cedric: (L) Yessir I bet I nailed up a thousand or a milliaon of em. I put a whole row of em along the side of the store out ther Mr. Edards.

Lum: Well I allowed that was what you was doin. I heard you poundin out ther. Might nigh give me a head ache . . Now tomorrey Cedric, I want you to do what I told [you] git a car from Dan Davis over ther and drive out on the road and nail em up on ever tree and barn you come to.

Cedric: Yessum, I left all the signs I had left over ther whal ago sos I can git a early start in the mornin.

Lum: Thats good.

Cedric: I jist wondered Mr. Edards if I got through early tomorrow, would you mind if I done a little squirrel huntin.

Lum: Why no that'll be alright I reckon.

Cedric: Well do you care if I use that old shot gun standin back ther in the corner.

Lum: Why I wouldn't minds fer you to use it Cedric but law me hits so rusty I doubt wher you could shoot it.

Cedric: Well I can take some coal oil and clean it up right good if you dont care fer me usin it.

Lum: (L) Go head then and clean it up. Take it out back of the store ther though I dont want you sloshin coal oil all over everthing.

Dick: Be careful tommorow too Cedric dont git yersef mixed up with no squirrell.

Cedric: (L) (faded) NO MAM I WONT.

Lum: (L) No mam. (L)

Dick: Well Lum I've got to be goin too. Tell Abner—

Lum: Set Down Dick Set Down. You aint in no hurry.

Dick: No I got to go Lum I locked the store up to come over——

Lum: Well wait a minit here comes Abner now.

Dick: Yea yea.

Lum: I grannies he looks up set about somp'n. WHATS THE MATTER OF YOU ABNER?

Abner: (FADE) I DOGGIES THATS A FINE HIDY DO. RIGHT HERE ON OUR OWN STORE TOO. LUM HOW COME YOU TO LET BUTCH DOLAN DO SICH A THING AS THAT—

Lum: Whats the mat- What you talkin bout?

Abner: Why whats all them Butch Dolan signs, advertisements doin nailed up all long the side of our store here?

Lum: Why them aint Butch Dolan Signs. Them's yours.

Abner: Aint no sich a thing. They got Butch Dolan fer sheriff right up accrost the top ther.

Lum: Well I swan to goodness. I aint seen em. Cedric went down to Dick's store and got em—Dont reckon you made a mistake Dick and give him the wrong signs?

Dick: No but I'm just wonderin . . He never opened up the

package while he was ther. The printin office might of accidental made a mistake and sent some Butch Dolan Signs stid of Abner's. (L)

Abner: Well Cedric ort to had more sence'n to put em up.

Lum: Well he caint read Abner. You ortent to blame him.

Abner: Well thats right. I wondered why bout half of em was upsided downaards.

Lum: Well he spent today puttin em up he can jist spend tommorey takin em down.

Dick: Have you found any clues yet Abner on the kinappers?

Abner: Well yes sorter. but I'm keepin it to mysef yet fer awhile.

Dick: Well I jist wanted to tell you if they's anyway I can hep Abner dont hesitate to call on me.

Abner: No I wont. Much obliged Dick.

Dick: Well I've got to go fellers. I've jist got to.

Lum: Well come over again and loaf with us Dick.

Dick: (faded) YEA I WILL LUM YOU FELLERS COME DOWN.

Lum: ALRIGHT DICK . . . Well I better go out and see Cedric and git him to take them signs down—

Abner: Wait jist a minit Lum. I want to talk to you a little.

Lum: Whats the matter?

Abner: Well in the first place I bleave Butch Dolan is mixed up in this kidnappin someway.

Lum: Butch Dolan (L) Why that couldn't be Abner. He's the sheriif.

Abner: I know but I was settin out on the road last night lookin fer a yeller sudan and one went by me headed thisaway goin so fast I couldn't tell fer shore but I'd might nigh bet money that Butch Dolan was a drivin it.

Lum: Oh (L) Fer the land sakes Abner dont be tellin that around. Fokes'll laugh at you.

Abner: Well he was out here in Pine Ridge last night I know that fer he called me on the telephone bout midnight and threatened me agin. Said if I never withdrawed from the race by today noon, I wouldn't live twenty four hours.

Lum: Well he coulda called you from in ther at the county seat.

Abner: Yea this call was made right here on the Pine Ridge party line. I know fer when the calls comes from the county seat the operater allus talks to you first and says who it is a callin you.

Lum: Yea thats right Abner. Thats good reasonin. Good reasonin. So Butch warned you agin did he?

Abner: Yea and he talked like he meant business this time Lum. I'm sorter oneasy bout mysef.

Lum: Oh fergit about it. Fergit about it. If he does come out here, I'll tell him wher to head in at. I'll show him a thin——

Abner: I doggies who's that comin up out ther in front.

Lum: Wherbouts?

Abner: Right yonder gittin outa that car. I doggies I bleave hits Butch—

Lum: Oh your nerves is on aige. Why—I GRANNIES THAT IS HIM JIST SHORE AS THE WORLD.

Abner: I knowed it. I'm goin out the back door here Lum. You tell him I've withdrawed from the race—

Lum: WELL WAIT A MINIT YOU AINT GOIN TO LEAVE ME HERE BY MYSEF AIR YOU?

Abner: I doggies I'm gone I tell you—

Butch: HOLD ON THER PARDNER. GIT YERSEF BACK IN HERE FORE I DRILL YOU. DONT TRY TO RUN FROM ME I'LL FILL YOU SO FULL OF LEAD YOU WONT BE ABLE TO RUN.

Abner: (fade in) Well Hidy do Mr. Dolan. I never seen you come in.

Lum: Was you wantin to see us about sompin?

Butch: Yea I want to see Peabody here. and I reckon you know what about. Dont bleave we'll be needin you round here Edards. You'd better make yersef scarse. Go on Scram. (two gun fires)

Abner: Do you want me to go too Mr. Dolan?

Butch: NO I WANT YOU TO STAY RIGHT HERE. I JIST NEVER WANTED NO WITNESS TO THIS SHOOTIN THATS GOIN TO TAKE PLACE. HAVE YOU GOT A GUN ON YOU?

Abner: Yessir but you can have it.

Butch: No I wont want it. Git it out . . NOW HOLD IT IN YER HAND.

Abner: What you want me to hold it in my hand fer.

Butch: Well I aint no fool. You dont think I want to do a stretch fer killin a varmit like you. Long as you've got that gun in yer hand I can claim self defence. (L)

Abner: You dont aim to kill me shore nuff do you Mr. Dolan?

Butch: What do you think I come out here fer to play drop the handkerchief. Now git over there against that wall over ther—So you been callin yearsef Able Abner Peabody, the peepuls peerless pertector have you?

Abner: Well Mr. Dolan I've already withdrawed from the sheriff's race. Jist fore you come in jist now.

Butch: Well you're too late Peabody. I give you plenty chances and you wouldn't take em. I told you what I was goin to do and I reckon you thought I was bluffin—

Abner: Yea but I—

Butch: Shut up. Now I'm goin to count three . . . ONE—TWO——

Abner: MR. DOLAN JIST A MINIT. WE'VE BEEN PUTTIN UP SIGNS FER YOU ALL DAY AN

Cedric: (FADED IN) WAIT A MINIT THER BUTCH DOLANS NOT SO FAST. FROW UP YER HANDS.

Abner: Well Cedric.

Cedric: I got this shot gun loaded with buck shot and I'm lible to pull the trigger any minit. If thats your car out ther you better git in it fore I lose my temper and dont you never show your sneakin honery hide round here no more——

DECEMBER 18, 1933

Lum: Now Cedric I want you to take this Christmas list over and give it to Evalener.

Cedric: You wrote down all the things you want er to give you fer Christmas huh?

Lum: No I wrote down what I dont want er to give me. I want to be shore she dont give me no nuther necktie like she give me last year.

Cedric: Well I'll tell er you dont want no necktie then.

Lum: No never mind I've got it down on the list here. Now if you want to tell er sompin that'll shore nuff hep me, I wisht you'd sorter reemind er while yer over ther about that old Edards sayin of mine bout it bein more gracious to give than it is to reeceive.

Cedric: Jist tell er hits more gracious to give than to receive on Christmas huh?

Lum: Yea thats right. Tell er that. I'll do sompin fer you sometime.

Cedric: You can do sompin fer me now if youns want to.

Lum: Whats that Cedric?

Cedric: Oh I dont like to ast you to do it.

Lum: Go head what is it?

Cedric: Reckon could you loan me a dollar till pay day. I want to buy my sweeheart a Christmas present.

Lum: Sweetheart? I never knowed you had one.

Cedric: (L) She dont know it neither but she is.

Lum: Who is it?

Cedric: Clarabelle Seestrunk. I'm sorter aimin on gittin er a pocket knife.

Lum: A pocket knife? That aint no fittin present fer a gurl. She caint use that.

Cedric: I know it thats the reason I'm goin to git that fer er. If she aint got no use fer it hersef she might give it back to me. I'm a needin one bad.

Lum: Fer goodness sake Cedric. Wait a minit though. That aint a bad idy though.

Cedric: There comes Mr. Huddleston yonder.

Lum: Yea. Better git on over ther with that list to Evalener.

Cedric: Aint you fergittin sompin?

Lum: Nope. I went over the list twiset I think I got everthing I dont want down there.

Cedric: I mean that dollar.

Lum: Oh yea. here you are. Now dont you fergit it.

Cedric: Nossir and I'll be back jist soon as I can git back.

Lum: WELL HIDY DICK COME IN COME IN.

Dick: (faded) HIDY LUM. Hello ther Cedric.

Cedric: (faded) Hidy Mr. Huddleston how you today?

Dick: Alright Cedric. How're you.

Cedric: Purty good how're you.

Dick: WHAT'RE YOU DOIN LUM?

Lum: Oh nuthin Dick. Jist settin. Come on back.

Dick: Wher's Abner?

Lum: Oh he went into the county seat to rent a kodak. He's aimin on takin some pitchers of his depultys fer newspaper plublicity.

Dick: Well thats the reason I come over here Lum to see if I couldn't talk Abner into withdrawin from the race.

Lum: Withdrawin. I thought you figgered he had a good chance of bein lected.

Dick: Well I bleave he does if nuthin happens to him. But I'm a little uneasy bout him. This Butch Dolan is a bad character. That fellow wouldn't stop at nuthin and if anything did happen to Abner I'd feel more or less responsible. You and I were the ones that talked him into runnin for Sheriff.

Lum: Yea. I thought about that some mysef. Special after Butch come out here last week and threatend to kill him . . Would have I reckon if hit hadn't been fer Cedric.

Dick: Yea cordin to what I heard about it Abner had a narrow escape.

Lum: Oh Butch woulda killed him in a minit if Cedric hadn't of come in here and throwed that shot gun on him and run him off.

Dick: Well how did Cedric know about Butch bein in here threatenin Abner?

Lum: Why he was out back of the store ther cleanin a shot gun, aimin on goin squirrell huntin the next day. So when Butch

run me out and fired that pistol at me a couple of times
Cedric heard it and knowed they was trouble.

Dick: Oh Butch shot at you huh?

Lum: Well . . yea he shot wher I had been . . Cedric jist run in
here with a empty shot gun and bluffed Butch clean outa the
store with it.

Dick: Well good for Cedric. That'd make a purty good story if
it'd git out on Butch. He's sposed to be such a bad——

Lum: Well ther's Abner drivin up out front now I reckon he jist
got back.

Dick: Yea. No listen Lum when he comes in lets both talk to him
git him outa this sheriff's race I think thats the safest thing for
him and I'd feel a whole lot better about it.

Lum: Dont look like abody'd have to do much arguin. I think
he's right on the pint of backin out now, jist wont admit to it.

Dick: Well I cant say that I blame him much at that—

Lum: WELL ABNER YOU MADE A QUICK TRIP.

Abner: (Faded) Yea Hit dont take abody long to git wher he's
goin in these New Ford V8s. WELL Hidy Dick I never seen
you settin ther.

Dick: Hidy Abner. I jist come over to talk to you.

Abner: Fine I'm glad you come over.

Lum: I see you got the kamery alright.

Abner: Yea I got it but I'm feard it aint goin to do us no good.

Lum: Whats the matter. Is it broke?

Abner: No but I stopped by Grandpappy Spears' place to tell him
I'd be over ther dreckly to take his pitcher and he's down in
bed sick.

Lum: Well I do know. I never knowed he was ailin.

Dick: Yea he's been sick for two or three days now.

Abner: I went in the bed room but hits so dark in ther a kamery
never would take a pitcher of nuthin in ther.

Lum: I grannies I reckon we'll have to wait till he gots well fore
we can take it. And right now is when we need the plublicity
too.

Dick: Well if you're in a hurry, you could let him set up and take a flashlight picture of him right ther in the bed room.

Lum: Yea you jist takend the words right outa my mouth Dick. I was jist fixin to say the same thing mysef.

Abner: Well thats the first time I ever heard of takin pitchers with flashlights. If I'da knowed that I've got a flashlight over at the house and I wouldn't a had to went after this camery.

Lum: Yea thats right.

Dick: Well you dont take em with a flashlight. Thats what they call it but all there is to it, they jist set a match to a little powder and when it flares up it makes it light enough to take the picture.

Abner: Have you got any of them powders down at your store Dick?

Dick: Well now I aint got no regular flashlight powder but I've got some black gun powder. That ort to work alright if you dont use too much of it.

Lum: Well we've got gun powder in the store here.

Abner: Yea I'll jist fix mysef up a sack full of that.

Dick: A sack full? Why you wont need more'n a tea spoon full Abner.

Lum: Why no. That'll be a suff—suffic—a plenty.

Abner: Well I better take plenty. May as well take a couple of pounds. And if I do have any left over I can fix up some caterdiges and hits good stock medicine too.

Dick: Well say I want to see that pitcher took. I'd like to go along with you.

Lum: Yea I better go along too and show you how its did Abner.

Abner: Well come on then lets go.

Dick: I caint go this afternoon Abner I've got to get back to the store dreckly.

Lum: Why dont you wait till tomorrow Abner if Dick wants to see it did. Grandpap'll still be ther.

Abner: Well I reckon I had better wait then fer I may need both of you fellers along to hep me talk him into it. He's awful skittish about new fangled idys thisaway.

Dick: Well Abner set down here a minit. Me and Lum wants to talk to you.

Lum: Yea you might not need no pitcher of Grandpappy.

Dick: I tried to see you yesterday at church and have a talk with you but you was so busy goin round shakin hands and all I never got a chance.

Abner: Yea I was politicin. Gittin votes.

Lum: I aimed to tell you Abner that was a good idy you heppin the wimmen fokes outa the automobiles and wagons and buggies and all.

Abner: Did I do it like you told me to?

Lum: Yea I couldn'ta did better mysef. That shakin hands with everbody and kissin the youngins is the best way in the world to git lected.

[A page of the script is missing.]

Lum: Yea thats the thing to do. I told Dick awhile ago you'd be glad of a excuse to git outa of it.

Abner: Well let me tell you fellers sompin. And this is final . . A time or two ther I sorter felt like withdrawin from the race but I've done made up my mind now and I dont aim to change it . . . I aint tellin all I know but I've got good reasons fer bleavin that Butch Dolan and his gang are the very ones that kidnapped that little Mullins girl in ther at the county seat last week and I'll have little Mary Mullins back with her mamma and pap before Christmas if hits the last thing I ever do and then I'm goin to clean up Butch Dolan's gang, but I caint do it long as he's in the sheriff's office. Thats jist the reasons I'm sayin I'm in this race fer sheriff and I aim to stay in it till the last vote's counted.

DECEMBER 20, 1933

Lum: No I told Cedric to tell you thats a list of the things I dont want fer Christmas. . . . You did? . . . Well course if you've done went ahead and got sompin thats on the list ther, I can use it . . . Did he tell you what I told him to bout hit bein better to give than hit is to receive on Christmas?. . . . Yea hit was a good thing I thought about that old sayin fore it was too late too. I was jist fixin to buy a whole batch of presents to give to you and if I had it woulda spiled your Christmas. . . . I want to make at as easy as I can fer you to give more'n you receive . . . Huh? . . Wait a minit Here comes Dick Huddleston. I tell you I'll telephone you back up dreckly after he leaves—

Dick: HIDY LUM I JUST THOUGHT I'D COME OVER AND—Oh excuse me.

Lum: Alright Evalener . . . Good bye. (click) . . WELL DICK HOW YOU FEELIN TODAY AFTER ALL THE EXCITEMENT.

Dick: Why I just came over to see how Abner is today?

Lum: Well I aint saw him today. He aint been down yit.

Dick: I reckon he's purty badly bunged up.

Lum: I was over ther last [night]. He peered to be feelin as well as could be expected. He's purty bad powder burnt around his face and hands. All his eyebrows and eyelashes is singed off and his chin whiskers was might nigh all burnt off.

Dick: Yea I couldn't hardly tell who it was when we picked him up over ther.

Lum: Dock Cook says he aint bad hurt. Worse scared than anything else.

Dick: Yea. I jist now come from Grandpappy Spears.

Lum: How's Grandpap feelin after the splosion.

Dick: Why tell you the truth I bleave it hepped him. He's up and around today. If it hadn't been for that he'd more'n likely still be layin over ther in bed sick.

Lum: Well hits a thousand wonders it never killed both of em aint it.

Dick: Yessir they're mighty lucky to come outa that alive.

Lum: When I heard that explosion and seen that smoke bilin outa that room I figgered they was both gonners.

Dick: (L) Well now that its all over and neither one of em is
serous hurt, it was right funny.

Lum: Yea twas. (L)

Dick: You know Abner musta put some more powder in that
thing after we left the room.

Lum: Yea didn't Grandpap tell you. After we left he put the
whole two pounds of black powder in that bucket lid and set
a match to it.

Dick: Well fer the land sakes. No wonder it caused so much
damage. I wondered how just a teaspoon full could knock
Grandpappy plum outa bed and tear up that kamary the way
it did.

Lum: Well Aint Charity said hit knocked her down and she was
clear back in the kitchen. And that room they was in was
plum ruirned.

Dick: Oh yea broke all the winders out and knocked the clock off
the wall and busted it.

Lum: Yea and the worst part about it was, that's a rented kamery
Abner was a usin. Blowed that thing into a thousand pieces.

Dick: Thats right that never blonged to him did it?

Lum: No, Abner rented in ther at the photographers at the
county seat. They aint a bit of tellin what it'll cost him.

Dick: Well say that little escapade'll cost Abner quite a bit wont
it?

Lum: Yea and he's needin ever cent he can git his hands on fer
his campaign too. Wouldn't sprise me none if that flashlight
pitcher of Grandpap cost him any way a hunderd and fifty
dollars fore its over and then the pitcher wernt no count.

Dick: Well he's lucky the whole house didn't burn down.

Lum: I grannies it would of if we hadn't been ther to douse some
water on them curtains and things.

Dick: (L) Wellsir that was more excitement than I've seen in
a long time. I tell you what tickled me though Lum. Was
Grandpap sposed to be sick in bed ther and claimin he never
had a nuff strenth to stand on his feet long a nuff fer youall

to get his pitcher and when that powder went off he picked hisef up offa the floor and jumped through the winder and takend out accrost the yard as agle as a kitten.

Lum: Yea that was a sight him runnin around ther barfooted with his night shirt jist a flappin.

Dick: Yea and old Abner layin over ther in the corner plum onconcious. Still had that rubber bulb in his mouth.

Lum: (L) Yea hits a wonder he never swollered it. I dont think he knowed what happened till we dashed that bucket of water in his face and brung him to.

Dick: (L) Well he was out of his head ther fer half a hour I reckon. Kept sayin "Look pleasant Please" "Look Pleasant please" over and over.

Lum: He peered to be alright in his head last night. I bleave I'll telephone up over ther and see how he's feelin.

Dick: Yea go head and do that Lum. He might of been hurt worse'n he let on like he was.

Lum: (((((TELEPHONE))))) I grannies I bet hit'd be hard to git Grandpap to pose fer arry nuther flashlight pitcher now—

Dick: (L) Yea he'll be kamery shy n——

Lum: HELLO. . . . . LIZZYBETH. . . . THIS IS LUM TALKIN. HOW'S ABNER FEELIN TODAY?. . . . OH HE DID . . MUST BE FEELIN ALRIGHT THEN (L). . . . . YES TIS HITS A WONDER HE WERNT BAD HURT. . . . WELL THAT WAS HIS OWN IDY? DONT TRY TO LAY THE BLAME OFF ON TO ME . . HE'S THE ONE THAT PUT ALL THAT POWDER IN THER HISEF. ME AND DICK TOLD HIM NOT TO PUT MORE'N A TEASPOON FULL IN THER. . . . YESSUM . . . WELL I RECKON HE'LL BE BY THE STORE FORE HE GOES HOME . . . ALRIGHT . . LIZZYBETH . . GOODBYE. (CLICK) (L) She says I ort to be shamed of mysef puttin Abner up to tryin sich stunts as that.

Dick: No ther's one mishap he caint blame nobody with but hisef. Wher'd she say he was at?

Lum: Said Cedric telephoned him up awhal ago and told him he had another clue on the kidnappin so he got up outa bed and went to meet him someplace.

Dick: Wellsir I bleave Abner's just wastin his time lookin for that little girl around Pine Ridge here. Wouldn't sprise me if them kidnappers aint got her hid a thousand miles from here. I jist noticed in the paper today where the kidnappers demanded the ransom be paid within the next 24 hours or they would [not] promise her safe return.

Lum: Well Abner seen in the newspaper wher the kidnappers headed out towards Cherry Hill and Pine Ridge and he's been snoopin round tryin to find a trace of her ever since. He's got Cedric heppin him.

Dick: What does Cedric know about clues and sich as that.

Lum: Oh him and Abner has been studyin that book on how to become a great detecitive and they been bout to run me crazy round the store here puttin on different disguises. Makin out like they're Sherlock Holmes and Dr. Watson.

Dick: Well what was they doin out here at the side of the store the other day with that old hound of Abners?

Lum: You mean old Blue? (L)

Dick: Yea.

Lum: Why (L) They's tryin to learn him to be a blood hound. Learn him to track down criminals. I bet they wasted ten pounds of salt pork meat outa the store here. The only way they could git him to foller em was to carry a piece of meat with em.

Dick: (L) Well what you reckon they think Old Blue could do after he trailed down a criminal. He aint got a tooth in his head.

Lum: Oh I dont know. Jist some more of their foolishness. Both of em carryin spy glasses around with em. Takin finger prints of everbody. Cedric's been hidin along the side of the big road from the county seat ever night this week watchin ever car that come by, lookin fer the kidnappers . . I reckon he thinks they're goin to have a big sign on the car sayin. KIDNAPPERS.

Dick: (L) Yea . . . Well Cedric aint got no business bein out at night this kinda weather. He dont look at all well to me. Looks like he might have the yeller jaunders.

Lum: Oh you mean that yeller complexion he's got the last few days?

Dick: Yea I was jist noticin yesterday. He looks bad.

Lum: (L) Why they aint nuthin the matter with him. Abner put that colorin on him down here at the store the other day. He's been tryin to disguise him as a indian. Put a bunch of turkey feathers in his hair and then rubbed walnut hulls all over his face (L) Now then Cedric caint git the walnut stain offen his face.

Dick: No that stuff wont come off at tall. Hit'll jist have to wear—

Lum: Wait a minit who's that comin yonder? . . Looks like Abner now.

Dick: Yea . . Runnin like sompin's after him.

Lum: I grannies. Dont reckon Butch Dolan is in after him again?

Dick: By geaorge his face is all bandaged up ther to wher he caint half see he's lible to stumble over sompin and break his neck.

Lum: Now dont josh him none about the flashlight pitcher he took Dick. He feels dreadful bad about it anyway.

Dick: Kind of a tetchy subject with him is it.

Lum: Yea, dont let on. Make out you dont even notice he's all wropped up with bandages . . . WELL COME IN ABNER. I GRANNIES I'M PROUD TO SEE YOU GITTIN AROUN SO PEERT——

Abner (fading in) I DOGGIES MEN I'VE DID IT. I'VE DID IT JIST SHORE AS THE WORLD.

Lum: Did what? . What you talkin bout?

Abner: I TOLD YOU FELLERS I'D FIND LITTLE MARY MULLINS IN TIME TO HAVE ER BACK TO HER FOKES BEFORE CHRISTMAS?

Lum: WELL KAM YERSEF DOWN . . YOU THINK YOU'VE LOCATED WHER SHE'S AT?

Abner: THINK NUTHIN. I DOGGIES I'VE FOUND ER.
I JIST NOW TAKEND ER OVER TO THE HOUSE.
LIZZYBETH'S FIXIN ER UP SOME HOT VITTALS RIGHT
NOW.
Lum: WELL I DO KNOW.
Dick: You mean you've found the little girl that was kidnapped
shore nuff?
Abner: Yessir. I told you I had some clues.
Lum: Well have you telephoned her mamma and papa yit and
told em you found er.
Abner: No thats the reason I run on over here I wanted to git you
to telephone em fer me.
Lum: Yea they'll be tickled plum to death. Let me call them up
first thing.
Abner: Yea git that did and then I want to organize a possie and
ketch the low down scoundrels that done that kidnappin.
Lum: Well didn't you ketch the kidnappers?
Abner: No but I know who done it. Butch Dolan is the ring
leader in it. Snake Hogan is mixed up in it too. CEDRIC IS
WATCHIN THE HOUSE WHER THEY HAD THE LITTLE
GIRL HID. (((((TELEPHONE)))))
Dick: Where did they have her hid Abner?
Abner: In the barn to the old Medford place. Aint nobody
lived ther fer over three years now. And Cedric seen some
automobile tracks leadin offen the road and we follered em
down the old Medford lane and seen wher they turned into
the old Medford place. I knowed all along that——
Lum: (faded) HELLO Wait a minit keep quiet you fellers . . .
HELLO IS THIS THE CENTRAL GIRL IN AT THE COUNTY
SEAT PLEASE MOM?. . . . WELL I WANT TO TALK TO MR.
MULLINS THE BANKER THER . . YESSUM. . . THE ONE
THATS HIS LITTLE GURL WAS KIDNAPPED . . . YESSUM
JIST AS QUICK AS YOU CAN GIT HIM——
Abner: TELL HIM SHE'S ALRIGHT. AND WE'LL TAKE GOOD
CARE OF HER TILL THEY CAN COME AFTER ER.

Dick: Seems to be alright does she Abner?

Abner: Oh yea. They aint mistreated er none. She said hit was awful cold up ther in that barn loft and they hadn't fed her nuthin to eat hardly.

Dick: Well wasn't ther anybody there with er when you found er?

Abner: No we jist hit it lucky. We seen this car there and hid till we seen em leave and Butch Dolan and Snake Hogan and one other feller come outa the barn and drive off in it and me and Cedric slipped up ther and found her and brung er on home. She was cryin agin we got ther she said them fellers had jist made her write a note to her pappy sayin——

Lum: Wait a minit . . HELLO . . . MR. MULLINS?. . . . THIS HERE IS LUM EDARDS OUT AT PINE RIDGE . . . WHY WE'VE GOT SOME GOOD NEWS FER YOU. WE'VE GOT YOUR LITTLE GURL FER YOU . . . SHE'S ALRIGHT. FEELIN FINE . . . NO THIS AINT THE KIDNAPPERS THIS IS LUM EDARDS JESTICE OF THE PEACE . . . I JIST FOUND YOUR LITTLE GURL UP IN A BARN LOFT OUT HERE AND YOU CAN COME AFTER [HER] ANYTIME. . . . YEA SHE'S OVER AT THE PEABODY'S. . . . . . (L) WELL I KNOWED YOU'D BE GLAD. . . . REWARD NUTHIN I WAS JIST ONLY PROUD TO DO IT. JIST DONE MY DUTY. . . . WELL JIST MAKE THE REWARD TO ABNER PEABODY. HE HEPPED A RIGHT SMART IN LOCATIN ER . . . ALRIGHT MR. MULLINS WE'LL BE LOOKIN FER YOU. (CLICK)

DECEMBER 27, 1933

Lum: Oh me, Hits allus a sort of a let down after Christmas this away, aint it?

Abner: Yea tis. Takes about a week to git back on the track agin. Git the Christmas tree throwed out in the yard and all.

Lum: Yea I notised two or three trees layin out in fokses yards as I was comin down to the store this mornin. I dont know

of anything that looks more lonesomer than a Christmas tree
bout a week after Christmas. Look like a outcast. Sompin
thats sarved hits purpose and aint wanted no longer.

Abner: Yea. Hit allus makes a tetch of sadness come over me agin
I look at one.

Lum: Reckon what ever becomes of all the old Christmas trees.
(L)

Abner: Wellsir I dont know. But I wisht they could git rid of the
turkey the same way.

Lum: Yea thats allus a problem.

Abner: Hits jist sort of a penalty we have to pay fer Christmas.
Gittin the turkey ett up.

Lum: Yeap. Hits a wonder I aint gobblin right now.

Abner: Wellsir when Lizzybeth brung that big turkey out and set
it on the table Christmas day I couldn't hardly wait to wade
into it but I doggies now if I never see anothern hit'll be way
yonder too soon.

Lum: Maybe thats the reason they have Christmases jist come
oncet a year.

Abner: Well Christmas dinner we started in on him. Christmas
night we had cold turkey sandwiches. Yistidy at noon we had
him warmed over again. Last night we had turkey hash and I
know in reason Lizzybeth'll study up some other way to use
him fer the next few days.

Lum: Oh they're harder to git rid of than dyptheria.

Abner: Why I'm might nigh afeard to eat my breakfast food,
feard hits turkey in disguise. To me this week right after
Christmas is the hardest week to git through in the whole
year.

Lum: Well I dont know though. This little spell twixt Christmas
and New Years allus gives the fokes time to look their
presents over again. See if they can find the price mark on em
again.

Abner: Yea Yea.

Lum: Then they can go through all their Christmas cards again

and see how many they fergot and left offen their list sos they
can send em a New Years card.

Abner: Yea and scratch the names offen the list of them that
never sent them no cards this year.

Lum: (L) Yea I've saw em take and rub their finger crosst the
readin on the cards to see wher they was engraved or not.

Abner: (L) Yea I allus do that mysef. Wellsir we never got as
many cards this year as we git ordinary.

Lum: No I never neither. But I never sent out as many neither
so hit was bout a stand off. You ort to sent out a lot of em
Abner on account of you runnin fer sheriff.

Abner: Yea I coulda put my advertisement right on em couldn't I?
Able Abner Peabody The Peoples Peerless Pertector. Canidate
fer Sheriff.

Lum: Hits too late to be thinkin about it now.

Abner: I was sorter thinkin bout strikin out again tomorrow Lum
and makin some more speeches. I jist wasted my time yistidy
makin them speeches in the wrong county.

Lum: Well now Abner they aint no uset to count on gittin out fer
a couple of days yit anyhow. We've got to take invoise of the
store here you know.

Abner: Yea but that wont take but a few minits will it.

Lum: A few minits?

Abner: Well what is that invoice anyway? I've heard the name
called a hunderd times I reckon but I never did know what
they meant by it.

Lum: Well what we've got to do is count the articles we've got on
the shelves and counters and set em down on a sheet of paper.
Thataway abody can tell how much money he lost last year.

Abner: I dont see how we could tell thataway.

Lum: Well you see we take what we've got now and then we
git the list we made up last year and then we deduct. The
difference is what we aint got. Course if we've got more this
year than we had last year why we deduct what we had last
year from what we've got this year and the difference would

be how much more we've got this year than we had last year, but now if we had more last year than we've got this year we'd have to take and deduct what we've got this year from what we had last year——

Abner: What do you mean this year and last year. We never even had the Jot Em Down Store last year.

Lum: Yea thats right that wont work will it. Well we'll have to take what we had when we started last spring.

Abner: Yea could do that but trouble of it is we never kept no list of what we started with.

Lum: Thats goin to make it hard too.

Abner: Might take them old invoices from the wholesale house and figger out what we bought to start with.

Lum: Yea that'd be fine if we had em but we aint got em.

Abner: Aint got em?

Lum: No I was lookin at em the other day and deesided we never had no use fer em and started a far with em.

Abner: We caint use them then can we?

Lum: No. But the easiest way to do it anyway. We know how much money we had to start with dont we?

Abner: Yea I put up a thousand dollars. And you never put up nuthin.

Lum: Yea but I paid you back five hunderd dollars outa the store though. Recollect the first five hunderd dollars profits went to you. I never got a nickle of it.

Abner: Thats right Thats right you shore did. I'd fergot about that.

Lum: Well then the thing to do is say we started with a thousand dollars.

Abner: Yea.

Lum: Well all we got to do then is count up and see how much we got on hand and deduct the thousand dollars from it and that'll show how much profit we made. (L) What would you do if you never had me to look after the business end of the business here.

Abner: Yea I wouldn't know how much money we made last
year.

Lum: Jist leave it to me I'll figger it all out fer you . . . Now lets
see . . First thing we got to do——

Abner: Lum what do you say agin we figger out how much we
made, we deevide it up and me and you take half the profits.

Lum: Yea I'd love to do that. Ort to have a big settlement oncet a
year anyhow. I dont know what we'll do with all that money
but we jist wells to git it and enjoy it.

Abner: Yea I can use it on my campain fer sheriff.

Lum: First thing we got to do is figger out how much money we
owe.

Abner: Yea.

Lum: Well I know what that is. Twelve hunderd dollars. That
wholesale house has been writin us a lot of letters reemindin
us of that. Facts is the last time they sent a statement they had
a pitcher of a man with big tears in his eyes sayin. Please.

Abner: Yea I seen that.

Lum: Well we owe them twelve hunderd dollars. I'll set that
down. 1200. Now we owe the hardware company three
hunderd and eighty dollars.

Abner: Thats all we owe aint it.

Lum: Yea we paid the bank. You know they wouldn't reenew.
That totals up 1580. Thats what we owe. Now then we got
to take the cash we got on hand and all the money we got
in the bank and add them two together . . See how much we
got in the cash drawer over ther, I'll call up the bank and git
em to give me our balance ther. I dont know what it is. I've
deposited so much dourin the hollidays I caint keep up with
it. ((((TELEPHONE))))

Abner: (faded) One . . Two . . Three . . Three dollars and fifty
sixty . . sixty five . . Sixty six sixty seven . . sixty eight.
THREE DOLLARS AND SIXTY EIGHT CENTS LUM.

Lum: Wait a minit. HELLO IS THIS THE CENTRAL GURL AT
THE COUNTY SEAT . . . WELL WILL YOU RING THE

UNION BANK FER ME PLEASE MOM? . . How much did
you say Abner?

Abner: THREE—Three Oh shuckens I'll have to count it agin
Lum.

Lum: HELLO. . . . IS THIS THE UNION BANK? . . . . UH HUH
. . I want to speak to the President Please. . . . Alright . . (to
Abner) Some two by four clerk in ther I reckon doin the
talkin . . I dont like to talk my business with jist anybody .
. HELLO . . . WHY THIS IS LUM EDARDS PRESIDENT
AND GENERAL MANAGER OF THE JOT EM DOWN
STORE OUT AT PINE RIDGE . . YESSIR. WHY I WISHT
YOU'D LOOK ON YER BOOKS AND SEE HOW MUCH
MONEY WE'VE GOT ON DEPOSITS AT YOUR BANK
IN THER. . . . YEA OUR BALANCE. . . . ALRIGHT I'LL
HOLD IT . . .

Abner: We got three dollars and sixty eight cents Lum.

Lum: Uh huh. Well count that out in two piles then, we may
as well start deeviding right—HELLO. . . . . YESSIR. . . .
HAH?. . . . . OH. . . . . ALRIGHT THANK YOU SIR. . . .
SIR?. . . . YESSIR WE WILL. YEA WE'LL WATCH THAT
. . . ALRIGHT (CLICK) Well Eight dollars and fifty cents
overdrawed. Thats goin to make it hard to figger this thing
out . . . May as well put the money back in the cash drawer
till I can do some figgerin here.

Abner: Dont want to deevide this huh?

Lum: No Not yit . . . Let me see. We owe 1580 and we've
overdrawed eight dollars and a half thats 1588.50 . . we owe
and we've got, we've got . . . I grannies we aint got but three
dollars and sixty eight cents . . Hit looks like we're goin in
the hole here.

Abner: What about that thousand dollars we had to start
with?

Lum: Yea thats right (L) That'll cut that down some . . . That
jist leaves five hunderd and eighty eight dollars and half not
countin the money in the drawer yonder.

Abner: Well thers that five hunderd dollars you give me fer your half intrust in the store.
Lum: Thats the time thats wher its at. I knowed we couldn't of—Now here though wait a minit.
[The final page of this script is missing.]

JANUARY 2, 1934

Lum: Abner put that pipe down. Uh uh uh.
Abner: Well I aint fixin to smoke. I was jist lookin at it.
Lum: Alright now. First thing you know you'll fill it up with terbacker and be a smokin unconcious.
Abner: Well I dont know what to do with mysef. I'm lost lesson I got that pipe in my mouth.
Lum: Well if you've got to carry a pipe in yer mouth you better whittle one out of a piece of wood, without no hole in it sos you caint fergit yersef and fill it up with terbacker.
Abner: Jist sompin to hold in my mouth huh?
Lum: Yea sorter like a passifyer they give babys.
Abner: Yea that might work. I tried puttin quinine on the end of this pipe stem sos hit'd taste so bad I couldn't put it in my mouth but I doggies I've ett so much quinine now my ears is ringin.
Lum: Trouble with you is Abner you aint got a nuff will power.
Abner: Aint got a nuff what?
Lum: Will power . . You know what will power is dont you.
Abner: No. What?
Lum: Well will power is . . You take fer instance . . Uh. You dont know what it means huh?
Abner: No I thought you was fixin to tell me ther.
Lum: Well I am. I'm tryin to splain it in little bitty words sos you can understand it. Lets see . . You know what . . Horse power is dont you.
Abner: You mean like they've got on automobiles.
Lum: Yea. Dont you know the new Ford v-8 fer 1934 has got . . _____ horse power.

Abner: Yea but you said I never had no will power.

Lum: Well on a man they call it will power and on a automobile
they call it horse power.

Abner: Well what they call it on a horse.

Lum: Why they call it . . . Uh . . . Now thats clean offen the
subject. We're talkin bout you needin more horse—I mean
will power to keep yer new year's resulition.

Abner: I aint busted it yit have I?

Lum: No but I'm jist tellin you the reasons hits so hard fer you to
keep is you aint got a nuff will power.

Abner: You say thats the same as horse power huh?

Lum: Yea. You'd be bout a fourcylinder automobile. And the
way you're goin now holdin that pipe in yer mouth, you're
hittin on bout one cylinder. Jist recollect now what its goin to
cost you if you break over.

Abner: Yea I know I said I'd buy you the best hat in town if I
busted my revolution and you said you'd buy me one if you
broke yourn.

Lum: Yea but you needin to worry bout me breakin mine. Talkin
bout that will power. Ther's sompin that I've got. Wher you're
a four cylinder I'm bout a v-8. and I'm hittin on all of em.

Abner: I doggies I bet you dont know what you're revolution is?

Lum: Yes I do. I've got it wrote down sos I wont fergit it. You
was sposed to do the same thing sos they wouldn't be no
argument if we busted em.

Abner: Well I've got mine wrote down too. Here it is right here
on this piece of paper.

Lum: Wher?

Abner: Right ther.

Lum: Well that aint drawed up right. Let me see what you said
ther . . I aint goin to smoke no more . . Well here you never
even signed yer name to it.

Abner: I know I never I'm sorter pertickler what I sign my name to.

Lum: Well this aint goin to work nohow. This aint no way to
draw up a resolution. This aint even bindin.

Abner: You mean I coulda smoked without bustin it?

Lum: Why course hit aint drawed up right.

Abner: Well I do know. Fer two days now I been sufferin to smoke and I coulda went right ahead and hit wouldn't a hurt nuthin.

Lum: Yea we better git yours drawed up like I done mine . . . Wher is that . Yea here . . Now here is the right way to draw up a new Year's resolution . .

Abner: Is that what that is? I seen that layin ther and thought it was some kind of a legal document.

Lum: Hit is might nigh a law the way I've got it drawed up ther . . See that Notary public seal on ther.

Abner: Yea.

Lum: That makes it official.

Abner: Whats all that readin ther? Hit dont take you that long to give your revolution does it?

Lum: Why hit does to do it right . .

Abner: Well you musta made some that I dont know nuthin bout.

Lum: No. It says here, KNOW ALL MEN BY THESE PRESENTS . . TO WHOEVER IT MAY CUNCERN, THAT I, LUM EDARDS? HEREINTO AFTERWARDS REFERED TO AS PARTY OF THE FIRST PART DO SOLOMONELY RESOLVE . . SWEAR OR AFFIRM TO WIT. WHEREAS; TRUTH CRUSHED TO EARTH IS BOUND TO RISE AGAIN AND THE OLD EDARDS SAYIN . . TRUTH WILL OUT I do hereby and herewith promise and state that from this the first day of January 1934 A D fer the balance of my days. will tell the truth the whole truth and nuthin but the truth. Witness my hand and seal Lum Edards . . . Subbscribed and sworn before me this 1st day of Jan. 1934 Lum Edards Notary Public.

Abner: Whats that other name down ther?

Lum: Oh thats a witness . . Lum Edards witness.

Abner: I doggies that makes it might nigh a penentintury offence to bust one of them dont it?

Lum: Oh yea thats drawed up proper.

Abner: Well Lum I dont bleave you'll ever keep it. Dont bleave you can.

Lum: You mean to set ther and say that hits goin to be hard fer me to tell the truth.

Abner: Yea I'm afeard you're goin to have trouble ther Lum I shore do.

Lum: You mean I aint been tellin the truth?

Abner: Well I wouldn't come right out and say you lied Lum. But you do git mighty closet to the edge sometime. You're jist sorter like old Uncle Henry Lunsford when he swopped off that old blind horse of his. (L)

Lum: What do you mean like Uncle Henry Lunsford?

Abner: Well he wouldn't come right out and tell the feller he was swoppin with that the horse was blind but he did say the critter never looked as good as he ort to.

Lum: Well I dont aim to even do that. From here on with me hits nuthin but the absolute truth.

Abner: You'll never make it.

Lum: Abner us Edardses has allus been knoted fer tellin the truth and will power all through the degenerations. Clean back to my decendents . . . King Edards the first——

Abner: Keerful now Lum. Keerful. Recollect yer revolution.

Lum: Well clean back to my Grandpap then.

Abner: Yea but what I'm talkin bout Lum you're goin to loose ever friend you got.

Lum: No I wont loose no real friens Abner. Recollect that old Edards sayin, the truth never hurt nobody.

Abner: Like when sister Simpson throwed her head in the air and prissed outa the store here this mornin. What'd you say to her that made er so mad.

Lum: Oh nuthin fer er to git mad about. I jist told er the truth . . She wanted to know how I liked her new hat and I told er it looked like a last years birds nest.

Abner: (L) Well you ortent to said that Lum.

Lum: Oh you seen her she wern't mad at tall. You ort to saw
   Kalup Weehunt's woman this mornin. She got mad a nuff to
   bite. Frothed at the mouth. Stamped outa the store here.
Abner: What was the matter with her.
Lum: Oh she was tellin me bout havin a birthday tomorrow and
   wanted me to guess how old she was and I tried to git around
   it told er I never had no idy and she says how old do I look
   and I says well puttin it thataway. You look a hundred but I
   dont think you're over fifty.
Abner: Why she aint but forty.
Lum: Well no wonder she got so mad. (L) Course now I've
   missed some sales here in the store, but I've got to tell the
   truth regardless.
Abner: Yea hits a good thing we both never made that revolution.
Lum: Yea thats the reason I called you over to wait on Ezry
   Seestrunk when he ast me if we had any fresh butter and
   eggs. I never wanted to break——
Abner: Well yonder comes Dick Huddleston.
Lum: Yeap. (L) Dick said he wern't goin to make no resolutions this
   year. He resolved not to make none. So he couldn't bust em.
Abner: I doggies I wisht I'da thought of that. I'd give four hats to
   smoke right now.
Lum: Well Abner hit aint the price of the hat. Hits the idy of a
   man not havin strenth to keep his word.
Abner: Yea but I'm gittin to wher I dont keer so much about
   that——
Lum: WELL HIDY DICK COME IN COME IN.
Dick: (FADE IN) HIDY MEN . . HOW YOU FELLERS TODAY.
Lum: Oh First rate I reckon Dick.
Abner: Happy new year to you. I aint saw you since last year.
Dick: Thats right Abner. Same to you.
Abner: Same to you.
Lum: Well Dick set down. Set down.
Dick: Yea I just heard awhal ago that they dropped them charges
   agin you in ther at the county seat.

Lum: Yea they called up this mornin said jist fergit about it. I
knowed they would though.

Dick: Why sure they never had no case against you. That was
just a scheme of Butch Dolan's to get back at Abner.

Lum: Yea.

Abner: I doggies thats a good lookin pipe you got ther Dick.

Dick: Yea. Yea that was a Christmas present. Coolest smokin
pipe I ever had in my mouth.

Abner: Well. That smells like right good terbacker too.

Dick: Yea thats a special blend I'm tryin out.

Abner: I doggies that shore does small good.

Dick: Well here Abner try a pipe full of it. If you like it I can get
you some.

Abner: Yea——

Lum: No Dick Abner wouldn't keer fer none.

Dick: You're welcome to it now if you want it.

Lum: No he wouldn't keer fer none. You see Abner has swore off
smokin.

Dick: Oh I see. New Year's resolution huh?

Abner: Yea. I reckon so.

Dick: Well thats fine. I'd hate to give my pipe up though. I get
more pleasure outa that than anything. There's nuthin more
restful than a good pipe of tobacco. Sorter sooths your
nerves.

Abner: Yea it shore does.

Dick: I'd give up might nigh anything before I would smokin.
Why I'd be lost if I didn't have my pipe in my mouth.

Lum: Nossir Dick that whole thing was a frame up to git Abner
outa the sheriff's race. I know in reason that Butch Dolan
hisef put that notice in the paper sayin the kidnappers would
return to the barn wher the little Mullins girl was found.
Wher you goin Abner?

Abner: (fading) You fellers scuse me a minit I got some work to
do back here.

Lum: Butch knowed that Abner would see that notice in the

paper and go over ther to catch the kidnappers and then he could arrest him and acuse him of doin it.

Dick: The prosecutin attorney throwed it outa court huh?

Lum: Oh yea. Quick as the little Mullins girl come down and seen me and Abner she said we never looked a thing like the men that done the kidnappin.

Dick: Well course Abner had a good alibi. It was only natural for him to be there. He's the constable here and when he seen the notice in the paper it was his duty to go over ther and try to catch em.

Lum: Oh I look back now and see wher hit was jist a trap.

Dick: Well I believe it will act as a boomarang.

Lum: Hit'll what.

Dick: I mean it'll git out. The word'll get passed around that Butch was tryin to frame Abner and it'll work out in Abner's favor. Hit'll get——

Lum: Wait a minit Dick. Looky yonder.

Dick: WHAT IS IT.

Lum: LOOK AT THE SMOKE BILIN OUTA THE FEED ROOM BACK THER.

Dick: (fading) YEA GRAB THAT BUCKET OF WATER LUM YER STORE'S ON FIRE.

Lum: I GRANNIES THAT FEED ROOM'S FULL OF HAY TOO.

Dick: WELL HURRY UP LUM MAYBE WE CAN SAVE IT.——

Lum: Wait aminit Dick. (L) Wait a minit. Smell that smoke. Thats terbacker smoke (L) I think I've won me a new hat. . . . COME ON OUTA THER ABNER. I KETCHED YOU.

January 3, 1934

Abner: No Lum you're goin to ruin the business here in the store if you dont quit that new years revolution.

Lum: Well Abner if jist tellin the truth ruirns our business. Hit ort to be ruirned. When hit gits to the pint wher abody has got to tell a pack of lies to keep customers, hits time we was gittin into sompin else.

Abner: Well now this is the third day you've been tellin the truth and I betcha we've lost twenty five customers . . In two weeks me and you'll be the only ones tradin here.

Lum: Looks to me like fokes'd preciate bein told the truth.

Abner: Yea and hit looks to me like you could see by now that abody caint tell the truth. Hit jist wont work.

Lum: I said I was goin to tell nuthin but the truth in 1934 and I aim to stick to my word.

Abner: Well thats alright fer you Lum but recollect I own half intrust in the store and I'm a sufferin fer sompin you're doin . . That new years revolution is as hard on me as it is on you.

Lum: You're jist tryin to git me to break it sos I'll have to buy you a new hat. Jist cause you never had the will powers to keep from smokin aint no sign I caint keep mine.

Abner: Well law me if that hat's all thats makin you keep it, we'll jist call the bet off. You wont even have to buy me one. Facts is I'll buy you a nuthern if you'll break it.

Lum: No I wouldn't want to do that.

Abner: Why hit'd be a heap cheaper on me. You've run off a nuff business in the last two days to buy fifty hats.

Lum: Who have I made mad sept The widder Abernathy and Sister Simpson and Mrs. Weehunt and Old Uncle Henry Lunsford?

Abner: Well you said sompin to one of the Mackmillan boys that made him stomp outa the store and I heard Marthy Gattlin holler back at you from the front door ther yistidy that she'd set foot in this store fer the last time.

Lum: You know what that was over. No reason at tall sept that I told er if she never started reducin she was goin to be big as a barn.

Abner: Well you ort to knowed how tetchy she is bout how fat she's gittin.

Lum: Well I was jist tellin er the truth. Like when I told Luther

Phillips yistidy He wanted some stuff ona credit and I told him I'd let him have it but I never spected to git the money fer it. And it was the truth.

Abner: Well I'll say one thing we aint did a nuff business since you started that truth tellin to mount to anything. Looks like 1934 is goin to be worse'n arry year we've had yit.

Lum: Well the only way I see out of it Abner is fer you to wait on all the customers.

Abner: You mean fer me to do all the sellin?

Lum: Yea I can set back here by the stove and make out like I'm asleep.

Abner: Yea. Yea. I bleave I see through the whole thing now. You want me to do all the work while you set back here and sleep.

Lum: No I dont Nossir . . Hit aint that. Why I never oncet thought—

Abner: Keerful now recollect yer revolution. You cain tell nuthin but the truth.

[A page is missing, in which Dick arrives, apparently bringing a letter for Abner.]

Lum: Oh yea they's some I reckon. But I'll tell you right now. When you see anybody that caint stand to be told the truth, you can put it down right then and there that they aint much to em. Shows a shaller character.

Dick: Well I dont know Lum. I dont bleave they's any of us that wants to hear the truth all the time.

Lum: Well now thers wher yer wrong. I do. And thats the reason I want you to tell me the truth about what them fokes said that quit us and started tradin with you.

Dick: Well I dont remember just exactly what all they said. I do remember that the Widder Abernathy said she wouldn't trade with you if this was the only store in town . . Said she'd go hungry first.

Lum: Well dad blame her soul we didn't want her business no how.

Dick: Now Lum I dont like to tell you these things cause I know its goin to make you mad and it aint necessary at tall.

Lum: I want to hear it. I aint goin to git mad. Thats one thing I can say fer mysef. I can stand to hear the truth told about me without gittin my back up.

Dick: Well (L) Old Uncle Henry Lunsford said if he was a few years younger he'd give you a whoppin—

Lum: I grannies he aint never saw the day he could give me no whoppin.

Dick: Martha Gattlin said she——

Lum: Why dad blame her. She caint talk about me like that—

Dick: And Luther Phillips. Said you was the biggest crook in town and said if Abner wasn't elected sheriff it'd be because you was managin his campaign. Said you never had a nuff sence to git in outa the rain—

Lum: Well he's a fine one to be talkin thataway. TalKIN BOUT BRAINS THAT LUTHER PHILLIPS AINT GOT——

Dick: Now Lum recollect what you said. Said you could stand to hear the truth.

Lum: WELL YOU DONT MEAN TO SET THER AND SAY THATS THE TRUTH DO YOU?

Dick: Well I dont know. I'm just tellin you what they said.

Lum: WHY DAD BLAME YOU DICK HUDDLESTON I BLEAVE YOU AGGED EM ON. ENCOURAGED EM IN SAYIN THEM THINGS.

Dick: (L) No Lum. I'm just tellin you what they said.

Lum: Dad blame onery outfits I hope they dont never come in this store agin—

Abner: Well I'll be switched I caint make no sence outa this letter here. I caint figger out what they're wantin.

Dick: What does it say Abner.

Abner: Here take it and read it. See if you can make any sence out of it Dick I caint. They want me to talk over sompin.

Dick: Well this is from the radio station in there at the county seat. I guess they want you to talk over the radio.

Abner: No it says they want me to talk over the Wilx.

Lum: Over the what?

Abner: Wilx, I reckon you call it. Hit's spellet WILX.

Dick: Oh thats the name of the station. Station WILX.

Lum: Go head and read it Dick. What is it they want?

Dick: (L) I thought you was mad at me.

Lum: No I never got mad.

Dick: Look out now Lum tell the truth.

Lum: Well I mighta got a little mad. What does the letter say?

Dick: Dear Mr. Peabody. To all the candidates seeking office in the January election, we are extending the privelege of speaking over station WILX. If you care to avail yourself of this opportunity of addressing the voters of this county and [t]outing your campaign please advise us immideately. We have taken the liberty of scheduling you at 6:25 Thursday evening, Jan. 4, for a five minute talk. Please advise if this time is satisfactory and does not conflict with previous laid plans . . . Yours very truly . . . A. W. Finley, Program Director . . . Well say thats mighty nice aint it?

Lum: Yea. That'll be a big help to you Abner.

Abner: Well what is it he wants me to do?

Lum: He wants you to make a speech over the radio tomorrow night at 6:25 in behalf of yer candidacy fer sheriff.

Abner: Well why didn't he say so.

Lum: He did. Thats what he says there.

Abner: Well I dont know nuthin bout talkin over one of them radios. I'd druther not have nuthin to do with em. I'd be skeerd to death.

Lum: Why hit ort to be a lot easier fer you. You're allus complainin that you hate to git up in front of a gatherin to do outloud talkin. The radio is jist the thing fer a feller like you. You dont have no audience settin ther in front of you.

Dick: Yea Abner, you sure want to take advantage of that. You can reach everbody in the county talkin over the radio.

Lum: I was jist thinkin Abner me bein yer campaign manager and all I bleave hit'd be a good idy fer me to introuduce you.

Dick: Well now Lum he's just got five minutes. You'll have to make just a short introduction. Just tell who it is thats goin to speak.

Lum: Oh yea. Shore. Jist a few words, about Abner tellin what a great sheriff he'll make.

Abner: Well if you're goin to tell em that, they wont be nuthin left fer me to tell em.

Lum: Oh you can tell em. What all you're goin to do agin you git in office. You know that stuff bout makin the County safe fer wimmen and childerns. I'll write yer speech fer you. And you can jist read it. Wont have to learn it by heart like you been doin fer nobody wont see (((((TELEPHONE))) you talkin over the radio.

Abner: I wont even have to dress up will I?

Lum: Why no. Not unless you want to.

Abner: I doggies if you'll write it fer me and I dont have to learn it by heart, I'll do it. I'll jist write and tell em I'll be there——

Lum: Wait a minit I bleave thats our ring.

Abner: Yea go head and answer it.

Lum: Yea if hits somebody wantin to buy sompin I'll let you talk to em. If I tell em the truth they allus—HELLO . . . YEA THIS IS HIM . . . WELL HIDY EVALENER . . . HUH. . . . YOU AND SISTER SIMPSON IN A ARGUMENT . . WHAT ABOUT. . . . WHY SHORE . GO AHEAD AND ASK ME. . . . . WHER THEY'RE GENUINE OR IMMYTATION HUH? . . . Wait a minit hold the receiver a minit.

Abner: Lum you're white as a ghost.

Lum: I grannies I'm into it now shore nuff.

Dick: Whats the matter Lum?

Lum: Why hits Evalener. She says her and Sister Simpson is in a argument bout them pearls I give her fer Christmas and she wants me to settle it. Sister Simpson says their immytation and Evalener says she knows they're genuine cause I told her they was. And she wants to know how much they cost.

Dick: You never paid but four dollars for em did you?

Abner: He never paid nuthin fer em. He got em on a candy deal.

Lum: I dont know what to tell er.

Abner: Jist recollect yer new year's revolution. Tell the truth the whole truth and nuthin but the truth.

Lum: Yea. Well. I aint goin to break it . . HELLO EVALENER . . THEM PEARLS IS IMMITATIONS AND I NEVER PAID NUTHIN FER EM I GOT EM AS A PREMIUM ON A CANDY DEAL I BOUGHT FER THE STORE . . . YEA . . . WELL YOU SEE . . WELL WAIT A MINIT . . . I-. HELLO HELLO. . . . (SHAKE UP PHONE) . . . WELL . . HUNG UP THE receiver on me.

January 8, 1934

Lum: Yea thats goin to tract lots of attention. Hit'll git Abner a manya vote.

Dick: Well I seen that parade comin down the street this mornin and I thought they was a circus in town.

Lum: Yea they went on over to Cherry Hill. They're goin to prade ther. Then they aim to circle round by Milltown and Mountainburg and put on parades ther.

Dick: Well thats a purty good stunt. Who thought that up.

Lum: Oh that was one of my idys. I was the one that painted them signs on the elephant.

Dick: (L) Buttercup come in purty handy after all didn't he?

Lum: Yea I spect Abner is the first canidate fer sheriff that ever made his campaign ridin on a elephant.

Dick: (L) If he didn't look a sight settin up ther on that elephants head. Looked like a turtle settin on a log. (L)

Lum: I grannies I thought I'd never git um started this mornin. Taken all the stove polish we had in the store to git Cedric blacked up like a slave.

Dick: Is that what Cedric was sposed to be—a slave?

Lum: Yea. Most pitchers you see of these fellers that rides elephants has got a slave walkin long by the side of the elephant to guide him, you know.

Dick: Yea course it aint none of my business Lum. You're Abner's campaign manager and you're doin a good job of it but I'm jist wonderin how its goin to look to these democrats around here for Abner to be ridin around on a elephant. Thats the republican emblem.

Lum: Well yea but thats the reason I had Grandpappy Spears follerin along behind ther on that donkey. See thataway we git the deemocrats and the reepublicans . . Abner's runnin on the demo-publican ticket you know.

Dick: Why sure I never thought about that. (L) How in the world did you ever get Grandpappy Spears to dress hisef up like a clown.

Lum: (L) I grannies I did have a hard time talkin him into it. He never wanted to do it. I told him he'd either have to ride in the parade or we wouldn't let him be deputy sheriff agin Abner's lected.

Dick: Well tomorrow's the big day.

Lum: Yea we'll soon know who's goin to be our next sheriff.

Dick: Well if I know anything about the politics of this county Abner'll be elected by a large majority.

Lum: I grannies I hope you're right. Abner'll be turible dissapinted if he aint.

Dick: Well here comes Dock Cook.

Lum: Yea, I wonder if he's been over to our store to buy sompin and found it all locked up.

Dick: Did you jist lock up to come over here?

Lum: Yea they wern't nuthin doin round ther. No business. I was gittin lonesome settin over ther by mysef. Abner wern't ther to play checkers with.

Dick: Why my business has been oncommonly good here lately.

Lum: Yea I reckon so. All of our customers has quit us and started tradin down here.

Dick: Yea and if you dont change that new years resolution of yours and not tell nuthin but the truth you aint goin to have no customers left at tall.

Lum: Well I aint goin to cut that out. I'll tell you that right now.
I said I aimed to tell the truth the whole truth and nuthin but
the truth this year and I aim to stay with it.

Dick: Alright Lum. It's your funeral. The more fokes you make
mad, the more customers it makes for me but I'm just tryin to
tell you for your own good. You caint tell customers the truth
and stay in business. They dont want to hear the truth.

Lum: Well I'm bout to decide that mysef.

Dick: WELL HIDY DOCK. COME IN.

Lum: HOWDY DOCK.

Dock: (faded) GENTLEMEN . . GENTLEMEN.

Lum: WaS YOU OVER THER AT MY STORE FER SOMPIN?

Dock: (faded) WHY YEA I COME BY THER JIST NOW
WANTED TO GIT A CAN OF TERBACKER. PLACE IS
LOCKED UP AINT IT?

Lum: Yea I jist come over here to loaf with Dick. They wern't
nuthin goin on to speak of.

Dock: Yea I spect things is purty quiet after the hollidays.

Dick: Sompin I can do for you Dock?

Dock: Yea. Can of smokin terbacker is all I reckon.

Dick: Well you know wher its at ther Dock, jist help yersef.

Lum: MUCH SICKNESS IN THE CAMUNITY NOW DOCK?

Dock: (faded) WELL NO MORE'N THEY IS ORDINARY I
RECKON FER THIS TIME OF THE YEAR. AINT GOT
NO SERIOUS CASES OF NO KIND . . . WHERBOUTS DID
YOU SAY THAT WAS AT DICK?

Dick: RIGHT THER AT YOUR LEFT DOCK . . NO NO ON
THE NEXT SHELF . . THATS IT.

Lum: Been hearin politics talked much Dock round at the places
wher you've called?

Dock: Well yes theys a right smart of talk about the sheriff's race.

Lum: How's it lookin fer Abner?

Dock: Well up till now I figgered Abner'd win in a walk but
after seein that article that Butch Dolan come out with in the
Sunday paper yesterday. I dont know. I aint so sure.

Lum: Yea I seen that. I think though I've got a way studdied up that'll take keer of that alright.

Dock: I dont know Lum. Butch said some awful mean things bout Abner in that. It's bound to have some influence on the voters.

Dick: The worst part about it is he waited till the last minit to do it and it dont give Abner no time to deny the things he said about him.

Lum: Yea that stuff about their bein a shortage in the Constable's office. The whole thing wern't a nuthin but a pack of lies.

Dock: A week ago it'd a been a landslide fer Abner. I was in at the county seat one day last week to a meetin of the Polk County medical society. Dock Rollins from down ther in the lower end of the county said Abner'd carry their presinct.

Lum: Well thats encouragin. Encouragin.

Dock: Facts is I made it a point to enquire from most of the Doctors that was ther. They all had a favorable report to make on it.

Lum: Well they ort to know. They round mongst the fokes as much as anybody I reckon.

Dick: Well now recollect Lum. That was before that article come out in the paper.

Lum: Well dont you worry none about that article.

Dock: Well I better be gittin along men. I got a call to make . . I got to try to ford that river if I can.

Lum: Got a call on the fer side of the river huh?

Dock: Yea I got to go to Uncle Henry Lunsfords.

Dick: Uncle Henry down Doc?

Dock: Well I dont know wher it's Uncle Henry or his horse. They both been sick.

Lum: Well.

Dock: Yea I was over ther Thursday night all night with Uncle Henry. He might nigh had the nemonia. Then Friday night I had to set up all night with his horse.

Lum: Not that big roan of hisen?

Dock: Yea. Thats the one. I thought they was goin to lose him shore as the world.

Lum: I grannies that'd be a shame. Thats a fine animal.

Dock: How you feelin Lum. Did that medicine I give you straighten you out alright?

Lum: Well . . . Tell you the truth Doc. I never takend it.

Dock: Never took it?

Lum: No.

Dock: Well why didn't you.

Lum: Well I dont like to answer that Doc on account of I made a new years resolution to allus tell the truth but long as you asked me . . I didn't take [it] cause I didn't bleave it'd do no good.

Dock: Dont you figger I've practised medicine long a nuff to know what I'm doin?

Lum: Well yes but on the other hand they's lots of folks over ther in the cemetary by the school house that took the medicine you perscribed.

Dock: Well if you've got to wher you know more bout medicine than I do, I'd jist soon you wouldn't call me over to your place no more . . . Jist doctor yersef from here out. (Fade out)

Lum: Well.

Dick: HERE WAIT A MINIT DOC DONT RUSH OFF THISAWAY.

Lum: No Doc.

Dock: WELL I'M TOO BUSY TO STAND AROUND AND BE INSULTED———(faded out)

Lum: Well I do know.

Dick: HURRY BACK DOC. Well Lum. Ther's another one of your friends that you've made mad.

Lum: Yea.

Dick: And another regular customer for the store here.

Lum: I grannies of all people I thought Doc Cook could stand to be told the truth.

Dick: No and nobody else can.

Lum: And I've allus heard that honesty is the best policy. And that the truth never hurt nobody. And all them old sayins—

Dick: Well its alright to be honest Lum. Its alright to tell the truth too. You dont have to be dishonest to be truthful, but once in awhile its best not to say anything or evade the question sometimes. If you haven't learnt it by now I dont know what it'd take to convince you.

Lum: I hope all these fokes thats got mad at me, over nuthin you might say, I hope they dont vote agin Abner tomorrow.

Dick: Oh I dont think they'd do that, I aint worried about that near as much as I am that big full page advertisement he had in the paper yesterday.

Lum: Sassafras I aint lettin that bother me one bit.

Dick: You said AWHILE AGO you had a way studdied up that'd take care of that article. What'd you mean.

Lum: Oh never mind you'll find out tomorrow.

Dick: Well now, you've got to deny those statements that Butch made some way or ruther.

Lum: Well I tell you Dick . . Dont say nothin bout this fer I dont want Abner to know I done it . . but I set home all yistidy afternoon and wrote a big article denyin everthing Butch said about Abner and tellin a lot of things on Butch I know he wont have time to deny them . . Beatin him at his own game.

Dick: And havin it printed in todays paper huh?

Lum: No Hit was too late to git it in the paper but I had big sheets of it printed and got some fellers round in ever presinct nailin em up right clost to the votin booth.

Dick: Well say thats a good idy Lum . . . Wher you goin to git the money to do all that with?

Lum: Well thats the reasons I never wanted you to tell Abner. Hit cost five hunderd dollars to git it did. But I figgerd Abner already had spent a thousand dollars on the race and he was beat lesson sompin was did and did quick so druthern to see him lose what he'd already spent I went into the county seat

this mornin and borryed five hunderd dollars on my farm.
Give em a mortgage in thar at the bank.

Dick: Well that was a fine thing for you to do Lum, I know
Abner'll preciate it but why dont you want him to know
anything about it.

Lum: Oh he wouldn't stand fer it a minit. He wouldn't let me
put none of my money in his race. I know a week ago when
we found out the campaign fund was all spent and we was
needin money and Abner never had none, I offered to borrey
some money then and he jist wouldn't listen to it.

Dick: Well course it is kinda risky business Lum. If Abner aint
elected he wont be able to pay you back and I know you
haven't got any way of payin it. Specially with your business
the way it is at the store. Losin all your customers . . . Your
makin too much of a sacrifice ther Lum. You stand a good
chance of losin yer place.

Lum: Well lets dont start worryin bout that now. The election
is tomorrow. If Abner aint elected he's goin to be turible
disapointed.

Dick: Yea and if he aint elected you're goin to loose your farm.

JANUARY 11, 1934

Announcer: In the final count of the votes in the Polk county
election for sheriff yesterday, it was discovered that there
were several thousand more votes cast than there were poll
tax receipts issued. The election board has ordered a new
election to be held January 25th. As we look in on Pine Ridge
today we find Lum and Abner down at the Jot Em Down
Store reading an account of the affair in the county paper.
. . . LISTEN

Abner: DID YOU FIND A NEWSPAPER LUM?

Lum: (faded) Yea I got one. Tells all bout the lection.

Abner: Well hurry up and read it. I caint wait to hear what it
says.

Lum: Look at them headlines crosst ther . . FRAUDELANT VOTING CHARGED IN SHERIFF'S RACE.

Abner: What do they mean by that?

Lum: Why jist what it says.

Abner: What does that word frogalant mean?

Lum: Fraudalant Abner . . Crooked work . . Cheatin . . Let me read it I aint had a chance to look it over mysef yit.

Abner: I bound you Butch Dolan'll be shamed to show his face now.

Lum: Yea that'll hurt him a lott this newspaper comin out and sposin him thisaway. Says . . Election Board claims Ballot stuffed and orders new election . .

Abner: I doggies I'm jist a good mind to call up the newspaper and thank em fer takin sides agin Butch Dolan thisaway.

Lum: Yea you ort to do that . . Final count in the general election shows there were more votes cast in the sheriff's race than there were poll tax receipts issued and James R. Donavin, chairman of the Polk County election board has ordered a new election to be held January 25.

Abner: That means that me and Butch is goin to run again on the 25th of this month huh?

Lum: Yea. By that time the word'll be passed round all over the county that Butch stuffed the ballot box and they wont nobody vote fer him.

Abner: Yea that artickle ther in the paper is a nuff to ruirn him.

Lum: Oh yea. You're same as lected right now. You've got the newspaper with you now. This is a lot of free plublicity.

Abner: Yea I'll have twiset as good a chance with them in behind me wont I?

Lum: Yeap . . Wait a minit whats this here? It was the opinion of the election board that both candidates are guilty of fraudelant voting—Well they're sayin you stuffed the ballot box too.

Abner: Why I never done no sich a thing.

Lum: I know you never but thats what they say here. An

investigation has been ordered and it is believed that
irregularities will be exposed which will reveal the most
illegal election ever held in the history of the county—Well I
do know.

Abner: Well now jist what do they mean ther by that. They're
usin words ther I never heard of.

Lum: Why the lection board must have the idy that you and
Butch both was mixed up in crooked votin and they're goin
to make a investigation.

Abner: I doggies I hope they dont.

Lum: Why let em investigate. Thats jist what we woant em to do.
They'll find out then that Butch Dolan was the only one that
done any crooked votin.

Abner: Well I dont know I aint so sure bout that Lum.

Lum: Why shore they'll go back over ever vote that was cast. see
jist who cast it and all.

Abner: I doggies if they do that I'm a ruirnt man.

Lum: Well here Abner you never done no crooked votin did you?

Abner: Well to be right honest about it Lum, I'm feard I did.

Lum: Well I'll swan to goodness Abner. You'da been the last
feller in the world I'da ever thought woulda did a thing like
that.

Abner: Well I—

Lum: Why I'da druther you'da got beat a thousand times than to
resort to sich low down underhanded methods as that.

Abner: Yea but Lum I—

Lum: I aint got a bit of use in the world with a feller that'll cheat.
Why if anybody'd a told me you'da did a thing like that I'da
fit em. I wouldn't bleave it from anybody but you. I [am]
ashamed of you.

Abner: Well you never let me explain—

Lum: You couldn't never splain that to me . . They aint no excuse
fer it . . Recollect that old Edards sayin. It aint whether you
won or lost but how you played the game—

Abner: Well dad blame it I never meant to do it—

Lum: Never meant to do it. Jist so anxious to git yersef lected you couldn't—

Abner: No it wernt that.

Lum: What all did you do. Maybe I can hep git you out of it.

Abner: Well I voted fer mysef twiset.

Lum: Well fer goodness sake. What good did you think that little old extry vote would do. Never helped you none but you're jist as guilty as if you'da voted a thousand times. How come you to ever do sich a thing anyway. What put the idy in yer head.

Abner: I dont know . . . I ort to knowed better.

Lum: Why course you ort. They aint no excuse in the world fer it.

Abner: If I'da taken time to set down and think it over I never woulda did it. I jist wasn't thinkin. Hits the penalty fer bein so fergitful . . absent minded. When I went in ther and voted the second time late that evenin I plum fergot about votin early that mornin.

Lum: Oh you mean you fergot and voted twiset?

Abner: Yea thats jist what I done Lum. Long late in the afternoon lection day I jist happend to think I hadn't voted fer mysef yet so I run over ther and voted and hit wern't till late that night that I happend to think I'd done voted oncet.

Lum: Well thats goin to be hard to splain. They'll never bleave but what you done it apurpose.

Abner: I dont know what to do bout it.

Lum: Well I tell you what I'd do if I was you. I'd step right ther to the telephone and call that chairmans of the lection board and tell him what you done and how come you to do it and all.

Abner: Yea I bleave thats the best thing to do. What was his name now, you read it ther in the paper—

Lum: Lets see. Let me look at that article again . . Yea. James R. Donavan. Tell him you nevr—No wait a minit hold on. I bleave I'd jist let it go Abner.

Abner: What'd you start to say fer me tell him.

Lum: Nuthin. Jist let it go.

Abner: Why you started to tell me sompin to say to him—

Lum: Jist let it go Abner. I dont bleave I'd say nuthin bout it. Hit was a honest mistake on your part. You never meant to do it. Facts is I jist happend to think, you talkin bout votin twiset jist called to my mind, blamed if I dont bleave I done the same thing mysef. Voted in the mornin and in the afternoon both.

Abner: Well I do know.

Lum: I can understand how you could make a mistake thataway. And I dont hold it agin you at tall Abner. ((((TELEPHONE)))) Excited over the lection and all. Yessir I recollect now. I was one of the first ones to vote and then I recollect votin jist fore they closed the polls—

Abner: I bleave that was our ring then Lum.

Lum: Yea. I grannies you dont reckon thats the lection board already found out what we've did do you.

Abner: Tell em we never done it a purpose.

Lum: You tell em.

Abner: No you can splain it a heap better'n I can.

Lum: Go on Abner answer it. You're the one that got us into this mess. You're the one that was runnin fer sheriff.

Abner: Well alright. What must I say.

Lum: Why jist admit to the whole thing. They aint no uset to deny it, The votes is ther to show fer therseves.

Abner: HELLO . . THIS IS ABNER PEABODY AND I JIST WANT TO SAY ME AND LUM AINT DENYIN VOTIN TWISET WE DONE IT BUT WE NEVER DONE IT A PURPOSE . . . HAH? . . . WHO IS THIS I'M TALKIN TO . . (L) WELL HIDY DICK I THOUGHT YOU WAS——HAH? . . OH NUTHIN. . . . . HE IS? . . WHATS HE COMIN OVER HERE FER? . . . . HE NEVER . . . WELL ALRIGHT MUCH OBLIGED DICK . . . ALRIGHT. GOOD BYE.

Lum: Whats who comin over here fer?

Abner: That was Dick. He said Butch Dolan is on his way over here to the store to see me, but I caint wait here to see him I jist happend to think I've got to go over to the house.

Lum: Go over to the house fer what?

Abner: Oh I jist thought maybe Lizzybeth might be needin me fer sompin.

Lum: You aint goin to leave this store, we caint both leave and jist lock the store up.

Abner: Well wher you goin?

Lum: Why I've got to go-Why I've got to go to—Got to go see Evalener.

Abner: I thought you said you wern't goin to tell nuthin but the truth.

Lum: Well I want to go see Evalener then. Thats tellin the truth. aint it?

Abner: Yea but ther's Butch Dolan comin up the front steps now.

Lum: Yea now look what you done. Standin round here arguin with me till I caint leave. You're jist about goin to git both of us shot now, jist by arguin.

Abner: Wait a minit . . here he is.

Lum: Yea . . . HIDY BUTCH. COME IN.

Abner: YEA COME ON BACK MR. DOLAN . . HOW'RE YOU TODAY?

Butch: (faded) FINE FINE HOW'RE YOU GENTLEMEN?

Abner: Oh tolably I reckon.

Butch: Have a cigar Judge Edwards.

Lum: Who oh yea yea. Much obliged. Dont care if I do.

Abner: Set Down Butch.

Butch: Yes thanks. Why what I came out here to see you gentlemen about . . I hope neither one of you hold any hard feelings against me over this sheriff's race. I want [to] be friends. I think a lot of both of you.

Abner: Well. I didn't think you liked me.

Butch: Oh yes. Ther's always some hard feelings develope in

pollitics but if I've done or said anything that offended you I want to apoligise for it.

Abner: Well I'll say the same thing.

Lum: Yea, Nice of you to come out here and offer to be friends. Sometimes we think we dont like a feller hits on account of we dont know him.

Butch: Yea. I jist wonder if I could talk to you alone for a few minutes Mr. Peabody.

Abner: Why yea I reckon so.

Lum: Why shore I'll git out. I've got to—er I want to go over to see Evalener anyhow . . . Glad you come out Butch . . . (fading) I'll be back after while Abner.

Abner: ALRIGHT LUM.

Butch: Wellsir ther goes a fine man. A mighty fine man.

Abner: Oh yea Lum's a alright feller.

Butch: Why what I want to talk to you bout is this Mr. Peabody. You know I guess that they're goin to hold the election over.

Abner: Yea we was jist readin it in the paper jist a minit ago.

Butch: Looked like both of our friends were a little too anxious to see us elected and put in a few extra votes.

Abner: Yea several thousand of em. (L)

Butch: Well they're goin to hold another election. That'll be a big expence to the county. If one of us should withdraw from the race they wouldn't have to have another election.

Abner: You aint aimin on withdrawin are you?

Butch: No but frankly Mr. Peabody if they hold this election over I'll carry the county four to one instead of three to one . . You haven't got a chance.

Abner: I dont know. Might nigh everbody I've talked with said they'd stay by me.

Butch: Oh yes you'll get a few votes around Pine Ridge here but here's what I'm willin to do and I wouldn't do this if I didn't think so much of you. I cant stand to see a friend of mine lose in nuthin. Now I know that you put a lot of money in this campaign.

Abner: Yea I spent over a thousand dollars on it.

Butch: And course Lum Edwards put that five hundred dollars in the day before the election to have them posters printed.

Abner: Is that wher the money come from to pay fer them posters.

Butch: Why sure a friend of mine in the bank there at the county seat told me this morning that Edwards mortgaged his home and farm for five hundred dollars to put in your campaign fund.

Abner: Well I do know. And he done all that fer me . . Unbeknowins to me.

Butch: Yea that'll be too bad when they foreclose on him and take his place. No place to live and all. Thats quite a sacrifice he's makin for you Peabody.

Abner: Well I'll pay it all back to him agin I'm elected.

Butch: Yea but what you goin to do if you aint elected. Now here's the proposition I've got to make to you. You cant afford to stand off and see your best friend lose his home and farm. What kind of a man would you be? Now you put a thousand dollars in this campaign and Edwards has put in five hundred dollars. If you'll take out, withdraw from the race, I'll hand you fifteen hundred dollars in cash, thataway you wont be out a dime on the race.

Abner: Nope I aint a goin to do it. I've wanted to be sheriff of this county all my life and I'd take the risk of losin everthing I got to git mysef elected. I want to sarve the good people—

Butch: Jist thinkin bout yersef huh? You're willing to set back and let your best friend lose his home and farm.

Abner: No I dont want to see Lum lose nuthin but—

Butch: You sign this agreement and I'll hand you the money and we can go right into the bank and pay off that mortgage Lum gave em.

Abner: I dont know what to do. I couldn't tell Lum nuthin bout it. He wouldn't stand fer it.

Butch: Well dont say nuthin to him about it. This will show him that you place his friendship higher than your own ambitions

.. He's made a big sacrifice for you and this is the least you could do to show your appreciation.

Abner: I dont know what to do about it. I wanted to be sheriff so bad.

Butch: Well I'm going to give you one minute to make up you mind—

Announcer: So we must leave Abner struggling between two conflicting emotions. Whether to accept Butch Dolan's offer and protect Lum against the possible loss of his farm or stay in the race in the hopes of realizing a life long ambition.

JANUARY 15, 1934

Dick: WELL COME IN LUM YOU'RE THE VERY FELLER I'M LOOKIN FOR.

Lum: (fading in) Lookin fer me?

Dick: YEA I CALLED UP OVER TO YOUR STORE JIST NOW AND NOBODY ANSWERED THE TELEPHONE.

Lum: Well I locked up a few minutes ago. I'm out lookin fer Abner. He aint been down all mornin.

Dick: Maybe he's over to his house.

Lum: No I called over ther. His woman, Lizzybeth said he left fer work right after breakfast same as usual. I'm sorter oneasy bout him, he's been actin awful strange fer the last day or two.

Dick: Well I think I understand why he's actin strange. Do you know anything about this?

Lum: What is it.

Dick: This is what I wanted to show you. This is the mornin paper from the county seat. Look at them headlines acrosst ther.

Lum: Peabody WITHDRAWS FROM SHERIFF'S RACE .. Well I do know. Reckon how that got in ther?

Dick: Why I suppose he put it in ther.

Lum: No thats a mistake. I know it is. I know Abner aint

withdrawed from the race. I grannies I'm goin to telephone up that newspaper and give them a piece of my mind startin sich tales as that.

Dick: Well I dont bleave the paper woulda printed it Lum if they ((((TELEPHONE)))) never had good reasons to believe it was so.

Lum: Well they ort to find out about sich things fore they print em. What do they think Abner'd be withdrawin now fer, right here when he's same as lected. HELLO . . IS [THIS] THE CENTRAL GIRL IN AT THE COUNTY SEAT? . . . WELL I DONT KNOW WHAT THE NUMBER IS BUT I WANT TO TALK TO THE NEWSPAPER IN THER PLEASE MOM . .

Dick: I was jist thinkin Lum, if you're sure Abner hasn't withdrawn, maybe Butch Dolan had that put in the paper.

Lum: I grannies thats jist about what happened. Butch Dolan's back of this whole thing. The dirty low down——

Dick: Ask em wher they got their information—

Lum: Hello . . THIS IS LUM EDARDS JESTICE OF THE PEACE. PRESIDENT OF THE SCHOOL BOARD AND CAMPAIGN MANAGER FER ABLE ABNER PEABODY THE PEOPLES PEERLESS PERTECTOR . . I JIST NOW SEEN THAT ARTICLE ABOUT ABNER PEABODY WITHDRAWIN FROM THE SHERIFF'S RACE. . . . . . WELL I'M HIS CAMPAIGN MANAGER AND I DONT KNOW NUTHIN BOUT IT. . . . . WELL WHERBOUTS DID YOU—Who told you SICH A OUTLANDISH STORY AS THAT. . . . . Uh hum . . Jist what I thought . . . WELL YOU FELLERS ORT TO HAVE MORE SENCE'N TO BLEAVE ANYTHING BUTCH DOLAN TELLS YOU . . I'LL GIVE YOU TO UNDERSTAND THAT ABNER AINT THE KIND OF A FELLER THAT'LL LAY DOWN ON HIS FRIENDS AT THE LAST MINIT THATAWAY . . I BLEAVE THE WHOLE SHEBANG OF YOU IS MIXED UP RIGHT IN WITH BUTCH DOLAN.

Dick: Lum.

Lum: THIS MISTAKE YOU'VE MADE IS GOIN TO HURT
ABNER IN THE NEXT LECTION THE LAST OF THE
MONTH AND IF HE DONT WIN WE'RE GOIN TO LAW
SUIT YOU TO THE LAST COURTS—

Dick: Lum. Careful now what you say—

Lum: YOU CAINT CORRECT IT. THE DAMAGE HAS
DONE BEEN DID AND YOU KNOW IT . . I RECKON
YOU FERGIT I'M A SORT OF A LAWYER. THATS A
OUT AND OUT CASE OF LIBILITIES. . . . . . . WELL
YOU BETTER STRAIGHTEN IT OUT. BIG HEADLINES
CLEAN ACROSST THE TOP . . . MISTAKE . . . ME
AND ABNER—MR. PEABODY'LL BE IN THER THIS
AFTERNOON TO SEE YOU BOUT IT. . . . GOODBYE.
(CLICK) I GRANNIES THAT ORT TO HOLD EM . . I'LL
LEARN EM HOW TO PRINT SICH STUFF AS THAT
ABOUT ABNER.

Dick: They said Butch Dolan told em that Abner had withdrawn
huh?

Lum: Yea, jist another one of his low down honery tricks. That
feller can study up more ways to be unhonest than arry feller
I ever seen.

Dick: Well looks to me like the newspaper woulda checked with
Abner on that. Confirmed it.

Lum: Well hit wouldn't sprise me none if Butch never slipped a
little money in their hands to git that put in ther . . . What
does the rest of that article ther in the paper say?

Dick: Why I read it jist says the election will be called off and
Butch Dolan will be reelected to succed himself because of no
opposition.

Lum: I grannies thats goin to break Abner's heart when he hears
that. He wanted to be sheriff so bad.

Dick: Yea I feel sorry for him. Course if you can get the paper to
correct that statement, it might be that he can still be elected.

Lum: Yea but hits like I told the newspaper awhal ago, the
damage has done been did.

Dick: Wellsir Butch had a lot of nerve to try to pull a stunt like this and get away with it.

Lum: Yea. You know he was out here one day last week to see Abner.

Dick: Yea what'd he want?

Lum: Why I was over at the store when he come in. He was oncommonly friendly. Said he jist dropped in to say they wern't no hard feelins over the sheriff's race [and he] wanted to shake hands and be friends.

Dick: That dont sound like Butch does it?

Lum: No hit was sprisin to me . . He wanted to see Abner bout a personal matter so I left out—Wait a minit I grannies . . I bound you I know what he was up to. Thats more'n likely what he come out here fer was to git Abner to withdraw. Thats jist about the size of it. Abner wouldn't do it so he went back into the county seat and told em he done it anyway.

Dick: Abner never did tell you what Butch wanted to see him personally about huh?

Lum: No I told you he's been actin turible strange last few days. Friday I went into the Wholesale house to buy some more stock fer the store and Satidy we was so busy I never got a chance to talk to him. I reckon Abner was feard to tell me what he was wantin feard I'd jump on Butch and give him a whoppin.

Dick: Well the thing to do Lum is get Abner and go into the county seat and go before the election board and get this whole thing straightened out.

Lum: Yea. Reckon wher he is.

Dick: Why dont you call his house again. See if he's back ther.

Lum: I'll call him but I tell you I shore hate to drap the news to him.

Dick: Yea I know ((((TELEPHONE)))) He's goin to be turible dissapointed but I dont think its goin to be too late yet to do sompin about it.

Lum: Pore Abner. I'd druther take a whoppin than to tell him. I know he's goin to—HELLO . . . ELIZABETH THIS IS LUM . .

Dick: Maybe you'd better jist tell him to come down here Lum. We can explain it to him a heap better down here.

Lum: Yea . . WHY IS ABNER THER?. . . . UH HUH. WELL HAVE YOU SAW HIM SINCE I TALKED TO YOU THIS MORNIN? . No. . . . No HE AINT SHOWED UP AT THE ST——

Dick: Wait a minit Lum I bleave thats Abner com—Yea HERE HE COMES NOW.

Lum: WELL HERE HE IS NOW LIZZYBETH . . . YESSUM . . . ALRIGHT THANK YOU MOM.

Dick: Well this is goin to be purty much of a shock to him Lum.

Lum: Yea. Better break the news sorter gradual . . You better splain it to him Dick I caint bear to tell him. He's got his heart set on bein sheriff—

Dick: Yea I'll tell him bout it.

Lum: I hope he dont break down.

Dick: WELL COME IN ABNER. WE GOT SOMPIN IMPORTANT TO TALK TO YOU BOUT.

Lum: YEA SOMPIN DREADFUL HAS HAPPENED.

Abner: (FADED) HIDY FELLERS. I JIST BEEN DOWN TO THE BLACKSMITH SHOP PITCHIN HORSE SHOES WITH Grandpappy Spears.

Lum: IS THAT WHER YOU BEEN ALL MORNIN. I BEEN LOOKIN EVERWHER FER YOU.

Abner: I swan that old skinflint is gittin to wher he cheats worse'n anybody I ev—

Lum: Abner set down. We've got some awful bad news fer you. Better take a chair sos you can bear up under it. . . . Now dont take it too hard.

Dick: Yea ther's been a turible mistake made Abner.

Lum: Go head and splain it to him Dick.

Dick: Why uh . . Well JIST TO MAKE A LONG STORY

SHORT ABNER. THEY COME OUT IN THE PAPERS
THIS MORNIN SAYIN YOU'VE WITHDRAWN FROM
THE SHERIFF'S race.

Lum: Thats what they did Abner.

Dick: We jist called the county newspaper and they said Butch
Dolan told them that you'd withdrawn.

Lum: (pause) I bleave you better come over that again Dick. I
dont bleave Abner got it straight in his head jist what has
happened.

Dick: Well all there is to it, they're jist accusin you of withdrawin
from the race.

Lum: You see Abner, That means that you're plum outa the
sheriff's race the way things stands now.

Abner: Yessir ther in that last game I throwed a ringer right smak
dab around the stob and Grandpap claimed it was hissen
. . Said I knocked one of hissen on . . . Luther Phillips was
standin right ther and said it was my ringer and Grandpap
wouldn't even bleave him . . . Got mad and stomped off—

Lum: Whats the matter with you. Whats eatin on you. Here you
are talkin bout pitchin horse shoes and that newspaper ther
accusin you of withdrawin from the sheriff's race.

Dick: Wait a minit . . Look here Abner . . . Did you withdraw
from the sheriff's race.

Abner: Well uh . . uh . . Yes I did. I shore did fellers.

Lum: Why Abner you never done no sich a thing and you know
you never.

Abner: Yea I shore did Lum. I hated to but they jist wern't no
way round it.

Lum: So you withdrawed did you.

Abner: Yea (L)

Lum: That newspaper was right. I never woulda bleaved it hearin
it from anybody else but you . . . AFTER ME AWORKIN
THE WAY I HAVE A HELPIN YOU WITH YOUR
CAMPAIGN . . WERN'T GITTIN A THING OUT OF IT.
JIST WANTED TO SEE YOU GIT THE OFFICE CAUSE

YOU WANTED IT SO BAD. WHY I JIST DONT SEE HOW
YOU COULD DO IT . . SLIPPIN ROUND BEHIND MY
BACK . . NEVER EVEN AST ME BOUT IT. NEVER EVEN
TOLD ME YOU'D DID IT—

Abner: Now Lum let me splain it to you. I had my reasons fer
doi——

Lum: Explain. EXPLAIN . . . WHY YOU COULDN'T EXPLAIN
TO ME IN A THOUSAND YEARS HOW YOU COULD
QUIT RIGHT HERE WHEN I HAD YOU SAME AS
LECTED. YOU'RE A QUITTER THATS WHAT YOU AIR.
A YELLER QUITTER.

Abner: No Lum dont say them things fer you jist dont know how
come me to do it.

Lum: I dont want to hear it. I dont want to have narry thing
to do with you. NOT NEVER . . I'VE DONE LOST
CONFYDENCE IN YOU. WHY YOU AINT FITTIN TO
SOSIATE WITH HONEST AND UPRIGHT PEOPLES.
ME AND YOU HAS BEEN PARDNERS IN THE JOT-
EM-DOWN STORE AND THE PINE RIDGE MOTOR
COMPANY. Well we're through now . . . WE'RE
THROUGH DO YOU HEAR . . I'M GOIN OVER THER
NOW AND LOCK THE DOORS. I dont never want to
have nuthin more to do with you as long as I live——(fade
out)

(PAUSE)

Dick: Well Abner I dont know that I can blame Lum much. How
come you to ever pull such a stunt as that anyway?

Abner: Well Dick I never woulda did it in this world but I done it
to save Lum losin his place. You know how bad I wanted to
be sheriff.

Dick: Yea. Thats why I caint understand it.

Abner: Well Butch Dolan come out here a Thursday and told me
what Lum had did. Told me Lum had mortgaged his farm
and house fer five hunderd dollars to pay fer them posters
and that advertisin he got out jist the day before elections and

I knowed if I was to lose the race I wouldn't have no way to pay him back and he'd lose his place.

Dick: Well withdrawin never helped none. You've shore lost it now.

Abner: Well after Butch told me what he'd done, he offered me fifteen hunderd dollars, jist the amount me and Lum both had put in the campaign fund if I'd withdraw.

Dick: Oh I see now . . You just saw where you could make a little money on it and you just sold out . . SOLD OUT. Sorry to hear that Abner. Sellin out is even worse'n quittin.

Abner: No I never done that Dick. I wouldn't take his fifteen hunderd dollars fer I knowed that'd be wrong. I never takend anuff to pay me back fer what I'd spent but as bad as I wanted the sheriff's office I couldn't let Lum take them chances on losin his place. He'd made a sacrifice to me when he borrowed that money and I wern't goin to let him lose it, so I taked five hundred dollars from Butch and went right straight to the bank and paid off that mortgage Lum give em and right here it is . . . I was aimin on givin it to him but I'm jist afeard I've lost the best friend I ever had——

JANUARY 16, 1934

Dick: Yea it jist makes me sick to think about it. Here we been tryin to get Butch Dolan outa that office fer years and you had him beat three to one and then went and withdrawed. Jist give the office right back to him.

Abner: Yea I see now I done wrong in withdrawin alright. I dont bleave Butch told me the truth out chere the other day.

Dick: What'd he say to you Abner anyway?

Abner: Why he jist come out here and told me that he'd took a turible likin to me and wanted to help me. You see he'd jist made a trip over the county hisef and he admited that he had me beat bad but he was willin to pay me back fer the money me and Lum had put in my campaign if I'd git outa the race.

Dick: So thats the way he talked you into it huh?

Abner: No, no I turned him down cold on that fer I knowed hit'd be wrong and I figgered I owed it to my friends to go ahead on even if I got beat.

Dick: Why sure you did. Fokes aint got a bit of use fer a quitter.

Abner: But Dick, when he told me bout Lum mortgagin his place and borryin five hunderd dollars to put in my campaign, I knowed I ortent to take any chance to wher Lum would be apt to lose his place. Course the way you're talkin here now, I reckon I mighta staid in the race and been elected and paid Lum back his five hunderd dollars without no trouble.

Dick: Why sure you could.

Abner: Well as Lum says, they aint no uset to cry over spillt milk.

Dick: Well I dont hold aginst you Abner. I know in reason it was a big sacrifice fer you to give up your chances of bein elected sheriff jist to save Lum from losin that five hunderd dollars, but Lum was your campaign manager an you ort to talked to him about it first.

Abner: Yea I reckon I ort to but the onlest reasons I never, I knowed he wouldn't stand fer it a minit and if I lost the race I never had no way to pay him back. Thats the reasons I jist takend five hunderd dollars from Butch, I wanted to have a clean conciousness.

Dick: Yea I bleave I understand jist how you felt about it.

Abner: Worst part about it Dick, I'm feard Lum never will be friends with me again. Everbody else is down on me. Grandpappy Spears come over to the place right early this mornin, he'd jist heard about me withdrawin, and was he mad, called me everthing mean he could think of.

Dick: Well I guess Grandpap's dissapointed cause he didn't get to be deputy sheriff.

Abner: Yea thats whats the matter with him. Said he'd worked hard fer me tryin to git me lected and I quit. Stood ther and shook his umbreller in my face and jist kept on.

Dick: Oh well I wouldn't pay no tention to Grandpap, he's gittin old and childish [and] he'll git over it.

Abner: Well he aint the only one. I went down to the black smith shop awhal ago and tried to git up a game of horseshoes and nobody wouldn't play with me. Facts is they all left me standin ther talkin to mysef. I started tellin a story I heard yistidy I thought was right funny and I doggies agin I got through they wernt nobody in ther sept a old lop eared mule that Luther Phillips was a shoein . . . and he never looked no too friendly.

Dick: Well the word has got passed around that you let Butch Dolan scare you out the race that's more'n likely what they're down on you about.

Abner: I dont care so much about the rest of em, what they think, but I would like fer Lum to give me a chanch to explain.

Dick: Well he's more'n likely cooled off now.

Abner: No he aint neither. I went down to the store this mornin goin to tell jist how come me to do it and he seen me comin and locked the door. I know he was ther fer I seen him. I knocked and hollered fer half a hour and he never would come to the door. I seen him peek his head out from hind the counter ther oncet so I know he was ther.

Dick: Well you cant blame Lum for bein mad. He dont know your side of the story. You see he's helped you for the last two or three months to win this race and you go and withdraw unbeknowins to him. He's got a right to be purty mad.

Abner: Dick I wonder if hit'd be astin too much to git you to speak to him bout it. He'll allus listen to you.

Dick: Why I'll be glad to Abner but I caint gitaway from the store jist now.

Abner: I wanted you to hand him this mortgage I paid off fer him.

Dick: I tell you what I'll do. I'll call him up and get him to come down to the store here then you can give it to him and I'll explain the whole business.

Abner: Yea telephone him up and get him to come down here. He can lock up the store.

Dick: Yea I reckon he's still over ther. ((((TELEPHONE))))) (((((BREAK)))

Lum: (Telephone)))))) (clears throat) HELLO THIS IS THE JOT EM DOWN STORE. LUM EDARDS. PRESIDENT AND LEFT AND RIGHT VICE PRESIDENT DOIN THE TALKIN. . . . WELL HIDY DICK. . . . OH JIST ONLY TOLABLY I RECKON. . . . . YEA I RECKON I COULD. I'll have to lock up though. Abne—Mr. Peabody aint here no more you know . . . What was it you was wantin to see me bout?. . . . . Oh he is? Well I aint comin down ther then fer I know I dont want to see him. I aint havin a thing to do with him no more. . . . . . . He wants to splain what?. . . . . . Well I dont keer nuthin bout hearin it. He couldn't never splain that to me . . . Nope, nope Dick me and him is through . . Wait a minit Dick here comes a customer in the store. Oh hits Grandpappy Spears . . WELL HIDY GRANDPAP. COME IN.

Grpap: (fade in) HIDY LUM. JIST THOUGHT I'D COME OVER AND SEE WHAT YOU THOUGHT ABOUT THE WAY ABNER DONE IN THE SHERIFF'S RACE.

Lum: Jist take a chair Grandpap. I'll be done talkin here dreckly.

Grpap: Yea go head.

Lum: HELLO DICK. . . . NOPE DICK JIST TELL HIM THAT I DONT WANT TO SEE HIM. . . . . . NO DONT YOU SEND HIM OVER HERE . . I TOLD HIM ONCET TO STAY WAY FROM HERE. THE LESS I SEE OF HIM THE BETTER I'LL LIKE IT. . . . . WELL THATS THE WAY I FEEL ABOUT IT ALRIGHT. . . . ALRIGHT DICK ALRIGHT. (CLICK)

Grpap: Was that Abner you and Dick was talkin bout?

Lum: Yea.

Grpap: Well I dont blame you fer feelin thataway after the way he done. That was the honerest low down trick I ever heard of him a doin.

Lum: Yea I was turible dissapinted in Abner. I never woulda
thought he'da laid down on his friends thataway.

Grpap: Well I wernt a bit sprised at him. They aint a thing to him
when it comes right down to a show down.

Lum: Well I dont know as I'd go so fer as to say that Grandpap.

Grpap: Nossir he's jist a double crosser thats all they are to it.
A feller that'd do what he done wouldn't stop at nuthin. Jist
aint got no principles I wouldn't trust him outa my sight.

Lum: Now looky here Grandpap. Dont go too fer with yer talk.
Course he done wrong in this sheriff's race but he's allus been
upright in his dealins.

Grpap: Upright. You dont call a feller that'll sell out to his
oponent upright do you.

Lum: No but Abner never sold out to Butch, he jist got cold feet
and withdrawed.

Grpap: You mean to say you dont know bout him sellin out?

Lum: I tell you he never sold out. I dont want you to say that
narry nuther time. Butch jist come out here and scared him
into withdrawin.

Grpap: That jist goes to show how little you know about him.
Snake Hogan told me he was in Butch Dolan's when Abner
signed a greement to withdraw from the race fer five hunderd
dollars and he seen Butch hand him the money. If that aint sellin
out I dont know what you'd call it.

Lum: Are you tellin the truth Grandpap.

Grpap: I wouldn't have no reasons fer comin over here and tellin
you that if it wern't a fact. I allowed you already knowed
about it.

Lum: And I mortgaged my place to git money to hep him on his
campaign. I jist cant bleave it. Caint bleave he'd do it.

Grpap: Why dont you ast him then. He'll have to own up to it.
He wont deny it in front of me.

Lum: Well I dont want to dispute your word Grandpap but I
jist couldn't bleave it lesson I heard him say it with his own
mouth.

Grpap: I tell you what we'll do, if you know wher he's at we'll go over ther and I'll prove it to you.

Lum: Well I know wher he's at. He's down at Dick's store but I dont want to go off down ther.

Grpap: Wait a minit. I'll jist call him up on the phone and let you hear him.

Lum: No Grandpap. You're jist wastin yer time I know he never sold out. ((((TELEPHONE)))) Thats more'n likely a tale Butch Dolan and Snake Hogans made up on him cause they dont like him.

Grpap: Well you'll bleave it if you hear him say it won—Wait a minit. HELLO . . WHO IS THIS DICK?. . . . . IS ABNER STILL IN THE STORE THER?. . . . . TELL HIM TO GIT UP TO THE PHONE I WANT TO TALK TO HIM . . (TO LUM) I JIST WANT TO SHOW YOU WHAT KIND OF A SNAKE IN THE GRASS THAT ABNER PEABODY HAS TURNED OUT TO BE. . . . . . HELLO ABNER. THIS HERE'S GRANDPAP? . (TO LUM) Here Lum git yer ear up hear clost to the receiver . . . Now listen . . (to Abner) WHY ABNER. HOW MUCH MONEY WAS IT BUTCH DOLAN PAID YOU TO WITHDRAW FROM THE SHERIFF'S RACE . . . HOW MUCH? . . (to Lum) Could you hear him alright?

Lum: Yea I heard him.

Grpap: WELL THATS ALL I WANTED ABNER. . . . GOODBYE. (CLICK)

Lum: So Abner sold out fer Five hunderd dollars. I never woulda bleaved it.

January 17, 1934

Grpap: Nossir if it hadn't of been fer Abner a sellin out, I'da been the deputy sheriff of the county.

Dick: Yea Abner'da been elected alright I dont think ther's any doubt about that.

Grpap: He was jist a thinkin about hisef. He never thought about us fellers that got out and worked so hard fer him.

Dick: Yes yes Grandpap its too bad he sold out but lets forget about it. Thats all I've heard all week, people talkin about Abner. Criticisin him for withdrawin from the sheriff's race.

Grpap: He ort to be critisized, ort to be rode outa town on a rail, tarred and feathered—

Dick: You been talkin to Snake Hogan I can tell that. He was down here yesterday runnin Abner down.

Grpap: Yea. Me and Snake was talkin bout it awhal ago, over at the blacksmith shop.

Dick: Well I wouldn't pay any attention to nuthin he says, Abody can tell he's just tryin to stir up trouble. He's not only been goin round talkin bout Abner turnin everbody against him but he's been goin to Lum and tellin him a batch of stuff Abner said about him and then goin to Abner tellin him a lot of stuff Lum said about him. Just makin it all up. He's got em so mad at one another right now they're might nigh ready to shoot on sight.

Grpap: Well I heard they was sorter feudin, packin guns fer one another but I never knowed Snake Hogan was the one that caused it.

Dick: Well he's the very one. I run him outa the store here yesterday. Told him I was tired of listenin to his gab.

Grpap: Well I do know. Come to think about it I bleave he was goin clean outa his way to turn me agin Abner. Told me I ort to talk to Lum about him too.

Dick: Thats what he's tryin to do. Tryin to bust them up sos they'll disolve partnership and sell the Jot Em Down Store. Thats what he's after. He figgers he can buy that store for bout half what its worth.

Grpap: Well the onery thing. I bound you thats what he's up to.

Dick: He was askin me in here yesterday what I thought it was worth.

Grpap: Yea and he was talkin to a big crowd down at the

Blacksmith shop this mornin tellin em he was sorter figgerin on goin into the store business and wanted to git their trade.

Dick: Well Grandpap stead of goin round repeatin these stories he's tellin bout Lum and Abner its up to his friends to put a stop to em. We've got to bring those two old fellows back together if we can.

Grpap: I reckon I done wrong yisterday. I was talkin to Lum and said some awful mean things about Abner but I was mad at the time.

Dick: Well I cant blame you for bein kinda put out over Abner withdrawin from the race right when it looked like he was goin to be elected and you woulda been deputy sheriff but its all over now. He's allus been a good friend of yours and right now is when *he* needs friends. Everbody has turned against him.

Grpap: Yea. Special if Lum has turned agin him.

Dick: Oh they're both mad now. I wouldn't be suprised to see some real trouble develope out of it. They're both as stubborn as mules you know—

Grpap: Wait a minit I bleave thats Abner comin up out front ther now aint it.

Dick: Yea, yea thats him.

Grpap: Looks mad a nuff to bite dont he?

Dick: Well I'm glad he's comin over. Maybe we can reason with him, get him to go over ther and make up with Lum.

Grpap: Yea we can git him in a good humor alright. Hits Lum I'm sorter worried about.

Dick: We can lead up to it sorter gradulal . . . WELL HIDY ABNER. HIDY.

Grpap: YEA COME IN ABNER. WE WAS JIST TALKIN BOUT YOU.

Abner (fading in) Hidy Men.

Grpap: Here have a seat Abner . . Take this chair.

Abner: No I dont want your chair. Whats come over you all of a suddent here.

Grpap: Oh nuthin, you jist look cold.

Abner: Last time I seen you you was wantin to give me a lickin.

Grpap: Oh I was jist joshin bout that.

Dick: You're not workin down at the store today Abner?

Abner: No and not tomorrow or the next day neither. I'ma gittin outa the store business and anything else that Lum Edards has got anything to do with.

Grpap: Why whats the matter with Lum. I thought he was a alright sort of a feller.

Abner: DONT CALL HIS NAME AROUND ME GRANDPAP. Evertime I hear it I git so mad I caint hardly stay in my boots.

Dick: Well now Abner you and Lum gotta fergit about this trouble you're havin and get your differences straightened up.

Abner: FERGIT NUTHIN. HE STARTED IT TELLIN A PACK OF LIES ON ME. I'LL SHOW HIM I AINT A SKEERD OF HIM.

Grpap: I bound you you been talkin to Snake Hogan.

Abner: Yea you bet I have. He's the only one in Pine Ridge thats good anuff friend to tell me what all Lum's a sayin bout me.

Dick: What is that under yor coat there Abner?

Abner: What that?

Grpap: Why Abner thats a pistol you're packin ther.

Abner: You dad blame right. And I got er loaded too. I'll show that Lum Edards how to go round talkin bout me to my back.

Grpap: You mean you're packin that gun fer Lum?

Abner: Yessir. If you see him you can tell him so. Tell him I'm ready fer him.

Dick: Well Abner you wouldn't shoot Lum. Why he's allus been your best friend.

Abner: Thats all you know bout it. I aint goin to stand up and let him shoot me full of holes thout someway of defendin mysef.

Grpap: You mean you think Lum's packin firearms fer you?

Abner: I know he is. Snake Hogan told me he was.

Dick: Well now Abner you caint believe everthing Snake Hogan tells you. Lum might be mad at you and all that but he aint carryin no gun for you I know.

Abner: Yes he is too. He sent word by Snake to tell me that he was a gunnin fer me.

Grpap: Oh he was jist sayin that to agg you on. I bound you he—

Abner: I dont keer what he was tellin me fer. I'm ready fer him. I aint takin no chances. I'm goin to shoot and ask questions later.

Dick: Now Listen Abner you did a fine thing payin off that mortgage for Lum, now dont spoil it by doin sompin that you'll regret the balance of your life.

Abner: Yea and I wisht I hadn't a paid off the blamed mortgage. I give up bein sheriff of this county jist to pay off that thing to keep him from losin his pesky five hunderd dollars. I wisht he hada lost it now.

Dick: What'd you do with the cancelled mortgage Abner.

Abner: I doggies I got it right here. I'm a good mind to jist throw it in the stove ther——

Grpap: No wait a minit dont burn it up Abner.

Dick: No let me have it Abner. That blongs to Lum I'll give it to him.

Abner: Well dont tell him I sent it to him. Dont tell him I had a thing to do with it.

Dick: Well I'll mail it to him. (fade) Put it in a plain envelope and not sign nobody's name to it.

Abner: If I git a good shot at him he'll never git the letter I'll tell you that though.

Grpap: Abner Peabody you ort to be shamed of yersef makin sich a remark———

Dick: (faded) Grandpap come here a minit.

Grpap: What do you want.

Dick: (faded) Excuse us just a minute Abner.

Abner: (fading out) Go head talk. But you aint goin to git me to change my mind I'll tell you that.

Grpap: (fade in) Whats the matter Dick.

Dick: (whisper) Git Abner outa here jist quick as you can.

Grpap: Git him out?

Dick: Yea I see Lum comin up out ther and it wont do fer them to meet the way they're feelin, they'll be a shootin spite of all we can do.

Grpap: Oh my goodness Lum's carryin a shot gun.

Dick: Yea git Abner out the back door quick as you can.

Grpap: Yea I'll git him ou . . . Uh Abner. IF YOU GOT A MINIT TO SPARE I CAN TAKE YOU OVER TO THE BLACK SMITH SHOP AND BEAT YOU A GAME OF HORSE SHOES.

Abner: I got a minit to spare but you'll never see the day you can beat me pitchin horseshoes.

Grpap: Git up from ther and come on then if you dont bleave it. Lets go out the back door here it's shorter.

Abner: (fading out) I'LL SEE YOU AFTER A LITTLE DICK SOON AS I GO OVER AND GIVE GRANDPAP A SKINNIN.

Dick: ALRIGHT ABNER. (sigh of relief) WELL HIDY LUM . . COME IN.

Lum: (fading in) HIDY DICK WHO WAS THAT JIST WENT OUT THE BACK DOOR?

Dick: Oh that was Grandpappy Spears Lum. WHER YOU GOIN. Rabbit huntin?

Lum: No I'm lookin fer a varmit but it aint a rabbit. Have you saw that holler headed Abner Peabody?

Dick: Yea he was in here a few minutes ago Lum.

Lum: WHER'D HE GO. WHER'D HE GO. RUNNIN FROM ME HUH. I'LL TRAIL HIM DOWN IF HITS MY LAST ACT ON THIS EARTH.

Dick: Wait a minute here Lum what you up to. You're not carryin that shot gun after Abner are you?

Lum: Yea I'm a carryin it fer him. They aint no way out of it. I got to do it to pertect mysef.

Dick: Protect yersef?

Lum: Why yea didn't you know it. Abner's totin a gun fer me.

Dick: Who told you that?

Lum: Why Snake Hogans was a tellin me. Said Abner was flashin a gun down here on the street makin his brags to everbody he seen bout how he was goin [to] kill off four or five presidents all with one shot. Said if they wanted to see him kill a dog jist to watch him shoot Lum Edards when he seen him.

Dick: Well did it ever occur to you Lum that Snake might be makin all that up. No you set down there and listen to me . . Snake Hogan is tryin to bust you and Abner up. He's goin to Abner tellin him a batch of lies about you and anyrthing he told *you* about Abner comes under the same headin.

Lum: Nossir Dick. Snake Hogan is my friend. He was jist tryin to help me. Thats more'n anybody else is doin. Why if it hadn't a been fer him I wouldn'ta a knowed bout Abner carryin a gun fer me and I mighta got shot in the back. I wouldn't put nuthin past that Snake in the Grass. Did you know Dick that he sold out in the sheriff's race.

Dick: Yea but you haven't heard all the perticklers.

Lum: Oh yes I did. I heard him admit to it with his own mouth. After me same as havin him lected, he seen a chance to git some cash money and he sold out to Butch Dolan fer five hunderd dollars.

Dick: Yea. Jist a minit. (fade) Let me show you sompin here.

Lum: WHERBOUTS DO YOU THINK THAT VARMIT WENT DICK?

Dick: (fading in) I dont know, here's a letter that might explain to you why Abner sold out for five hundred dollars.

Lum: Well who's this from. Aint got no After five days reeturn to nobody on ther.

Dick: You see Abner found out that you mortgaged your place Lum to get five hundred dollars to put in his campaign fund and he got to thinkin that he might not be elected and if he wasn't neither one of you wouldn't have no way to pay that note off and you'd lose your place.

Lum: Yea but—
Dick: No wait a minit. So he give up his chances of bein lected
  sheriff of this county just to be sure that you wouldn't lose
  your place.
Lum: Wait a minit. This here's that mortgage I give to borrow
  that money on. They's ondoubtly some mistake here.
Dick: No. Dont you understand now. Abner used the five
  hundred dollars he got from Butch and went right straight to
  the bank and paid off that mortgage you give em.
Lum: Well I do know . . and he done all that fer me. I've made
  a plum eediot of mysef thats what I've did. I'M GOIN
  RIGHT STRAIGHT TO ABNER THIS VERY MINIT AND
  POLOGISE FER ALL THE THINGS I'VE SAID AND DID. I
  never had the least idys—
Dick: WELL HERE WAIT A MINIT LUM . . . HOLD ON . .
  YOU BETTER STAY AWAY FROM ABNER TILL I CAN
  SEE HIM AND GIT A CHANCE TO TALK To him——

January 18, 1934

Dick: No Cedric you're workin fer Lum and Abner over ther in
  the Jot Em Down store and I couldn't hire you long as you're
  workin fer them.
Cedric: Yea but I'm goin to quit over ther.
Dick: Quit?
Cedric: Yesmam.
Dick: Whats the matter?
Cedric: Well they dont need me no more. Since Mr. Edards made
  that new years resolution not to tell nuthin but the truth they
  aint gittin a nuff business to keep one man busy much less
  three.
Dick: Oh is Lum still stickin to that resolution?
Cedric: Yessum, he made two customers mad this mornin and
  they stomped outa the store and said they never would come
  back no more.

Dick: Abner showed up over there today?

Cedric: Nomam he aint been down all week. Mr. Edards told him not to come round ther no more on account of him withdrawin from the sheriff's race.

Dick: Yea I know about that.

Cedric: Did you know Mr. Peabody was packin a gun fer Mr. Edards?

Dick: Yea thats what I heard but I dont think he'd really shoot Lum.

Cedric: Well Mr. Edards thinks he would. He's skeerd to death of him. Evertime any body comes in the store he dives under the counter and stays hid till I find out who it is.

Dick: (L) Well I've been tryin to find Abner and talk to him. He thinks Lum's carryin a gun for him too. If I can see him and talk to him I think I can get this all smoothed over.

Cedric: I dont know wher you can or not. He's actin awful funny. Was last time I seen him.

Dick: Well Snake Hogan has been talkin to both of em aggin this trouble on. He's got Abner to thinkin Lum's gunnin for him goin to shoot him on sight and Abner's sworn he's goin to git him first. Thats what I'm afraid of fraid Abner'll shoot before I get a chance to talk to him and explain that Lum is alright now.

Cedric: (L) I'd sorter like to see them two shoot it out jist to see whichin——

Dick: Wait a minit yonder comes Lum now. Maybe he's already talked to Abner and got their differences straightened out.

Cedric: No they aint neither I can tell by the way he's walkin . . Look at him bout half walkin and half runnin tryin to watch on all four sides at once like he was spectin somebody to jump out on him.

Dick: (L) Yea he's scared to death alright you can tell that.

Cedric: Dont say nuthin to him bout me wantin to go to work down here fer you Mr. Dick. I dont want him to know I'm threatinin to quit him. He's havin a nuff troubles thout losin me.

Dick: Yea that'd be bout the last straw I guess if you was to quit over there now Cedric. (L) WELL HIDY LUM. COME IN COME IN.

Lum: WELL HIDY DICK. CEDRIC WHAT YOU DOIN OFF DOWN HERE. I BEEN LOOKIN EVERPLACE FER YOU. WE GOT SOME DELIVERS TO MAKE—UH DELIVER I MIGHT SAY.

Cedric: I [was] jist settin down here talkin to Mr. Huddleston sorter restin.

Dick: Yea Cedric's been keepin me company down here Lum.

Lum: Well you better git yersef on over to the store wher you blong. Might accidental be somebody come in ther and want sompin. I had to lock up to come over here. Here, here's the keys. . . . I'LL BE BACK OVER THER DRECKLY.

Cedric: (FADED) YESSUM.

Dick: Come back agin Cedric.

Cedric: (FADED) YESSUM I WILL.

Dick: I swan that Cedric is a sight.

Lum: Dick What I come over fer. Have you saw Abner?

Dick: No I haven't Lum. Haven't had a chance to talk to him.

Lum: Well I wisht you'd see him. I've stood this bout as long as I can. I'm might nigh a narvous wreck.

Dick: Oh I dont think you've got any reason to be nervous Lum.

Lum: I grannies you git somebody out after you with a gun and see wher you're nervous or not.

Dick: Oh I dont think Abner would really try to shoot you Lum.

Lum: I dont know if Snake Hogan told him half the stuff bout me that he's told me about him I know he'd shoot.

Dick: Well I've been tryin to locate him all day. I've called up his house two or three times and Elizabeth says he aint been ther since right early this mornin.

Lum: No I know he aint. I been tryin to git hold of him on the telephone mysef.

Dick: Well I sent word to Luther Phillips over at the blacksmith shop to tell him to come over here if he showed up over ther.

Lum: Well if he aint been over here or over there at home neither. Wher is he at?

Dick: I dont know wher he could be.

Lum: I grannies thats scares me worse'n ever. Not knowin wher he's at. Gives a feller sort of a strange feelin knowin they's sombody's gunnin fer you and not knowin when and wher he's goin to step out and start shootin.

Dick: You're not carryin a gun are you Lum.

Lum: No, after I heard the perticklers yistidy, how Abner had sold out to Butch sos to git money to pay off that mortgage fer me I put my gun up. I couldn't bear the thoughts of shootin even if I knowed he was packin a gun fer me.

Dick: Well now you're not goin to help matters none by goin round scared to death.

Lum: Why I aint skeerd.

Dick: Why me and Cedric was talkin bout the way you was actin comin up out ther awhila go. You acted like a scared rabbit.

Lum: No hits jist a sort of a narvous strain. You see Dick they's more to this than abody might think jist off hand . . . You know they's allus been bad blood between the Edardses and the Peabodys.

Dick: Yea I've heard stories bout the old feuds between the two families back in the early days fore I come to this country but I thought you and Abner had allus been good friends.

Lum: Oh we have. Best of friends. I'll say right now they aint a better man livin nowhers than Abner Peabody. That is when he's hisef. He's allus been plum docile but this little mixup has brung out the bad side of him.

Dick: You dont mean to say you think this little trouble you're havin now will revive that old feud do you?

Lum: Well I dont know. The trouble the Edardses and Peabody's had before started over nuthin you might say.

Dick: Oh well you and Abner understand one another too well for sompin like that. Why you've been clost friends ever since I've lived here.

Lum: Yea but you know the old sayin old friends make the worst
   kind of enemys.
Dick: Why you've been pardners in business and all. I'd like to
   see you hurry up and get things straightened out.
Lum: Well I'm tellin you the truth I dont bleave I can stand this
   suspense much longer. Abner's dangerous the way things is
   now.
Dick: Oh he'll be alright soon as I can see him and talk to him.
Lum: I caint understand him gittin so het up over nuthin you
   might say.
Dick: Why its that Snake Hogan thats stirrin up the trouble. He's
   got Abner to bleavin that you're goin to shoot him on sight.
   Abner thinks now his only chance is to beat you to the draw.
Lum: Yea and he'll do it now. Me not even havin no gun on me.
Dick: Oh I wouldn't worry bout him. I dont bleave he could hit if
   he took a shot at you.
Lum: Yea Dick they's a lot of my anchesters over ther in the
   graveyard now that thought the same thing about some of
   Abner's kin.
Dick: Yea but that was years ago. What ever started that old feud
   in the first place you reckon?
Lum: Why the Edardses claimed they caught some of the
   Peabodys robbin their steel traps and the Peabodys claimed
   they caught the Edardses butcherin some of their hogs.
Dick: You reckon they did shore nuff Lum?
Lum: Well I dont know I've heard my own grandpap say that the
   mark branded on a hog never had nuthin to do with the way
   it tasted.
Dick: Oh well back in them days all the stock run loose a feller
   could make a honest mistake ever once in awhile.
Lum: Oh yea. But thats what started the feud they say. Me and
   Abner was the first ones of them two families that ever got
   along at tall.
Dick: Well I declare.
Lum: Yea I recollect when me and Abner first went in pardners

runnin the grist mill. My old Grandpap was still livin at the time. He wouldn't let Abner come on the place and told me I'd have my reegrets some day gittin mixed up with the Peabodys.

Dick: Well if I can see Abner I can—

Lum: Wait a minit. Dick. Wait a minit. Thats him comin up out ther now aint it?

Dick: No that aint Abner COME ON BACK HERE LUM THATS Grandpappy Spears.

Lum: Yea. I see now. I grannies Dick I've stood this jist long as I can.

Dick: Well just calm yersef down. Look at yoursef, shakin like a leaf. You're goin to have yoursef down sick the first thing you know.

Lum: I grannies what'd you say?

Dick: I said if you didn't stop this worryin you was goin to have yourself down in bed sick.

Lum: Yea. Wellsir thats a good idy . . In bed sick . . I'd have a excuse to stay in doors thataway. Yessir thats a——

Dick: WELL COME IN GRANDPAP COME IN.

Grpap: (faded) Hidy Men. Hidy. How you Richard?

Dick: Purty good Grandpap. Come on back and set down.

Grpap: (faded) Hidy Lum. How're you today?

Lum: Oh jist only tolably Grandpap. Only tolably. You aint saw Abner round no place today have you?

Grpap: No I aint. Aint saw him all day. Have you and him got yer troubles patched up yit?

Lum: Nope. I heard all the perticklers, how come him to withdraw from the sheriff's race and all but Dick aint had a chance to see him to tell him that I aint mad about it no more and I reckon he's still packin fararms fer me.

Grpap: Yea more'n likely he is. Fer I never seen Abner so mad in my life than he was yistidy. Evertime he'd pass a tree he'd draw that gun out and take aim on it. Said he was practisin up so when he seen you he could beat you to the draw.

Lum: He did huh?

Dick: Wher do you reckon Abner could be Grandpap? I been tryin to see him to talk to him all day.

Grpap: I aint got the least idys ((((TELEPHONE)))) He might be hidin out sommers sorter figgerin on takin a pot shot at Lum—

Dick: Hello. This is Huddleston's store Dick talkin. . . . . Yea he's here . . hold the phone. . . . Lum its for you.

Lum: Is it Abner?

Dick: No talked sorter like Cedric.

Lum: Now reckon what he's a wantin? HELLO. . . . YEA. . . . OH HE IS. WELL I'LL BE RIGHT ON OVER THER THEN . . YEA TELL HIM TO WAIT . . . ALRIGHT. (CLICK) Well I gotta go men.

Dick: Dont rush off Lum.

Lum: Oh Ezry Seestrunk is over ther wantin to pay some on his bill and Cedric dont know nuthin bout the books . . I'll be back dreckly.

Dick: WELL NOW JIST FERGIT ABOUT THIS TROUBLE YOU AND ABNER'S BEEN HAVIN LUM. THEY AINT NO USET TO WORRY OVER IT HE AINT GOIN TO DO NUTHIN.

Lum: (fading out) NO I AINT WORRIN BOUT [IT]. BUT YOU SEE HIM IF YOU GIT A CHANCH.

Dick: Alright Lum (L)

Grpap: Old Lum's sorter narvous bout Abner packin——

Dick: Wait a minit. What was that Grandpap? . . .

Grpap: What was what. I never heard nuthin.

Dick: I thought I heard a shot then . . LOOK AT LUM.

Grpap: WAIT A MINIT THEYS SOMPIN WRONG WITH HIM HE'S FELL DOWN THER ON THE PORCH—

Dick: LUM . . WHATS THE MATTER LUM. . . . BRING THAT BUCKET OF WATER GRANDPAP.

Grpap: Alright. See if hes hurt Dick.

Dick: WHAT IS IT WHY LUM YOUR SHOT . . . LET ME SEE . . . GRANDPAP PHONE DOCK COOK TO GIT OVER HERE JUST QUICK AS HE CAN. LUM'S BEEN SHOT.

JANUARY 22, 1934

(((((TELEPHONE)))))

Cedric: Thats the Jot Em Down store ring again aint it Grandpappy Spears?

Grpap: Yea, yea I'll answer it. You go on with yer work. Straighten up all that can goods ther in the shelf. . . . HELLO . . THIS IS THE JOT EM DOWN STORE . . NO THIS IS MILFORD SPEARS TALKIN. . . . . WHY I AINT HEARD SINCE THIS MORNIN BUT HE WAS GITTIN ALONG AS WELL AS COULD BE EXPECTED. . . . YESSUM. . . . Well they dont know who shot him. . . . . Why he was shot right on the front porch. . . . hah?. . . . . No (L) The front porch of Dick Huddleston's store . . . Yessum . . . Well I dont know wher Dock Cook's lowin any visitors over ther or not . . .

Cedric: YEA THEY'RE LETTIN MR. LUM HAVE VISITORS NOW.

Grpap: Shut up Cedric. This is Sister Simpson I know Lum dont want her over ther she'd worry the life out of him. talk his arms off . . . Why Sister Simpson I bleave I'd wait till Dock says its alright fer him to have company. . . . Yessum. . . . . I'll let you know if he takes a turn fer the worse. Alright. . . . Alright. Not a tall . . . Good bye . . (click) I swan to goodness that makes about the two hunderth one thats called up today wantin to know how Lum is.

Cedric: Why dont you announce over the party line bout once ever hour how he's gittin along . . Like him and Mr. Peabody used to broadcast the sociable ever Friday night.

Grpap: Yea thats what I ort to do (((((TELEPHONE))))) I aint had time to do nuthin all day sept answer this telephone . . . Ther it goes again. . . . . Hello . . This is the Jot Em Down Store. . . . This is Milford Spears talkin. . . . No Abner aint here today. . . . . . Well nobody dont know. He aint been saw since Friday. Well . . Nome I dont know but natural I've got my spicions. . . . . Well everbody knows that he was packin a

gun and had made his brags about how he was goin to shoot
Lum on sight so since Lum's been shot and Abner caint be
found nowher hit dont take no detecitive to figger out why
he caint be found. . . . . . Well Lum's gittin long as well as can
be expected. . . . Oh yessum Doc thinks he can pull through
alright . . You see the bullet went through his right shoulder
and whilst hit done a right smart of damage, hit aint nigh
as bad as it woulda been if hit'da been on his left side. . .
. . Well they're keepin him quiet . . My woman Charity is
over ther heppin look after him . . . Well (L) Yes she's allus
the first un ther whenever they's sickness or distress. Doc
Cook says hisef he never seen a better hand at lookin after
the sick. . . . Well she says she's havin a turible time keepin
Lum quiet. . . . Yea he wants to git up and stir around, you
know he feels like the weight of the world is right ther on
his shoulders. . . . Yessum well alright I will, if theys anything
you can do anyway you can hep I'll telephone you up. Alright
good bye (Click) . .

Cedric: Who was that called up Grandpapp?

Grpap: Why that was Ezry Seestrunks woman . . Marthy.

Cedric: (L) Thats funny cause she got mad at Mr. Lum down here
the other day and haint been speakin to him.

Grpap: What'd she git mad at him about?

Cedric: Oh sompin he said to her. You know he's made might nigh
everbody he's saw this year mad on account of that New Year's
resolution he's got to Not tell nuthin but the truth this year.

Grpap: Yea . . Well that jist goes to show, that frienship is a heap
deeper'n little ol squabbles and misunderstandins. They was
a lot of fokes thought they was mad at him but you notice
quick as he had that accident they all fergot bout him makin
em mad. He's got lots of friends . . Lots of friends Lum has.

Cedric: Grandpap. Wher is Ambush?

Grpap: Wher's what?

Cedric: Wher is Ambush? . . I keep hearin em talkin bout Mr.
Lum gittin shot from Ambush.

Grpap: Oh Cedric you dont understand. They mean Lum was shot by sombody that was hidin. They dont know who done the shootin.

Cedric: Well I bound you I know who done it.

Grpap: Well yes I've got a purty good idy mysef.

Cedric: I never woulda thought Mr. Abner woulda shot his best friend thataway.

Grpap: Well I dont think he would neither ordinarry Cedric but the word had got passed around that they was both packin guns fer one another and I reckon Abner jist shot to pertect hisef.

Cedric: Mr. Lum wasn't carryin no gun the day he was shot.

Grpap: No I know he wasn't but Abner never knowed he wasn't. Dick Huddleston tried to git in tetch with Abner to tell him but he couldn't find him no place.

Cedric: Snake Hogan was tryin to git up a posse awhal ago down at the Blacksmith shop to scour the woods and find Abner.

Grpap: He was?

Cedric: Yea. He had em all so mad down ther [that] they're figgerin on lynchin Abner if they can find him.

Grpap: Oh fer garden seed. Why ((((TELEPHONE)))) Didnt you tell me bout that Cedric. That wont never do . . . I wisht you'da told me bout that sooner. Wait a minit. . . . . HELLO THIS IS THE JOT EM DOWN STORE. . . YESSUM THIS IS MILFORD SPEARS. . . . . . WELL LUM TOLD ME TO COME DOWN HEP CEDRIC FER A FEW DAYS HERE IN THE STORE. . . . . . OH HE'S A RIGHT SMART BETTER. I WOULDN'T WORRY BOUT IT NOW LIZZYBETH. . . . . . NOME THEY'VE GOT THE REECEIVER SET OFFEN THE HOOK OVER THER. THATS MORE'N LIKELY THE REASON YOU COULDN'T GIT UM. SO MANY PEOPLE WAS CALLIN UP TO FIND OUT HOW LUM WAS GITTIN ALONG HIT WAS A RIGHT SMART OF BOTHER. . . . . YESSUM HE WAS RESTIN EASY LAST REEPORT WE HAD. . . .

.. WELL I DONT KNOW OF A THING LIZZYBETH.
.... THE NEIGHBORS HAS BROUGHT IN ANUFF
BROTH AND CUSTARDS AND FRUIT AND ONE
THING AND ANOTHER TO KILL HIM (L) YESSUM.
... WHY I THINK HIT'D BE ALRIGHT FER YOU TO
GO OVER THER AND SET WITH HIM AWHILE ..
YESSUM. HE'LL BE GLAD TO SEE YOU. . . . . . OH NO.
... HE WOULDN'T HOLD THAT AGIN YOU. . . . NO
HE KNOWS THAT ABNER MUSTA THOUGHT HE WAS
CARRYIN A GUN TO SHOOT HIM SO HE AINT EVEN
MAD AT ABNER BOUT IT . . . YEA IT WAS A NARRY
ESCAPE. . . . . WELL IF YOU CAN GIT IN TETCH WITH
ABNER LIZZYBETH TELL HIM I WANT TO SEE HIM
THE VERY FIRST THING. . . . AND LUM WANTS HIM
TO COME OVER AND SEE HIM TOO. . . . . YESSUM . . .
ALRIGHT . . . YEA I WIST YOU WOULD. . . . . ALRIGHT
(CLICK) . .
Cedric: I reckon Mrs. Peabody feels awful turible bout this.
Grpap: Yea. Cedric what time was it when you heard em talkin
over at the blacksmith shop about findin Abner and lynchin
him.
Cedric: Oh I dont know hit was when I was on my way back
from deliverin them groceries over to the Widder Abernathys.
Grpap: What time did they say they was goin to start out with
the posse?
Cedric: Well they was talkin bout goin jist quick as the whistle
blows this evenin and the mill hands gits off work.
Grpap: I wonder if Dick Huddleston knows about this . . I'm
goin to telephone him up (((((TELEPHONE)))) Hit'll never
do to let that posse git a holdt of Abner.
Cedric: Yea I'd hate to see anything happen to him.
Grpap: HELLO . . . HELLO . . . HUDDLESTON'S STORE?.
. . . . YEA HIDY DICK THIS IS GRANDPAP TALKIN . .
WHY CEDRIC WAS JIST TELLIN ME THAT HE HEARD
A BUNCH OF FELLERS OVER AT THE BLACKSMITH

SHOP THIS MORNIN PLANNIN TO ORGANIZE A
POSSE AND LYNCH ABNER FER SHOOTIN LUM. . . .
Cedric: YONDER COMES SNAKE HOGAN OVER HERE
NOW GRANDPAP.
Grpap: WAIT A MINIT DICK. WHAT'D YOU SAY CEDRIC?
Cedric: BETTER BE KEERFUL HOW YOU'RE TALKIN HERE
COMES SNAKE HOGAN UP OUT FRONT THER. HE'LL
BEAT MY HEAD OFF IF HE KNOWS I TOLD YOU BOUT
THAT.
Grpap: HELLO DICK . . . (WHISPER) SNAKE HOGAN IS
COMIN IN THE STORE . . I'LL HAVE TO CALL YOU
BACK DRECKLY. . . . HAH?. . . . YEA DO THAT. COME
RIGHT ON OVER. WE'VE GOT TO DO SOMPIN AND DO
IT QUICK . . . ALRIGHT DICK . . . (CLICK).
Snake: (faded in) Well Hidy . . Spears. . . .
Grpap: Hidy Snake . . You're the very feller I want to see.
Snake: Wher's Peabody?
Grpap: I dont know as fer as I know he aint been saw since
Thursday.
Snake: Yes you do know Spears and hit aint goin to be healthy
fer you if you dont tell.
Grpap: Now listen to me Snake Hogans. You might bluff some
of these fokes around Pine Ridge here but you aint scarin
me one bit. You aint nuthin but a big bluff . . . I told you I dont
know wher Abner's at and even if I did know I wouldn't tell
you. . . I know what you want with him. . . . I know bout you
tryin to git up a posse to hang him. But let me tell you right now
you caint right a wrong with a wrong.
Snake: Why you dried up old fossil. I never come in here to listen
to you preach . . . I want to know wher Abner Peabody is and if
you caint tell I'll find out from somebody else . . . We'll find him
. . (fade) and when we do its goin to be too bad fer him——
Grpap: Alright Cedric. We got to act quick. Lock them back
doors . . . We're closin up the store . . . We've got to find
Abner . . We've got to find him.

JANUARY 23, 1934

Lum: Well jist let the store go Grandpapp. I'd a heap druther you and Cedric would spend yer time a lookin fer Abner. Jist lock it up till you find him.

Grpap: Well I jist dont bleave Abner's in this part of the country. Me and Cedric trapsed all over these mountains alookin fer him and Snake Hogan and that mob never got in till right early this mornin, looked fer him all night and they never got no trace of him. They're goin out again tonight they say.

Lum: Pore Abner. I hope you can git word to him and warn him fore them fellers finds him.

Grpap: Oh yea they'll hang him shore. I tried to argue with Snake Hogan yistidy evenin tried to show him wher hits the wrong thing to do told him you caint right one wrong with anothern but hits jist like arguin with a stump on fire to talk to that feller.

Lum: Wellsir I caint understand why Snake is so bound and determined to see that Abner is punished fer what he done. I'm the one that ort to demmand his arrest if anybody does but I grannies I've made up my mind if they arrest him fer shootin me I'm goin to defend him in court.

Grpap: I bound you if Abner knowed that he'd come back home and face the music.

Lum: I feel sorryful fer Abner. I hate to think about him havin to hide around like a crimminal. Out in this kind of weather, no tellin wher he's sleepin and what kind of vittals he's gittin to eat . . . Lizzybeth was over here yistidy evenin, natural she's all tore up about this. Hits right pittyful. Her and Pearl is might nigh grievin therseves to death. They dont know what has became of Abner.

Grpap: I hope nobody dont tell Lizzybeth bout Snake Hogan and that mob lookin fer him, she *will* have sompin to worry er then.

Lum: Wherebouts did youall look fer Abner last night Grandpap?

Grpap: Well we looked all through that holler back of his farm over ther and then took a round clean on the other side of Old Piney Mountain then we circled back by the old gaddis place. We never even seen no trace of him.

Lum: Wellsir I dont know wher I dreamt it or wher I got the idy in my head but I caint hep but bleave Abner's hidin over torwards the river. You know theys several old farms that they aint nobody livin on now over in ther. Them old delapidated houses and barns would make a fine place fer a feller to hide out in.

Grpap: Yessir they shore would. I never thought about lookin over ther . . Well Lum if you think hits alright jist to lock up the Jot Em Down store, I'll go by and git Cedric and we'll take a jaunt down through the bottoms there, see if we can find him.

Lum: Yea (((((TELEPHONE))))) I wisht you would Grandpap. I jist wisht I was stout a nuff to go with you . . Wait a minit I bleave thats my ring there . . Would you minds to answer the telephone fer me fore you go Grandpap.

Grpap: Yea. More'n likely somebody else wantin to know how you're feelin today.

Lum: Tell em I'm a heap better.

Grpap: HELLO. . . . . YES. . . . THIS IS MILFORD SPEARS TALKIN. . . . . . WHO . . OH HIDY DICK . . . OH HE'S A HEAP BETTER TODAY . . . YEA. (to Lum) Hits Dick Huddleston Lum.

Lum: Well (L) Tell him to come over and set with me when he gits time.

Grpap: HOWS THAT DICK?. . . . UH HUH. . . . . WELL? YEA I'LL TELL HIM. . . . . ALRIGHT DICK. WHY LUM SAYS TO TELL YOU TO COME OVER AND KEEP HIM COMPANY WHEN YOU GIT TIME. . . . . . . ALRIGHT GOODBYE. (CLICK)

Lum: What was it he was a wantin?

Grpap: Why he said they was a stranger down at the store a few

minits ago lookin fer Abner and he's on his way over here to
see you to see if you can hep him locate him.

Lum: Lookin fer Abner huh?

Grpap: Yea.

Lum: I grannies thats more'n likely a detecitive alookin fer him.
Well I'll tell him right now he wont find out nuthin from me.
I'll swear Abner aint the one that shot me.

Grpap: Well now Lum. Course I know you dont want Abner to
git in no trouble over this and we've got to do our best to find
him to keep Snake Hogan and that mob from findin him and
doin sompin they'll all have their reegrets over but we caint
stand in the way of the law.

Lum: Well I may be a goose fer thinkin it but I still caint bleave
Abner would shoot me. I jist dont bleave he done it.

Grpap: Why who else could ita been Lum. Everbody knows he
was packin a gun fer you and had made his brags about how
he was goin to shoot you.

Lum: Yea I know.

Grpap: And then him dissapearin right after the shootin aint been
saw since.

Lum: I wont bleave Abner shot me lesson I hear him say it with
his own mouth.

Grpap: Why Lum you know he done it. He more'n likely done it
to pertect hisef cause Snake Hogan told him you was carryin
a gun fer him but I bleave he can git off with a light sentence
claimin self defence.

Lum: I jist caint bleave he done the shootin though. I dont bleave
he coulda shot me no easier than I coulda shot him and I
know I couldn't a shot him. We've been friends too long.
Besides Abner aint that gooda shot. He couldn't hit the side
of a barn if he was inside with the doors all locked.

Grpap: Lum I reckon thats that feller comin up out ther now.

Lum: Lets see . . . OOOH . . I caint move . . . What does he look
like?

Grpap: Oh he's a city feller abody can tell that by lookin at him.

Turible dressed up. Looks like he's about forty or forty five year old.

Lum: Yea I betcha thats what he is . . a detecitive. (((KNOCK))) (((KNOCK)))

Lum: Go to the door Grandpap and let him in.

Grpap: Well I bleave I'll go on Lum. I'll go by and git Cedric.

Lum: Alright GRANDPAP. I HOPE YOU FIND ABNER.

(DOOR OPEN)

Grpap: (faded) HOW YOU DO SIR.

Gibson: I am looking for a Mr. Lum Edwards.

Grpap: Well you've come to the right place.

Gibson: I am Mr. Gibson Mr. Edwards. I'm told that you might be able to help me locate Mr. Abner Peabody—

Grpap: Oh I aint Lum Edards. He's here in bed. Jist step right in, he's sorter spectin you.

Gibson: Oh I see. Thank you.

Grpap: Thats him over ther bed rid. He got shot last week.

Gibson: Well I'm sorry to hear that. I am Mr. Gibson Mr. Edwards.

Lum: Proud to make yer quaintance. Have a chair and set awhile.

Gibson: Thank you. Thank you. Mr. Edwards I am looking for——

Grpap: (faded) Well Lum I'll drap back by yer place agin we git back.

Lum: Alright Grandpap.

((DOOR CLOSES))

Lum: What was it you started to say Mr. gabson.

Gibson: Why I am here to see Mr. Peabody and I find that he has not been seen since last Thursday.

Lum: No.

Gibson: I have tried to obtain information from his wife Mrs. Peabody but she has repeatedly slammed the door in my face. I am told that you and Mr. Peabody have been associated together in business for sometime and I thought perhaps you might be able to give me information that would lead to his whereabouts.

Lum: What was it you was a wantin to see him about?

Gibson: Well . . The nature of my business is such that I cannot discuss it with anyone but Mr. Peabody and then only after I have seen and talked with him.

Lum: Well I dont know wher he's at and if I did I wouldn't tell you. Now they's some that may have the idy that Abner is the one that shot me last week but I'll tell you right now he wern't the one.

Gibson: Oh your assailant hasn't been apprehended then?

Lum: Huh?

Gibson: I just learned that you had met with an accident, that you had been shot but I didn't hear the particulars. You say it is generally believed that Mr. Peabody was your assailant.

Lum: Well yes but I know he never done it.

Gibson: Well I'm glad to know that. You're positive are you Mr. Edwards?

Lum: Why yes.

Gibson: To be perfectly frank. Quite naturally I had heard that Mr. Peabody was the one who shot you last week and that is why he has been hiding out. I have come to you because I knew you would know if anybody did, if this a[ccusation] is just. You say you do not believe Mr. Peabody is the one who shot you?

Lum: Nossir.

Gibson: Do you think he had any reason to attempt to take your life?

Lum: Noosir.

Gibson: Is Mr. Peabody in the habit of carrying a gun?

Lum: Well yes. You see he's the constable here in Pine Ridge and he can carry firearms legal.

Gibson: I see. Did it ever occur to you Mr. Edwards that Mr. Peabody might have used his office of constable to disguise his own crimminal habits?

Lum: What do you mean? crimminal habits?

Gibson: Mr. Edwards the world is full of just such cases.

Men who were upright citizens by day that gave vent to a supressed vicious nature at night.

Lum: Well Abner never could do nuthin like that . . not [at] night. He's too big a sleepy head. Why Abner couldn't stay awake to do any prowlin around after eight oclock.

Gibson: Ah but the magic hour of midnight . . There are cases Mr. Edwards—

Lum: Well I'll tell you right now you've got Abner down all wrong.

Gibson: Well I hope I have . . Thats why I'm asking these questions. I want to know what kind of a man I'm dealin with . . . But I believe even you have been mislead by his cunning. I believe you will discover that Mr. Peabody has a side to him that even you dont know . . . A crimminal side . . . That man is a dangerous fiend.

Lum: Wherebouts did you git sich idys is them in yer head.

Gibson: Well I have been making inquiries.

Lum: Somebody's been talkin to you that dont know a thing about him. If anybody knows Abner Peabody I (((KNOCK KNOCK)))) do . . Wait a minit . . Thats somebody at the door . . . COME IN COME . .

(door Opens)

Snake: (faded) Well Hidy Edards . . How you feelin?

Lum: Well Howdy Snake.

Gibson: Well how do you do Mr. Hogan.

Snake: (faded) Hi Gibson. They said I could find you here . . . Are you still looking fer Peabody?

Gibson: Why yes I thought perhaps Mr. Edwards might assist me in locating him.

Snake: Well git on yer hat and coat . . . We've got him located.

Lum: You've—You've located Abner?

Snake: Yea, I told you I'd find him. He's been hidin in that old cave on the east side of Eagle Mountain. . . .

Gibson: Thats fine. I'm glad you have him located. . . . My trip to Pine Ridge then has not been in vain . . . Mr. Edwards I want

to thank you for your information . . . You will soon know
the reason for my being here to see Mr. Peabody.
Lum: Thats alright . . . Uh Snake. Are you shore Abner's hidin in
that cave?
Snake: Yea we found wher he's been sleepin and ther's a place
wher he's been cookin his grub in ther. We'll catch him. He'll
come back and we'll nab him . . . Well Edards you'll more'n
likely find your friend hangin to a tree in the mornin.
Lum: Snake dont do nuthin you'll have yer reegrets over. Abner
never done it. He never shot me. I know he never.
Gibson: Good day Mr. Edwards.
Snake: So Long Edards. (DOOR CLOSES)
Lum: I've got to git word to Abner . . I've got to do it . . .
If I can git to the telephone . . . Uh . . . Ooooh . . Uh . .
I'll call Grandpap . . . Maybe he can git to him first . . .
(((TELEPHONE))) Hello. . . . Hello. . . . GRANDPAP. . . .
GRANDPAP . . . I'M SO WEAK . . I . . . I'M GLAD YOU
AINT GONE YIT . . . GIT TO ABNER Tell him They're
after him . . . They know wher he's at . . . He's in the—He's in
the—cave. . . . Falls.

JANUARY 24, 1934

Grpap: Yea Abner told me to be shore and tell you he never shot
you. Said the reason he was hidin out was cause he knowed
everbody'd think he done it.
Lum: Well fer some reason or ruther I never did think he was the
one.
Grpap: Well I told him that and it jist tickled him to death. He
wanted to know how you was gittin along and if you was
bad hurt and all.
Lum: Well that was thoughty of him.
Grpap: I told him bout you gittin up outa bed to telephone
me yistidy evenin to tell me Snake Hogan and them fellers
knowed wher he was hidin out at and bout you faintin and

fallin while you was talkin on the phone and he might nigh broke down and cried.

Lum: Well hit was the only thing I could do. They wernt nobody here jist then to call you sept me.

Grpap: Well Doc Cook says that was the worst thing you coulda did, weak as you air.

Lum: How was Abner lookin Grandpap. Did he look like he was gittin plenty to eat?

Grpap: Well yes I reckon so, abody couldn't tell much about him. He hadn't had no shave since he hid out and his clothes was all torn and all. I never hardly knowed him . . Looked more like a wild man . . He was jist fixin to cook some eggs in a sort of a stove he had rigged up ther in the cave when me and Cedric walked up on him.

Lum: Hits a wonder he never put up some kind of a fight. Youall sprisin him thataway.

Grpap: Well he started to run but I hollered and told him we had some good news fer him.

Lum: Well hits jist a blessin you and Cedric got to see him fore Snake Hogan and his gang got ther.

Grpap: Oh they'd a hung him shore.

Lum: Did you tell him bout that feller bein here to see him.

Grpap: Yea I told him he'd better stay hid fer a few more days that they was a deetecitive here lookin fer him.

Lum: Wellsir Grandpap I caint figger our wher that feller's a detecitive or not. I caint figger him out.

Grpap: Well what else could he be here in Pine Ridge lookin fer Abner fer then?

Lum: Well I dont know thats jist it. Strangest actin feller I ever seen. Acts like he's skeerd of Abner to me. He went with Snake Hogan and that mob yistidy evenin.

Grpap: I bet that was a dissapinted bunch. Looked all night fer Abner. Thats two nights now they've been out. Had the rope they was goin to hang him with and everthing.

Lum: Well Dick Huddleston was over here a few minits ago and said he found out who all was in that bunch and he seen most of em this mornin and talked to em. Reasoned with em, said they wasn't goin to bother Abner now.

Grpap: Why Snake had talked to em and got em all worked up they never stopped to think what they was doin.

Lum: I was jist thinkin if it wern't fer that Mr. Gipson, that detecitive or whatever he is, Abner could come on in home now.

Grpap: Yea they aint a bit of—Wait a minit . . Well I swan to goodness. Ther's Cedric comin up out ther. I wonder what in the word he's wantin. I told him not to leave that store while I was gone.

Lum: More'n likely somebody wantin sompin and he dont know wher its at.

Grpap: I swan that boy, that boy. He ort to know better'n to jist pick up and leave that store.

Lum: Well he does the best he knows how. He (((KNOCK))) tries mighty hard . . COME IN . . COME IN.

Cedric: (FADED IN) WELL HIDY MR. EDARDS. HOW YOU FEELIN TODAY.

Lum: Well I dont think I heped mysef none by gittin outa bed yistidy.

Cedric: Well I wisht you'd hurry up and git well. Shore miss you down at the store. Things jist aint the same when you aint ther.

Lum: Well thank you Cedric thats thoughty of you to say them things . . . Agin you go back to the store, hep yerself to a couple of pieces of candy.

Cedric: Well I knowed you'd say that so I went ahead and got it first.

Lum: Oh you did huh? Well Cedric if you must eat that candy I do wisht you'd sorter pick on that bucket of Christmas candy we had left over.

Cedric: Well I did till I ett it up.

Grpap: Cedric what are you doin leavin the store thisaway when I told you not to leave till I got back.

Cedric: Well the Widder Abernathy telephoned up and wanted

me to deliver some groceries and I jist come over to git you to stay in the store while I made the deliver. I told er I couldn't deliver em till you got back.

Grpap: Well fer goodness sake you locked up to come off over here. You may as well delivered the groceries. Hit'd take you a heap longer to come over here than it would to go to the Abernathys.

Cedric: Yessmam I never thought about that.

Grpap: Well lets go on over ther then and—WELL Lum you got some more company comin up out ther in front.

Lum: Who is it?

Grpap: Why hit looks like Evalener . . Yea. Thats who it is.

Lum: Evalener comin to see me? . . . (L) Well I do know. I thought she was mad at me. Hand me that comb and bresh ther Grandpap . . . Cedric git me that mirror ther on the dresser. Now dont drop it. My luck's jist now gittin good. So Evalener's comin to see me . . I jist been wishin she would.

Grpap: That shows right ther Lum she's bound to be in love with you else she wouldn't be comin to see you.

Lum: I grannies hits gittin shot that done it. I knowed they'd be some good come outa this . . . Lets see how can I prop mysef up here sos that bandage'll show good . . I'll look like sort of a hero to her all bandaged up thisway.

Grpap: Yea now you're lookin fine. I spect we'd better be goin Cedric. I know Lum and Evalener'll have a lot of personal matters to discuss.

Cedric: Yessum. If they's anything you need brought up from the store Mr. Edards, jist have somebody call me up and I'll fetch it over fer you.

Lum: Alright Cedric. But what ever you do dont bring no custard over here. (((((KNOCK))))) GO HEAD AND LET EVALENER IN GRANDPAP.

Grpap: ((OPENS DOOR)) WELL HIDYDO EVALENER . . HOW'RE YOU?

Evalena: JUST FINE. HOW IS MR. EDWARDS TODAY?

Grpap: Oh he's jist as piert as a young colt.

Evalena: Do you think it will be alright for me to talk with him a few minutes.

Grpap: Yea shore. We seen you comin up out front. Come on in.

Evalena: THANK YOU MR. SPEARS.

Lum: YEA COME IN EVALENER. COME IN PROUD TO SEE YOU.

Evalena: (Fading in) Oh how are you Lummy? I've been so worried about you.——

Grpap: (faded) WELL I'LL SEE YOU AFTER WHILE LUM.

Cedric: (faded) I'll be over late to feed and bed down yer stock fer you Mr. Edards.

Lum: ALRIGHT FELLERS. MUCH OBLIGED.

(door Closes)

Evalena: How are you feeling Lummy?

Lum: Well (L) I'm feelin a heap better now that you've come to see me.

Evalena: Well I would have been here sooner but Doctor Cook told me he thought it best that you not have too much company for a few days. But I've thought about you a lot.

Lum: Well thats nice.

Evalena: Oh I nearly forgot. I brought you something.

Lum: Brou—Welll.

Evalena: Something I made with my own hands.

Lum: Thats bound to make it a heap nicer. What is it?

Evalena: Look some nice custard . .

Lum: CUSTARD?

Evalena: Yes why?

Lum: Why I was jist thinkin. They aint nuthin I like better'n custard . . Facts is I was jist sayin awhale ago, I wisht somebody'd send me over some. . . .

Evalena: I hope you like this.

Lum: Wait a minit though. Hit aint got no nutmeg sprinkled on it has it?

Evalena: Why yes. I thought you'd like nutmeg . . . I put a lot of
it on it.

Lum: Well thats fine . . Oh yes, I was goin to say I caint hardly
stand custard without a good sprinklin of nutmeg. Jist set it
over ther on the dresser and I'll eat it dreckly.

Evalena: Why dont you want to eat it now?

Lum: Oh I'd druther save it . . .

Evalena: No I insist on you eating it now while I'm here. I want
to see how you like it. Let me feed it to you.

Lum: Well the only trouble I wanted to spend all the time while
you're here talkin to you.

Evalena: No No. Now open your mouth. . . . There.

Lum: Uhh . . . Thats fine . . . Yea thats the best I've tasted yet.
((((Telephone)) Now lets save the balance of it till after you've
gone—

Evalena: Oh have other women been sending over custard to you?

Lum: Would you minds to answer the telephone fer me Evalena. I
think that was my ring.

Evalena: . . . Certainly. . . . . . HELLO. . . . WHY THIS IS
EVALENA SCHULTZ. . . . . YES I'M HERE WITH HIM
NOW. . . . . . OH HE SEEMS TO BE GETTING ALONG
FINE. . . . .

Lum: Who is it Evalener?

Evalena: Its Mrs. Peabody. She wants to know if you want her to
send over some more baked custard.

Lum: TELL ER NO.

Evalena: What. I thought you liked custard?

Lum: Yea I like it but since I tasted that of yours I know I dont
want to eat nobody elses . . . SHE PUTS nutmeg—I mean too
much nutmeg on hers. Tell er I'm hungry fer Fried Chicken if
she's bound and determined to fix sompin.

Evalena: Why Mr. Edwards says he would rather have fried
chicken Mrs. Peabody. . . . . . Yes. . . . Of course not. They
never know what they want . . . I think the custard would be
better for him too. . . . . Alright I'll tell him. . . . Wait just a

minute and I'll see . . . (to Lum) Mrs. Peabody wants to know
if you've heard anything from Abner yet?

Lum: Tell er to call up Grandpappy Spears down at the Jot Em
Down store. He seen him last night.

Evalena: Why Mr. Edwards says Mr. Spears saw Abner last night
and I'm sure if you call him he can tell you all about him.
((((KNOCK))))) Alright Mrs. Peabody . . . ((((KNOCK)))
ALRIGHT GOOD BYE. (CLICK)

Lum: I bleave they's somebody ther at the door now Evalener.

Evalena: Shall I ask them in?

Lum: Yea see who it is Please . .

((Door Opens))

Evalena: (faded) How do you do?

Gibson: (faded) How do you do. I wanted to see Mr. Edwards please.

Lum: WHO IS IT?

Gibson: THIS IS MR. GIBSON.

Lum: WELL COME IN COME IN.

Evalena: Come right in. May I take your hat and coat?

Gibson: I just want a moment Mr. Edwards. I came by to tell
you that I will have to go back to the east without seeing Mr.
Peabody.

Lum: Well I dont know wher he's at. I told you so yistidy.

Gibson: It seems impossible to find him . . . JUST TELL HIM
THAT I WAS HERE IN CONNECTION WITH THE
PROBATION OF A WILL BUT I CANT WAIT ANY
LONGER. IF HE EVER RETURNS TO PINE RIDGE
TELL HIM . . . IF HE CAN PROVE HE IS THE PROPER
PERSON HE IS THE HEIR TO A PORTION OF THE
PEABODY WILL IN SALEM MASSITUETS.

Lum: Well Wait a minit hold on.

Gibson: Too bad you dont know where he is. Well Goodbye Mr.
Edwards. (slam Door)

Lum: Go after him Evalena. Get him back—

JANUARY 25, 1934

Lum: Well didn't Abner give you no idy wher he was goin to hide?

Grpap: No he jist tore out when we told him Snake Hogan and that mob was lookin fer him. Me and Cedric jist come on back home.

Lum: Thats a shame him hidin out sneakin around over them mountains when he wern't even the one that done the shootin.

Grpap: Yea if we jist had some way of knowin wher he was at we could git word to him that they've done found who it was that shot you and he could come on in.

Lum: I jist wisht I had my strength. I'd strike right out a lookin fer him mysef.

Grpap: Well they's a bunch of us goin out tonight see if we can find him. He's bound to be over ther round Eagle Mountain sommers.

Lum: How did they find out that Snake Hogan was the one that done the shootin?

Grpap: Well Dick Huddleston got spicious that he was the one on account of him tryin to git up a mob to lynch Abner. And Dick has been sorter investigatin ever since you was shot.

Lum: Oh I can look back now and see hits bound to been Snake. He was the one that told me that Abner was packin a gun fer me and then he went to Abner and told Abner I was carryin a gun fer him . . After he got Abner to gunnin fer me hit was plum easy fer him to do the shootin and lay the blame on Abner.

Grpap: Yea but I dont see why he was wantin you killed off.

Lum: Well I caint reason that out neither. The only thing I can think of is, he's been tryin to buy the Jot Em Down store offen us and maybe he thought if one of us was out of the way, he could git holdt of the store without no trouble. You know he wont stop at nuthin that feller wont.

Grpap: I reckon then thats the reason he was tryin to git that mob to hang Abner after he seen you was goin to git well alright he tried to git shud of Abner.

Lum: More'n likely. More'n likely. The onery critter.

Grpap: Hit was his own wife that told it on him too.

Lum: Hit was?

Grpap: Yea she told Dick that she tried her best to git him not to do it and he threatend to kill her if she told it on him. She said the reason he had it in fer you was on account of you sendin him to the pennitentury bout a year ago.

Lum: Yea . . Wellsir I hadn't thought about that. I know he said at the time he'd git even with me agin he got out.

Grpap: Well he's headin back fer the pennintury now jist shore as the world. They aint a chance fer him to come clear. His own wife swearin he done it.

Lum: I grannies if he goes to the pennintentury again he will try to git revenge the next time he gits out.

Grpap: Oh well you aint got nuthin to worry bout. You more'n likely wont be livin by the time he gits out noway.

Lum: You mean you dont think I'm goin to git well.

Grpap: No but this is a serious charge he's facin this time. Attempted murder. They'll more'n likely keep him in ther the balance of his life.

Lum: I grannies I hope so. ((((TELEPHONE))))) We never had so much peace and quiet in Pine Ridge as we did while he was in ther bef—Answer that will you please Grandpap.

Grpap: Well . . . I see you've moved the telephone.

Lum: Yea. I had it took down offen the wall so's I could talk right here in bed.

Grpap: Yea thats a good idy . . . HELLO. . . . THIS IS MILFORD SPEARS DOIN THE TALKIN . . . WHY HE'S RESTIN EASY THIS AFTERNOON DICK. . . . . . WELL HERE I'LL LET YOU TALK TO HIM . . . (To Lum) Here Lum hits Dick Huddleston. Says he's got sompin important to tell you.

Lum: Alright . . Hand me the reeceiver . . Thankee . . . HELLO

DICK . . . OH FEELIN A HEAP BETTER DICK. I'LL BE
UP AND AROUND IN A DAY OR TWO I THINK. . . . . . .
WHATS THAT. . . . . . . HE IS. . . . . TILL FOUR OCLOCK
HUH? . . . Well caint you talk him into waitin till tomorrow
to leave. . . . He caint?. . . . . . Well I dont see no chance to
git in tetch with him. Nobody dont know wher he's at. . . .
No he dont neither I was jist now astin him. He said he never
told em wher he was goin to hide. . . . . . Alright Dick . . . Oh
say . . I want to tell you. That was mighty fine work you done
findin out who it was done the shootin . . . Yea Grandpap
told me bout it. . . . . No I wernt at tall sprised fer I never did
think Abner shot me. I jist couldn't bleave he'd do it some
way or ruther. . . . Oh yea I can look back now and see wher
Snake was jist aggin me and Abner on. Tryin to git one of
us to do the shootin and I reckon he seen we wern't goin
to do it so he takend a shot at me hisef. . . . . . . Yea I hope
they do. The pennitentury is wher he blongs. . . . . Alright
Dick. . . . Huh? . . . Yea I'll do the best I can but I dont know
how in the world we can git word to him. You know he still
thinks this stranger thats here is a detecitive. . . . . . Why
Grandpappy told him that when him and Cedric seen him. .
. . . Yea . . . And he still thinks Snake Hogan and that mob is
lookin fer him. . . . . . . Well alright Dick . . . Much obliged. .
. . GOOD BYE. (CLICK)

Grpap: Dick wantin to git some word to Abner?

Lum: Yea . . . Said that feller Gibson thats here is goin to leave at
four oclock. Dick said he tried to git him to stay over another
day and see if Abner dont come in but he says he's got to git
back.

Grpap: Yea well.

Lum: I had a long talk with that feller Gibson yistidy evenin. He
come in here to say he was leavin, Evalener was here at the
time and she got him to come back and we talked him into
stayin over today and wait . . . He's a purty nice sort of a
feller agin abody gits to know him better.

Grpap: Well I jist dont like a feller that'll come in the way he did and not come out flat footed and tell his business. He's too secret.

Lum: Yea if he hada told me at first what he was after you coulda told Abner when you and Cedric seen him over on Eagle Mountain. I thought he was a detecitive all the time and done all I could to keep him FROM findin Abner.

Grpap: Yea I know you did.

Lum: They aint no tellin what this might mean to Abner . . He may be a millionare and not even know it. Looks like they ort to be someway fer us to git word to him.

Grpap: The only way I know would be to jist comb these mounrtains round here till we find him.

Lum: Might could git Kalup Weehunt to git out ther in the mountains and call fer him. He's the champion hog caller of the county.

Grpap: Well if he ever heard Kalup out in ther he'd think it was some kind of a varmit. Better not try that he'd go the other way. Scare him so far away he never would come home.

Lum: I tell you what we might do Grandpap. We might make a nouncement to everbody on the party line to be on the look out fer him. Somebody might run accrost him and tell him hits alright to come home now.

Grpap: Well course hit wont hurt nuthin to try it.

Lum: Hand me the telephone Grandpap. I'll call Doc Cook's number and I know everbody'll pick up their receivers and listen to see if I've took a turn fer the worse.

Grpap: (((TELEPHONE))) Oh yea. Everbody allus listens in whenever they hear Docs ring on the partyline.

Lum: (L) I can hear fokes pickin up the reeceivers all up and down the line. HOWDY EVERBODY. . . . THIS IS LUM EDARDS. I JIST WANT TO ASK YOU FOKES ON THE PARTY LINE TO BE ON THE LOOK OUT FER ABNER PEABODY . . IF YOUNS SEE HIM TELL HIM THEY'VE FOUND OUT SNAKE HOGAN IS THE ONE THAT SHOT

ME AND FER HIM TO COME ON HOME. THEY'S
SOME IMPORTANT NEWS HERE FER HIM. WHILE
I'M TALKIN I WANT TO THANK ALL YOU WIMMIN
FOKES THATS COOKED VITTALS AND SENT OVER
FER ME WHILE I'VE BEEN SICK . . HIT WAS MIGHTY
THOUGHTY OF YOU . . . Now if any of you have saw
Abner I wisht you'd call me back dreckly . . Thank you.
(Click) (L) Sorter reminds me of when we was puttin on our
sociables talkin over the party line thataway.

Grpap: I notice you was thankin the wimmen fokes fer the vittals
they've brung over fer you. I thought you was complainin
yistidy cause they'd sent so much boiled custard.

Lum: Well I dont like the stuff but hits mighty nice of em to go
to the bother to fix it up fer me. I preciate it jist the same.
Evalener brung some over yistidy evenin and I had to set here
and eat it till I might nigh choked. She insisted on feedin it
to me. ((((TELEPHONE))))) I tried to git er to set it on the
dresser, told er I'd—Thats my ring again.

Grpap: MAYBE THATS SOMEBODY THATS SAW ABNER.

Lum: Yea go ahead, SEE WHO IT IS Grandpap.

Grpap: HELLO. THIS IS LUM EDARDS PLACE. . . . NO THIS
[IS] MILFORD SPEARS TALKIN. . . .

Lum: I grannies I bound you they've located him. Ast em wher
they seen him Grandpap.

Grpap: Well alright I'll tell him . . . Yessum. I know he'll be glad
to hear it.

Lum: Course I'll be glad.

Grpap: Alright . . . GOOD BYE. (CLICK)

Lum: Wher's he at Grandpap?

Grpap: Why that was the Widder Abernathy. Says she's sendin
over a nice big bowl of Boiled Custard.

Lum: Oh my goodness Gracious . . . I hope she trips and—no I
dont wish that. But why caint somebody think to send over
some fried Chicken, corn bread, turnip greens, black eyed
peas, buttermilk and sich as that . . They aint nuthin wrong

with my appetite. Hits my shoulder that got shot not my appetite.

Grpap: I tell you what I'll do Lum. I'll git the woman to fetch you over a plate of real vittals tonight.

Lum: I wisht you would. I hate to ask anybody to do it. But you could do it thout nobody thinkin nuthin of it. ((((TELEPHONE))) Aint Charity has shore been nice to me Grandpap. I dont know how I ever will be able to thank— Yea go head and answer it and if its anybody wantin to send some more custard over here tell em that I've foundered on the stuff . . . I know what they mean by Custard's last stand now.

Grpap: Hello. . . . Yea this is Lum Edards place. . . . . . . WHO?. . . . . . WELL FER THE LAND SAKES.

Lum: WHO IS IT Grandpap?

Grpap: Hits Abner. Hits Abner.

Lum: Here let me have that telephone . . . LET ME TALK TO HIM. . . . YEA . . . HELLO ABNER. . . . WELL WHER IN THE WORLD ARE YOU AT. . . . . . WELL WHAT YOU DOIN OVER THER WHEN DID YOU GIT HOME. . . . . . . WELL HERE WE BEEN LOOKIN EVERWHER FER YOU TO TELL YOU . . . THEY'S A FELLER BEEN HERE IN PINE RIDGE FER MIGHT NIGH A WEEK ALOOKIN FER YOU AND HE'S LEAVIN AT FOUR OCLOCK . . . YEA HE'S GOT SOME GOOD NEWS FER YOU HE SAYS . . . I TELL YOU. YOU GIT YERSEF OVER HERE JIST AS QUICK AS YOU CAN AND I'LL TELEPHONE HIM UP AND HAVE HIM MEET YOU OVER HERE JIST AS——